ALICE LECCESE POWERS

Italy in Mind

Alice Leccese Powers is co-editor of the anthology *The Brooklyn Reader: Thirty Writers Celebrate America's Favorite Borough* (Harmony, 1994). A freelance writer and editor, she has been published in *The Washington Post, The Baltimore Sun, Newsday,* and many other newspapers and magazines. Ms. Powers also teaches writing at the Corcoran School of Art and Georgetown University. She lives in Washington, D.C., with her husband and three daughters.

Italy in Mind

Italy in Mind

AN ANTHOLOGY

Edited and with an Introduction by
Alice Leccese Powers

VINTAGE DEPARTURES

VINTAGE BOOKS
A DIVISION OF RANDOM HOUSE, INC.
NEW YORK

A VINTAGE DEPARTURES ORIGINAL,
MAY 1997
FIRST EDITION

Library of Congress Cataloging-in-Publication Data
Italy in mind : an anthology / edited and with an introduction by Alice Leccese Powers.—1st ed. Vintage departures
original.
      p. cm.—(Vintage departures)
    ISBN 0-679-77023-2 (pbk. : alk. paper)
   1. American literature—20th century. 2. Italy—
Literary collections. 3. English literature—20th century.
4. American literature—19th century. 5. English literature—19th century. 6. Italy. I. Powers, Alice.
        P S 509.I73I83   1997
    810.8'03245—dc21   96-47864
            CIP

Random House Web address:
http://www.randomhouse.com

Designed by Cassandra J. Pappas

Manufactured in the United States of America
20 19 18 17 16 15 14 13 12 11

For Brian

Acknowledgments

WITH GRATEFUL ACKNOWLEDGMENT to my editor, LuAnn Walther, and my agent, Jane Dystel; to my extended Italian family, both Sicilian and Barese, especially my parents Gaetana and Vito Leccese; to my sister, Maria Leccese Kotch, and my brother, Michael Leccese, who both shared my split-level childhood; to Kem Sawyer, Erich Parker, Marcy Rothblum, and Joyce Muis for their friendship and counsel; to my husband, Brian Powers, for his unfailing support; and to my patient Irish-Italian-American daughters, Alison, Christina, and Brenna Powers. Molte grazie.

Contents

Introduction

There are places where lips touched lips for the first time ever, or pen pressed paper with real fervor.
—JOSEPH BRODSKY
"December in Florence"

*I*TALY IS a contentious alliance of opposites—the North and the South, the Mediterranean and the Alps, the ancient and the modern, the Christian and the pagan. It encompasses crowded Neapolitan cafes and solitary Tuscan trattorias, the haunting stillness of Venetian passageways and the cacophony of Roman roundabouts; the high fashion of Milanese couture and the ubiquitous black dresses of Sicilian widows. Incongruity does not confound Italians. They thrive on chaos. Their astonishing ability to cope with disaster, wrote Gore Vidal, is equaled only by their complete inability to deal with success.

Italy both lures and baffles Anglo-Saxons. For generations they have tried to discover her secret, for foreigners often believe that she has some elusive internal consistency. Every few years an observer claims to have found the last piece of the Italian puzzle, the solution. But this European jigsaw has been worked for centuries, and the Italians withhold key pieces. A writer is, by nature, a puzzler, and the authors in *Italy in Mind* provide important clues. No one completes the picture, but collectively they come close.

This anthology offers many, sometimes conflicting, opinions. "My Italy is now a tangle of flight times, suburbs, superimposed cultures, a country caught up in an affluent hysteria, modern, but hoping that the modern was something that could be played at" offers Harold Brodkey. Joseph Brodsky exults in the Florentine winter, R. W. B. Lewis in its summer. Mary McCarthy found Venice "a little pale and moribund," while Gore Vidal concludes it is a "place outside of time." They are all right.

Italy in Mind is a collection of writing by British and American writers. This both narrowed the selections to a manageable number and confined the contributors to those with something of a shared sensibility. As Eleanor Clark wrote in *Rome and a Villa,* "for the Anglo-Saxon mind, ruled by conscience and the romantic, rigid in its privacies, everything [in Italy] is shocking—an endless revelation and immersion."

The Italian writer Luigi Barzini theorized that Italy has a special appeal for Anglo-Saxons because when in Italy they can take a holiday from their national virtues. "In the heart of every man," he wrote, "there is one small corner which is Italian, that part that finds regimentation irksome, the dangers of war frightening, strict morality stifling, that part which loves frivolous and entertaining art, admires larger than life-size solitary heroes and dreams of an impossible liberation from the strictures of a tidy existence."

In the nineteenth century no British or American education was complete without the "Grand Tour" of the Continent. France and the Netherlands were often on the itinerary, sometimes Austria and Germany, but the prime destination was always Italy. The neoclassical movement that swept the Victorians mandated direct knowledge of that country's cultural past. Visitors were initially drawn by the art and music and once there were enchanted by the coffee houses, the casinos, and the courtesans. Then, as now, tourists came to study dead Italians, wrote Barzini, but were entertained by the live ones.

Italy's somewhat licentious reputation afforded many writers sanctuary from Victorian morals. Both Byron and Shelley escaped ostracism in England for a more hospitable social climate. Elizabeth Barrett and Robert Browning fled to Italy after their secret wedding. Elizabeth, a virtual invalid dominated by her family, thrived in Italy, embracing marriage, motherhood, and Italian nationalism. She and Robert lived almost all their married life in Florence and raised their son in a villa, Casa Guidi, immortalized in her poetry.

Modern Italy continues to lure literary refugees. Ann Cornelisen arrived in the 1950s to do social work among Sicilian women. She is there still. Matthew Spender moved to Italy in the late 1960s for a brief adventure and never left. Both Mary Taylor Simeti and Tim Parks married Italians and stayed, struggling with their dual identities. Gore Vidal, grandson of a United States Senator, lives in a villa near Ravello.

Other writers visited and returned home, renewed physically, spiritually, and financially. Both Twain and Dickens moved their families to Italy to save money and made fortunes penning accounts of their travels. R. W. B. Lewis has spent a total of six years in Italy since World War II. His passion for Florence allows him to understand "Duomo-sickness," an ailment peculiar to Florentines who stay away from their city for too long. Bernard Malamud took his academic sabbatical in Rome and produced his wondrous short story collection *Pictures of Fidelman*. Herman Melville was an exception to these enthusiastic pilgrims. His in-laws feared for his sanity and sent him on a restorative tour of Italy and the Holy Land. Once there he wrote poetry, including the lyrical "In A Bye Canal," and researched his lecture "Statuary in Rome," but he proved to be a pedestrian tourist. In his journal he wrote of a Roman street, "Could hardly tell it from Broadway. Thought I was there." Viewing a painting of Lucrezia Borgia he notes: "Good looking dame. Rather fleshy."

There were other writers who, like Melville, failed to be enchanted by Italy. Complaints abound about the weather, the government, the customs, the food, the intolerance for change or the disregard for antiquity. Mark Twain wrote "I can not understand how a bankrupt Government can have such palatial railroad depots and such marvels of turnpikes." Tim Parks, entrapped in the tentacles of Italian bureaucracy, theorized that officials simply invent serpentine regulations on the spot, forcing the public into even more complex evasions. Mary Morris despaired, "I am not a cynic and I love Italy. But I have discovered that time and space are relative notions there."

Italy's duality reflects my own. In America, I am Italian; in Italy, I am American. Editing this collection provided pieces to my personal Italian puzzle and also revealed my prejudices. I knew that I had to include John Hersey's *A Bell for Adano* when Victor Joppolo said, seeing Italy for the first time, "I feel like I'm going home"—just my response. And I instantly empathized with Kate Simon's explanation of Italy's male mating ritual. Leering from car windows and catcalling to their prey, Italian men, she wrote, simply believe they are irresistible to women. Hemingway's description of rowing across Lago Maggiore from *A Farewell to Arms* touched me because, twenty-five years after my first sight of it, the spellbinding Isola Bella in the middle of that lake still inhabits my dreams.

The writers in *Italy in Mind* celebrate, analyze, interpret, and even chide Italy and her people. But Italy, that "Circe in silken landscapes," eludes—and ultimately seduces—both her admirers and her critics. E. M. Forster wrote, "The traveler who has gone to Italy to study the tactile values of Giotto, or the corruption of the Papacy, may return remembering nothing but the blue sky and the men and women who live under it."

Italy in Mind

HOMER BIGART

(1907–1991)

Homer Bigart was one of a remarkable corps of journalists who followed the Allied Army through Italy during World War II. His stories brought the war home to Americans with a startling immediacy and power. Bigart for the Herald Tribune and his colleagues, including John Hersey for Time and Walter Bernstein for Yank, filed stories from the front that established a standard for war reporting.

Bigart started at the Herald Tribune as a copyboy and by 1933 he was a reporter. He was assigned to Europe as a correspondent in 1942 and moved to Asia in 1944. When the Korean War broke out, he covered it, again for the Tribune. After more than twenty years with the Tribune, Bigart moved to The New York Times, reporting on the Middle East, the Eichmann trial, and the war in Vietnam. His writings were collected posthumously in Forward Positions: The War Correspondence of Homer Bigart.

Bigart wrote this story about the devastation of the town of Cassino, southeast of Rome, on May 20, 1944.

Cassino, Once Thriving, Is Turned Into a Scene of Unrelieved Grimness

NEW YORK HERALD TRIBUNE, May 20, 1944

With the 8th Army in Cassino, Italy, May 19.—Cassino is a bleak, gray, smoking ruin, which, with a little sulphur added, would be more grim than a Calvinist conception of hell.

The city, when we entered it at 12:30 P.M., was silent. For the first time since January no shells crumped down amid the skeleton walls of the few score buildings still erect.

I have seen all the devastated towns on the road to Rome—Capua, Mignano, San Pietro, San Vittore and Cervaro. But not even ghostly San Pietro compares with the utter ruin of this key citadel of the Gustav line.

This once prosperous district center of 15,000, roughly midway between Naples and Rome, is a phantom place of windowless shops and crumbled hotels. Not one Italian crawled from the ruins to cheer the British troops pressing onward for the battle against the Adolf Hitler line. Even in San Pietro part of the population had remained, but here in Cassino none could have endured the four hellish months of siege. The few safe shelters—shallow tunnels and caves along the bleak chalk slopes of Monte Cassino—were exclusively for the young fanatics of the 1st Parachute Division.

Kenneth L. Dixon, of The Associated Press; George Silk, a "Life" photographer; and I were the first reporters to enter the western part of the town, where German paratroopers threw back the American 34th Division in the mid-winter offensive and stalled the New Zealanders in the March assault.

Yesterday two British reporters approaching the abandoned German defenses along Highway No. 6 were killed by mines when they stepped off the road to avoid a sudden spate of enemy mortaring. Today we were lucky—not one shell landed within Cassino during our three hours in the town.

The uncanny stillness, broken only by the rumble of bulldozers wrestling with drifted rubble, intensified rather than lightened the uncompromising grimness of the scene. From the desolate cathedral on the southern outskirts of Cassino we looked across stagnant pools of water to where the ruined shops and houses rose tier on tier against the steep bare slopes of Abbey Hill. The terraced olive orchards rising almost to the monastery were reduced to successive levels of blackened stumps. Not one flower, not one blade of grass, lived in the gardens of the town.

The Germans had diverted the Rapido River, blasting the levee above Cassino so that a considerable stream flowed between the cathedral and the central square, flooding the gutted buildings on the edge of the town and swamping the fields in front of the Hotels Continental and de Rosa, the outposts of their line.

Twisted trees, defoliated by the fragments and concussion of thousands of bombs and shells, reached dead limbs out of pools covered with greenish slime. Across the swamp the scene was solid gray—the gray honeycomb of ruins, then the gray slope of Monte Cassino merging imperceptibly with the steely sky. Only the jagged black outline of the abbey wall, topping the crest 1,300 feet above Cassino, showed where sky and horizon met.

British sappers had thrown a road across the bog. Before crossing we looked inside the cathedral crypt, which served as a command post and first-aid station for the advance spearhead of the three Allied assaults. First, the 100th Battalion of Hawaiians had quartered its wounded there during the opening days of the siege. Then the chapel was intact, but soon enemy guns were reducing it bit by bit. Burial vaults, high up in the walls of the nave, were ripped open. Skeletons disturbed after centuries had rolled down on the startled troops.

After the Hawaiians departed the New Zealanders took over, remaining through the bloody futility of the March assault. When the British forces took over late in March there was nothing left except the underground vaults where fresher corpses lay. The British endured a month of ghastly stench, hanging sticky paper from the walls to arrest the spring invasion of flies. From this loathsome dungeon no one dared move during daylight hours, for all approaches were swept by machine-gun fire from the Hotel Continental across the bog.

Few tourists will remember the Continental, a three-story, limestone building of perhaps thirty rooms. Baedeker ignores it. But it was the only hotel in town that had a guest.

The guest squatted black and ugly in the vaulted lobby. Ever since Feb. 3, when the Americans penetrated the heart of Cassino, this Mark IV tank had slept there, rousing at intervals to poke its nose into the street and fire at the crypt or the buildings in the center of the town.

One American patrol got inside the hotel, starting room by room to mop up the Germans before a counter-attack set them back. They claimed the destruction of the tank, but it looked quite formidable today when viewed from a four-foot pile of rubble at the massive lobby entrance. Its career ended definitely on March 15, when waves of Allied bombers threw great drifts of debris against the hotel wall, imprisoning the tank until the British closed in on the last German strong points early yesterday.

Sixty yards up Via Casilina in the direction of Rome was the Hotel de Rosa, another enemy stronghold somewhat less badly smashed than the Continental. Rooms along the rear wall were bulwarked with sandbags, and in front of the side entrance were heaps of discarded clothing and a battered German bazooka.

That was the last building on Highway 6, but across the fields and abreast of the hotel were a half dozen stone houses that seemed to have escaped direct hits during the great air raid, although their walls were punctured by shelling. Elsewhere the Air Force had done a truly remarkable job of flat-lining Cassino.

There was a stench of death near the smoldering rubble of the Hotel Continental, but we saw only one German corpse, which lay near a steel pillbox on the western edge of the town.

The pillbox was embedded on the left side of the road where it curved northward along the slope of Hangman's Hill. It protruded only a foot above the curb and was so well camouflaged with rocks that it looked like a heap of crushed stones left by a road-repair gang. Its gun had been removed. Through a slit the Germans had an excellent view of the bare flats across which Allied troops must move to enter Cassino from the east.

Half a mile from the town, toward Rome, were two more German fortresses—on the left of the road, the colossal remains of an ancient amphitheater used by the Germans as a tank park, and opposite the ducal palace a square ruin of considerable dimensions with stone walls three feet thick. Here the Germans had their medical station and a storeroom filled with mortar ammunition.

Except for the Mark IV tanks and a portable pillbox abandoned near the Hotel de Rosa the Germans had left very little equipment of importance. The portable pillbox, mounted on heavy wooden wheels, was designed for a mortar, being opened at the top. Its walls were steel, three inches thick.

All sidestreets leading from the Via Casalina were posted with warnings of mines and booby traps, but a British captain commanding a company of sappers told us that surprisingly few mines were found. However, a considerable part of the town was still unexplored, though by mid-afternoon sappers had cleared a path up the slope through the barbed wire and mine-fields reaching Castle Hill, a barrier that three great assaults had failed to storm.

Behind Castle Hill is a shallow vale between the ruined castle and Monastery Hill where the Japanese-American battalion had been isolated for nine days while American tank destroyers tried vainly to reduce the thick citadel built in the Hohenstauffen era.

After the Americans withdrew, bombers completed the destruction of the castle, but even then its ruins continued to harbor German machine gunners. Across the vale high up on the slope of Monastery Hill was the celebrated Yellow House, a large stone mansion from which enemy automatic fire took a fearful toll among the attackers trying to advance over the boulder-strewn pass below.

Neither the castle nor the Yellow House were ever stormed. When the British and Poles closed their trap around the town and monastery two days ago, most of the defenders had vanished.

Fewer than 150 prisoners were taken in Cassino. Many came down the road from the abbey when the Poles approached, preferring to surrender to the British.

Thus ended the bitterest battle of the Italian campaign. In today's quiet, a party of New Zealand tankers returned to Cassino and found the bodies of three comrades killed in the armored thrust following the March 15 air raid. The lead tank halted by drifted rubble was easy prey for German guns.

The New Zealanders dug three graves beside the road, while swallows came back to a town forever dead.

HAROLD BRODKEY
(1930–1996)

Italy provides parentheses to Harold Brodkey's literary life. In 1958, as a young writer with an acclaimed short story collection, First Love and Other Stories, *he won the Prix de Rome. In 1992, near the end of his career, he went to Venice at the invitation of the Consorzio Venezia Nuova, a group charged with saving the city's heritage. Under their patronage he wrote his last novel,* Profane Friendship, *published in 1994 after his announcement that he had AIDS. In the years between, Brodkey's writing production was episodic; he worked for almost thirty-two years on his novel* The Runaway Soul, *finally published in 1991. His short stories are collected in* Stories in an Almost Classical Mode. *At the time of his death, literary critics were divided about Brodkey's talent. Though some have found his work self-indulgent and self-promotional, others consider him a genius: Harold Bloom called him "an American Proust," and said he was one of the best American writers since Faulkner.*

Set in Venice, Profane Friendship *is the story of a homosexual love affair. In the book's epilogue Brodkey wrote, "I did not dare attempt a serious representation of Venice but tried only to hint at only a small experience of love in this setting, in the marvelous water-shine and amoral sunlight of this place that is so dear to me. . . . I drew on the city's centuries old indulgence in the profane and its invention of secular grace."*

from PROFANE FRIENDSHIP

The airplane's course from Rome to Venice—a long crosswise swirl and then a spike going north with a small half-circle at the end—went from side to side of the peninsula from the Tyrrhenian to the Adriatic and up half the length of the boot of Italy past Ravenna and Ferrara to the foot of the Alps.

At one point, the plane banking over the Adriatic in clear air was suspended above the dimpling and restless glare of the sea, one sun-washed section of which was a dancing, unpictorial, pallidly gold mosaic, unimaginably far below.

All in all, the ancient ages and the Gothic moment and the *Rinascimento,* all the historical past, whispered briefly, foreshortened and terrifying below—the stone monuments and deaths—a moment of flight time here, a few seconds there—in the plane's raven-like shadow. The flight lasted an hour, actually sixty-three minutes. It represented a new Italian meaning of eagles and gods, *dei ex machinis* and angels-turned-demons spilled from the realized City of God and become air travellers in the wan hubris of vacationing or on business jaunts. Or returning to their childhoods.

My Italy now is a tangle of flight times, suburbs, superimposed cultures, a country caught up in affluent hysteria, modern but hoping that the modern was something that could be played at.

But the modern moment is unforgiving, no matter whether it is also unforgiveable.

When the plane landed, the old-fashioned clock tick before quartz, or even medieval time animated by brute noise and church bells, seemed for a moment to have been restored and to

rule still over footsteps and travellers and my life. We had returned to the other story, the other story still existed—or might
resume—at any moment. But I realized soon that here, too, even
on earth, on dry land, time was modern.

On the motorboat I hired to bring me into Venice, where I
had lived for a large part of my childhood and then again in ado-
lescence, the heavyset boatman, the water chauffeur—dressed
like Humphrey Bogart in *The African Queen*—opened up the
engine, opened the throttle when we came near the mouth of
the airport inlet, and the bow lifted; and we went skidding and
sliding thumpingly across the gray water of the Lagoon in the
lane set out by new channel markers. And apartment complexes,
factories, smokestacks, bridges, and the chemical pall of terra
firma were dimly visible in the distance all around the shore of
this part of the Lagoon in the gray light. A rainy, clouded afternoon with motionless, shroud-like light, weighted as if by rain.

So, the story here too was of a new order, much as I would
have liked to be comfortably held by the old description.

The motionless almost-stillness of the gray light is an illusion.
One knows the light is unstill, more unstill than the boat or
plane, more unseeably unstill than the mind which broodingly
ticks or sput-sputs and glides and slimly speeds and flatters itself
that the light of thought is swifter and steadier than light itself.
To be honest, one's eyes, not as young as they had been, do see
the raindrop-clouded light as a haze of grayly luminous motions, see this while my body is shaken by the mechanically solid
jazz of the motorboat engine and while I hear the not entirely
muffled noises of other engines in other boats not far off from
us in these channels.

And the whisking movements of the eyelids, and the shift of
images on the retina and in the mind, are part of the web of
restlessness in which one approaches Venice, part of the variable
and moist and tickling instantaneities of dimmed and jostling
rhythms and emotions . . . Here is the self and the hovering moment; here is the trembling, nervous, seemingly near motion-
lessness of the surface of the water; here is the rustling bow-wave

and wake; here they are in subduedly echoing canals in Murano; then here is the Lagoon again, Venice ahead obscured; here is *San Michele* on the left pretending that the dead are silent and are not numberless; here is the gouging and choppy passage of the white motorboat over gray fluidities, the lighted grayish rain-teased air holding a glow as of a decomposing moon, and I am enveloped in flitters of memory which I resist of the canals in Venice itself, the wrinkled water in the *rio* behind our house, the secret hushes and whispers there, time's indescribable motion on a Venetian afternoon. I was a child here. And here is my history of love. I see eternity-in-reverse now, welling up as reality, a reality which is particularly Venetian and which is mine, no part of which is eternal, my Venetian reality in a modern moment.

It is a sense of time and of my own life on which my mind is sailing so wildly, time emerging from *the direction* of my father and moving in the direction of my death and bearing and containing my life.

The day brightens infinitesimally, and here is the *Sacca della Misericordia,* in which at once the motorboat slows and the bow comes down. To the left, quite high, are statues in the air, on the roof on top of the delicately subsiding fabric of the *Gesuiti,* stone versions of angels riding in wonderful absurdity and suggestive of belief in the gray-blue air—blue because it is brightening somewhat, only a little, but somewhat. In the damp air, in the pause in the rain, buildings here rise on either side in pink and worn rosy walls and terraces forming abrupt, closed-in, yet somehow grand perspectives. Proud Venice. When I was adolescent I woke sensually each morning nearly always as an experience of falling into this world. In the narrow *Rio Noale,* the wind kept out and light obscured, the boat putt-putts in the shadow. At the end of the long open-roofed shadowed tunnel of this *rio* is a half-strongly lit, horizontal-but-as-if-tilted slab of wavery water in the Grand Canal, into which after a moment or two of heartbeat we ride. Which is to say, into the wider view we come.

And the motorboat slues and heaves in the bright, sharp chop

of the *Canalazzo,* in a sudden unfurling of a broad reality of
gray-lit water and tilted palaces. Really, it is like a gathered
thought, the scene, half-worded, incompletely visible, greedy
toward reality, to hold it, and full of a will to display itself, and
beautiful.

The boatman let me off at *Sant' Ortellia.* The porter sent
from the palazzo where I will stay waits with a two-wheeled
hauler where he stows my suitcase and my briefcase and my
notebook-computer. I hurried ahead of him.

Now I move into the narrow shadow of the *calle* and I come
at once into the shade of a number of fragments of memory,
and then after a hundred yards or so to a narrow canal, the *Rio
Piotin,* with water too low for the motorboat and with thin
sheaves of somewhat brightish, somewhat yellowish light visible
here and there among the walls. On the heavy, tossing silk of the
unclean water, seabirds, white, and black-headed, beaked, float:
small, living gondolas. Jiggling necklaces of light move on the
damp lower walls of the palazzi. An ocean has been funnelled
into greenish mirrors among walls softly and narrowly lit like
this. In this city much of the direction of my life was established.

In the cold shadow where I stand, I grin inwardly and move
over the high-backed curve or stone curl of a *ponte storto*—distorted bridge—and I come to the *Campo Marinention.* (I am
giving it a fictional name.) The old, many-windowed, double-
loggia'd palazzo, handsomely bent and cleverly restored and so
gently conceited and airy, bears the Venetian imprint, is an expression of the Venetian theme of secular grace. It has two trees
in front of it, leaves fluttering in the wind, and a Renaissance
wellhead; and part of the façade and the center of the *campo* is
touched by a spread of clear light.

I gaze at the palazzo façade in the light. I move toward the
light, and my heart shifts its weight when I pass into it, into the
clear light—I feel myself in Venice to be at home in the amoral
grandiloquence of the light.

I have come to Venice to write a little book . . . And it will be
about these things.

JOSEPH BRODSKY
(1940–1996)

Joseph Brodsky once said, "I am the happiest combination you can think of. I am a Russian poet, an English essayist, and an American citizen." Brodsky was born in Russia and was forced to emigrate in 1972. He became poet-in-residence at the University of Michigan and an American citizen in 1977. On his first university break he fulfilled his lifelong desire to go to Italy. "I used my first university salary to enact the better part of that dream and bought a round-trip ticket, Detroit-Milano-Detroit," he wrote. "The plane was jammed with Italians employed by Ford and Chrysler and going home for Christmas. When the duty-free opened mid-flight, all of them rushed to the plane's rear, and for a moment I had a vision of a good old 707, flying over the Atlantic, crucifix-like: wings outstretched, tail down." Brodsky's love affair with Italy began with that trip and he traveled there as often as possible—especially in winter—to write or translate. Italy became one of the central themes of his work.

Brodsky wrote in both English and Russian and translated his own poems into English. He was best known for his books A Part of Speech *(which includes the poem "December in Florence"),* Less Than One, To Urania, *and* Watermark, *a prose account of his passion for Venice. He won the Nobel Prize for literature in 1987 and was appointed United States Poet Laureate in 1991. Brodsky died in New York and was buried in Venice.*

December in Florence
from A PART OF SPEECH

"*He has not returned to his old Florence, even after*
having died . . ."
—ANNA AKHMATOVA

I

The doors take in air, exhale steam; you, however, won't
be back to the shallowed Arno where, like a new kind
of quadruped, idle couples follow the river bend.
Doors bang, beasts hit the slabs. Indeed,
the atmosphere of this city retains a bit
of the dark forest. It
is a beautiful city where at certain age
one simply raises the collar to disengage
from passing humans and dulls the gaze.

II

Sunk in raw twilight, the pupil blinks but gulps
the memory-numbing pills of opaque streetlamps.
Yards off from where the Signoria looms,
the doorway, centuries later, suggests the best
cause of expulsion: one can't exist
by a volcano and show no fist,

though it won't unclench when its owner dies.
For death is always a second Florence in terms of size
and its architecture of Paradise.

III

Cats check at noon under benches to see if the shadows are
black, while the Old Bridge (new after repair),
where Cellini is peering at the hills' blue glare,
buzzes with heavy trading in a bric-a-brac.
Flotsam is combed by the arching brick.
And the passing beauty's loose golden lock,
as she rummages through the hawkers' herd,
flares up suddenly under the arcade
like an angelic vestige in the kingdom of the dark-haired.

IV

A man gets reduced to pen's rustle on paper, to
wedges, ringlets of letters, and also, due
to the slippery surface, to commas and full stops. True,
often, in some common word, the unwitting pen
strays into drawing—while tackling an
"M"—some eyebrows: ink is more honest than
blood. And a face, with moist words inside
out to dry what has just been said,
smirks like the crumpled paper absorbed by shade.

V

Quays resemble stalled trains. The damp
yellow palazzi are sunk in the earth waist-down.
A shape in an overcoat braves the dank
mouth of a gateway, mounts the decrepit, flat,
worn-out molars toward their red, inflamed
palate with its sure-as-fate

number 16. Voiceless, instilling fright,
a little bell in the end prompts a rasping "Wait!"
Two old crones let you in, each looks like the figure 8.

VI

In a dusty café, in the shade of your cap,
eyes pick out frescoes, nymphs, cupids on their way up.
In a cage, making up for the sour terza-rima crop,
a seedy goldfinch juggles his sharp cadenza.
A chance ray of sunlight splattering the palazzo
and the sacristy where lies Lorenzo
pierces thick blinds and titillates the veinous
filthy marble, tubs of snow-white verbena;
and the bird's ablaze within his wire Ravenna.

VII

Taking in air, exhaling steam, the doors
slam shut in Florence. One or two lives one yearns
for (which is up to that faith of yours)—
some night in the first one you learn that love
doesn't move the stars (or the moon) enough.
For it divides things in two, in half.
Like the cash in your dreams. Like your idle fears
of dying. If love were to shift the gears
of the southern stars, they'd run to their virgin spheres.

VIII

The stone nest resounds with a piercing squeal
of brakes. Intersections scare your skull
like crossed bones. In the low December sky
the gigantic egg laid there by Brunelleschi
jerks a tear from an eye experienced in the blessed
domes. A traffic policeman briskly

throws his hand in the air like a letter X.
Loudspeakers bark about rising tax.
Oh, the obstinate leaving that "living" masks!

IX

There are cities one won't see again. The sun
throws its gold at their frozen windows. But all the same
there is no entry, no proper sum.
There are always six bridges spanning the sluggish river.
There are places where lips touched lips for the first time ever,
or pen pressed paper with real fervor.
There are arcades, colonnades, iron idols that blur your lens.
There are streetcar's multitudes, jostling, dense,
speak in the tongue of a man who's departed thence.

1976 / Translated by the author

ELIZABETH BARRETT BROWNING

(1806–1861)

Italy was Elizabeth Barrett and Robert Browning's refuge. Her overprotective family opposed their marriage and the couple eloped, eventually setting up their household in Florence. Their home was immortalized in her work "Casa Guidi Windows." Although Casa Guidi remained their base for fifteen years, they traveled constantly. Elizabeth became involved in Italian politics and championed Italian nationalism. Political themes crept into her work, which critics found increasingly "unwomanly." Saddened by the death of the Italian leader Cavour, she died and was buried in the Protestant Cemetery in Florence. Her final work Last Poems, *edited by her husband, was published in 1862.*

Although Elizabeth Barrett Browning produced a great deal of poetry in Italy, including "Aurora Leigh" and "Poems Before Congress," she is still best known for "Sonnets from the Portuguese," written during her courtship.

The following letter was written in 1851 by Elizabeth Barrett Browning to her friend Mrs. Ogilvy and details the exigencies of her travels in northern Italy—with her husband, baby, and servants in tow.

Letter 8

PARIS. JULY 2. [1851]

My dear friend, if indignation at my silence has not turned away your kind thoughts from me altogether, you, yet, will not have been thinking certainly that I should write (at last) to you from Paris. Listen to the explanation of the silence, & understand how it was not an ungrateful or unfeeling one. Both your letters were most welcome, of course, . . (& we made use of your information & carried the ms.s. in a pocket of Murray, side by side with the map) but I did not answer the first, intending to be in time with a letter to meet you in London, . . and when the second came, we were in such a confusion of plan, that I could not tell you where to write back to me, & waited & waited till I could. Dear bewitching Venice, which charmed me to the last, agreed very ill with Robert & worse with Wilson. He lay awake night after night, suffering nervous pains in the face & head,— and she could eat nothing without agonies of indigestion, & grew so thin & looked so ill & haggard that it would have been homicide to have kept her there. She says now that if she had stayed a month longer she should have died. Venice is as bilious as it is beautiful. Also our rooms proved, as I feared they would, very oppressive when the heat set in—not tenable by any manner of means. Yet I was savage enough to grow fatter & fatter while we remained & others were perishing—the place agreed with me in body & soul. More's the pity—for I had to lean down an immense height in order to sympathize with Robert,

& be glad when we went away. And, do you know, the first day at Padua restored everybody—Robert began to sleep again, & Wilson to eat, . . . while Wiedeman & I continued to sleep & eat . . . and so there was nothing more to be complained of . . . *except leaving Venice.*

After you went away, we found out that Murray was right about the gondolas & that the universal charge (apart from imposition) is, a swanziger the first hour, & half a swanziger for every hour after. So we "swam in gondolas" to our heart's content—yes, and we went to the Lido, and we went to Chioggia (and we were kept out till two in the morning & frightened Wilson) and we went a second time to the opera, & twice to the play, and twice, besides, to the Malibran day-theatre—and, once, I teazed Robert into taking Wiedeman, (as we paid eight pence for our whole box, & the performance was over at eight oclock) and we repented it afterwards, both of us. The play turned out to be an heroic melodrama, in verse, in five acts, tremendously tedious to us all—but I assure you it was only in the fifth that Wiedeman gave signs of being a little tired, by putting up his small heels on the edge of the box & singing his favorite song about "Papa & Mama" a thought too loud. What pleased him most was the music, the drawing up & down of the curtain, & the clapping of hands— He shouted out "Heigh" to the audience, & clapped his own hands to show how they were to do it again. But he didn't much like the putting into chains of Odolinda's father, . . (was on the point of a roaring cry after some excruciating sensibility on the part of the prisoner—) and Robert said rightly that it was quite wrong to expose a young child to the shows of grief, before he could possibly discern the meaning of the imitation of Art. So, I wont take him to see Mad<u>lle</u> Rachel—you need not apprehend it.

Well—we left Venice, . . Wilson & the gods crying out . . on a friday; the natural consequence of which was a series of misfortunes. In the first place, we were too late for the train by five minutes & had to wait some three hours in the café before we could get on—secondly, we arrived at Padua just as St Anthony's feast had raised all the prices, & paid, for two poor bedrooms, *fourteen swanzigers,* after being asked sixteen! Had it been only for Giotto (noble as Giotto is at Padua) we should have proceeded to Vicenza, so scared were we by these prices, but we had both set our hearts on doing pilgrimage to Argua & seeing Petrarch's house, & I tenaciously clung to this purpose. So, leaving Wilson & Wiedeman at the inn, we set off in a caleche, . . and misfortune the third was, that our driver turned out a 'birbone' & set us down a mile from Argua in the burning sun, protesting the inability of his horses to drag us up the hill. As ignorant victims we groaned & resigned ourselves . . when lo, & behold, the road proved excellent, the mountain not more than a gentle slope, & the villagers lifted up their hands & eyes in astonishment at the iniquity of the Paduan. To reach the carriage again, I had to be set on a donkey, and, even so, I arrived as exhausted as a pilgrim might. But oh, how worth everything was the sight of Argua!— and Petrarch's tomb & his house . . & the little, little room, out of which the great soul issued into its spiritual sphere. We were both moved to tears . . even Robert was . . by the homely look of that little room. There are depths which a small pebble dropping down, gives notice of. It was very affecting—but then, you know, we have great organs of reverence & a taste for old slippers & such gear. Yet we never saw Titian's house at Venice. Titian is not Petrarch! And then you beat us to pieces in the ordinary energies of sight seeing, &, do you know, after you left us disconsolate at Venice, we fell into a sort of enchanted somnolence & went to see scarcely anything more.

To continue this confession, Juliet's tomb was not once enquired after . . it was through infidelity, that want of curiosity. But I am really afraid of your scorn, when I add that we passed through Brescia at night, & so tired that I was scarcely alive enough to enjoy the vision of the town glorified in the brightest moonlight possible, beautiful as the vision was. We took the diligence in sixteen hours from Verona to Milan, arriving there at nine I think, in the morning, & stopping at Brescia one hour at midnight . . Wiedeman in the highest spirits & the most soup-devouring mood. Think of that child! He has adapted himself to every circumstance, & satisfied even Robert's exigences with his perfection of goodness. Again, we were four & twenty hours in diligence from Strasbourg to Paris, the railroad intermissions being nought, (as the carriage was only placed on the rail) and he slept at night & laughed in the day while we were all groaning round. I was very afraid for him & rather for myself—but, without sacrificing the coupé, & indeed the security of places altogether, there was no way of escaping that last four & twenty hours of continuous fatigue. And now, though charmed with the Paris shops, he is apt to talk longingly of the "cavalli" and the "vapore"—he doesn't like to be done with travelling. How I wander. My story has broken its own back. We stayed two days at Milan, & I climbed to the topmost pinnacle of the cathedral. That cathedral is almost worthy of standing face to face, as it does, with the snow Alps: it impressed me deeply. Milan, indeed, delighted us altogether—the pictures, exquisite—and the famous Leonardo keeping its promises to the full. At Como, I was suffering rather from the cathedral, & was not fit the morning after our arrival, to go to Colico as we meant . . so we slept at Cadenalbia, opposite Bellaggio, & took a caleche from Menaggio to Porlezza, & a boat across that beautiful lake to Lugano. Slept at Lugano, & went by vettura next morning to Bellinzona. Slept there, &, leaving Wilson & Wiedeman to take care of themselves, spent the next day on the Lago maggiore. So we did a good deal, you see, in spite of some omissions,—and you will agree that we couldn't have done much more when I add that Robert had an overplus of exactly ten francs on his arrival at Lucerne. . . .

Oh—let me remember to tell you that we saw Mr. Reade two days before we left Venice. He asked after you earnestly. I never saw anybody looking so ill, or more ill, than when he took coffee with us in the piazza of St Mark the last evening. Venice had evidently seized him by the throat. He was on his way to the German water cure. Also, in the course of those last days, we met in the street M. de Goethe, & spent a good deal of time together in gondola & out of gondola. Few persons have interested me as much as he does.

ROBERT BROWNING
(1812–1889)

Robert Browning spent his marriage in his wife's shadow. Elizabeth Barrett Browning was more famous than her husband, whose poetry was considered obscure and obtuse. It was not until his wife's death in 1861 that Robert Browning was acknowledged as a poet in his own right. A century after his death, his reputation has superseded hers. Both husband and wife thrived in Italy, and Browning's volume of poetry Men and Women reflected his enchantment with its landscapes, cities, and history.

Browning's Italian idyll ended with his wife's death. He and their son returned to England, where he lived for his last twenty-eight years. He led a gregarious social life and a productive literary one. Browning died in Italy at the Palazzo Rezzonico in Venice, his painter son's home. Although he wished to be buried next to his wife in the Protestant Cemetery in Florence, Browning was interred in Westminster Abbey.

"Up at a Villa—Down in the City" is an example of Browning's characteristic use of dramatic monologue. One critic wrote that although Browning did not invent the dramatic monologue, he established it as a norm.

Up at a Villa—Down in the City

(As Distinguished By an Italian Person of Quality)

1

Had I but plenty of money, money enough and to spare,
The house for me, no doubt, were a house in the city square;
Ah, such a life, such a life, as one leads at the window there!

2

Something to see, by Bacchus, something to hear, at least!
There, the whole day long, one's life is a perfect feast;
While up at a villa one lives, I maintain it, no more than a beast.

3

Well now, look at our villa! stuck like the horn of a bull
Just on a mountain edge as bare as the creature's skull,
Save a mere shag of a bush with hardly a leaf to pull!
—I scratch my own, sometimes, to see if the hair's turned wool.

4

But the city, oh the city—the square with the houses! Why?
They are stone-faced, white as a curd, there's something to
     take the eye!
Houses in four straight lines, not a single front awry;
You watch who crosses and gossips, who saunters, who hurries by;

Green blinds, as a matter of course, to draw when the sun gets
    high;
And the shops with fanciful signs which are painted properly.

5

What of a villa? Though winter be over in March by rights,
'Tis May perhaps ere the snow shall have withered well off the
    heights:
You've the brown plowed land before, where the oxen steam
    and wheeze,
And the hills over-smoked behind by the faint gray olive trees.

6

Is it better in May, I ask you? You've summer all at once;
In a day he leaps complete with a few strong April suns.
'Mid the sharp short emerald wheat, scarce risen three fingers
    well,
The wild tulip, at end of its tube, blows out its great red bell
Like a thin clear bubble of blood, for the children to pick and
    sell.

7

Is it ever hot in the square? There's a fountain to spout and
    splash!
In the shade it sings and springs; in the shine such foam-bows
    flash
On the horses with curling fish-tails, that prance and paddle
    and pash
Round the lady atop in her conch—fifty gazers do not abash,
Though all that she wears is some weeds round her waist in a
    sort of sash.

8

All the year long at the villa, nothing to see though you linger,
Except yon cypress that points like death's lean lifted forefinger.

Some think fireflies pretty, when they mix i' the corn and
    mingle,
Or thrid the stinking hemp till the stalks of it seem a-tingle.
Late August or early September, the stunning cicala is shrill,
And the bees keep their tiresome whine round the resinous firs
    on the hill.
Enough of the seasons—I spare you the months of the fever
    and chill.

9

Ere you open your eyes in the city, the blessed church bells begin:
No sooner the bells leave off than the diligence rattles in:
You get the pick of the news, and it costs you never a pin.
By-and-by there's the traveling doctor gives pills, lets blood,
    draws teeth;
Or the Pulcinello-trumpet breaks up the market beneath.
At the post office such a scene-picture—the new play, piping hot!
And a notice how, only this morning, three liberal thieves were
    shot.
Above it, behold the Archbishop's most fatherly of rebukes,
And beneath, with his crown and his lion, some little new law
    of the Duke's!
Or a sonnet with flowery marge, to the Reverend Don So-
    and-so
Who is Dante, Boccaccio, Petrarca, Saint Jerome, and Cicero,
"And moreover," (the sonnet goes rhyming) "the skirts of
    Saint Paul has reached,
Having preached us those six Lent-lectures more unctuous
    than ever he preached."
Noon strikes—here sweeps the procession; our Lady borne
    smiling and smart
With a pink gauze gown all spangles, and seven swords stuck in
    her heart!
Bang-whang-whang goes the drum, *tootle-te-tootle* the fife;
No keeping one's haunches still: it's the greatest pleasure in
    life.

10

But bless you, it's dear—it's dear! fowls, wine, at double the
    rate.
They have clapped a new tax upon salt, and what oil pays
    passing the gate
It's a horror to think of. And so, the villa for me, not the city!
Beggars can scarcely be choosers: but still—ah, the pity, the
    pity!
Look, two and two go the priests, then the monks with cowls
    and sandals,
And the penitents dressed in white shirts, a-holding the yellow
    candles;
One, he carries a flag up straight, and another a cross with
    handles.
And the Duke's guard brings up the rear, for the better
    prevention of scandals:
Bang-whang-whang goes the drum, *tootle-te-tootle* the fife.
Oh, a day in the city square, there is no such pleasure in life!

GEORGE GORDON, LORD BYRON

(1788–1824)

George Gordon, Lord Byron, was another of England's exiles who found a haven in Italy. From 1816 to 1822 Byron lived in Italy, championed Italian nationalism, and often took part in its crusades. In 1819 he won the affections of a twenty-year-old married countess, Teresa Guiccioli of Ravenna. Teresa and the radical Italian separatist movement, the Carbonari, inspired Byron's passions and poetry. During this period he wrote the dramatic poems "Marino Faliero," "Scardanapalus," and "The Two Foscari." While there, Byron often lived with Percy Bysshe Shelley, his wife Mary Shelley, and her half-sister Claire, who became Byron's lover. Shelley and Byron spent many afternoons together sailing off the Ligurian coast, until Shelley's death in 1822.

Byron's enthusiasm for Italy waned with the end of the Carbonari movement. He took up a new cause, Greek liberation from Turkey, armed a brig, The Hercules, and set sail for Greece in 1823. Less than a year later he died of rheumatic fever. His heart was buried in Greece and his body was returned to England and buried in the family vault.

The following four stanzas are from Byron's poem "Childe Harold's Pilgrimage," published in 1811. The quotations in the opening lines of the third stanza are from Gibbon's history The Decline and Fall of the Roman Empire.

On Rome

from CHILDE HAROLD'S PILGRIMAGE,
CANTO IV

A ruin—yet what ruin! from its mass
Walls, palaces, half-cities, have been rear'd;
Yet oft the enormous skeleton ye pass,
And marvel where the spoil could have appear'd.
Hath it indeed been plunder'd, or but clear'd?
Alas! developed, opens the decay,
When the colossal fabric's form is near'd:
It will not bear the brightness of the day,
Which streams too much on all—years—man—have reft away.

But when the rising moon begins to climb
Its topmost arch, and gently pauses there;
When the stars twinkle through the loops of time,
And the low night-breeze waves along the air
The garland-forest, which the gray walls wear,
Like laurels on the bald first Cæsar's head;
When the light shines serene but doth not glare,
Then in this magic circle raise the dead:
Heroes have trod this spot—'tis on their dust ye tread.

'While stands the Coliseum, Rome shall stand;
'When falls the Coliseum, Rome shall fall;
'And when Rome falls—the World.'
    From our own land

Thus spake the pilgrims o'er this mighty wall
In Saxon times, which we are wont to call
Ancient; and these three mortal things are still
On their foundations, and unalter'd all;
Rome and her Ruin past Redemption's skill,
The World, the same wide den—of thieves, or what ye will.

Simple, erect, severe, austere, sublime—
Shrine of all saints and temple of all gods,
From Jove to Jesus—spared and blest by time;
Looking tranquillity, while falls or nods
Arch, empire, each thing round thee, and man plods
His way through thorns to ashes—glorious dome!
Shalt thou not last? Time's scythe and tyrants' rods
Shiver upon thee—sanctuary and home
Of art and piety—Pantheon!—pride of Rome!

To the Hon. Douglas Kinnaird

Venice, April 24th, 1819

. . . I have fallen in love, within the last month, with a Romagnuola Countess from Ravenna, the spouse of a year of Count Guiccioli, who is sixty—the girl twenty.

She is as fair as sunrise, and warm as noon, but she is young, and was not content with what she had done, unless it was to be turned to the advantage of the public, and so she made an éclat, which rather astonished even the Venetians, and electrified the Conversazioni of the Benzona, the Albrizzi, and the Michelli, and made her husband look embarrassed.

They have been gone back to Ravenna some time, but they

return in the winter. She is the queerest woman I ever met with, for in general they cost one something one way or other, whereas by an odd combination of circumstances, I have proved an expense to HER, which is not *my* custom, but an accident; however it don't matter.

She is a sort of Italian Caroline Lamb, except that she is much prettier, and not so savage. But she has the same red-hot head, the same noble disdain of public opinion, with the superstructure of all that Italy can add to such natural dispositions.

She is also of the Ravenna noblesse, educated in a convent, sacrificed to wealth, filial duty, and all that.

I am damnably in love, but they are gone, for many months— and nothing but hope keeps me alive *seriously*.

Yours ever, B.

JOSEPH CALDWELL

(1928–   )

*Like his protagonist Michael Ruane, Joseph Caldwell was born in the
American Midwest. Besides* The Uncle From Rome, *he is the author
of several other novels, including* In Such Dark Places, The Deer at
the River, *and* Under the Dog Star. *Caldwell won the Rome Prize
awarded by the American Academy of Arts and Letters and twice received a playwriting fellowship at Yale. He now lives in New York.*

In The Uncle From Rome *Caldwell's protagonist Michael Ruane
has come to Italy to recover. His ex-lover has died of AIDS, and opera
stardom in the United States has eluded him. He is in Naples as a comprimario, a singer of secondary roles, in* Tosca *at Naples' Teatro San
Carlo. As a favor, Ruane agrees to be the "uncle from Rome," an es-
teemed position at a Neapolitan wedding. Unexpectedly, his life takes a
dramatic turn worthy of an opera libretto.*

from THE UNCLE FROM ROME

Michael Ruane—Indianapolis born, Indianapolis bred—had
planned to climb Vesuvio that morning and look down into the
volcanic crater, but he was persuaded instead to go to a wedding
in the basilica of Santa Chiara and present himself as the "uncle
from Rome." Persuaded is perhaps too weak a word. Actually,
he was there by the near-royal dictate of Aganice Calefati, the
soprano in whose *Tosca* he would sing a minor role the week after next at Naples's Teatro San Carlo.

La Calefati had had no less than the stage director of the production phone Michael early the morning before and "beg"—a soprano's word for command—beg him to see her at the opera house in an hour. She would be having a costume fitting, and he'd find her in the costumer's atelier. Michael had other things he wanted to do, but he was a *comprimario*—a singer of secondary, even tertiary, roles in opera—and it wouldn't hurt to have a lead soprano, and one of Calefati's presumed ascendancy, in his debt.

Calefati, after asking his honest opinion about her costume and accepting somewhat skeptically his nods of approval, got down to business. Would he please, for her sake, and as a favor to her—which would excite no end of gratitude—go to a wedding as the family's "uncle from Rome"? It was, she explained, an old Neapolitan custom, not that much in favor anymore, but what it came down to was this: To impress one's friends and neighbors, one would ask—even pay—a distinguished-looking person, a man, to attend an important family function and be pointed out in tones of reverence and respect as the "uncle from Rome." That the family had connections to the capital and possibly to the Vatican would ensure a status obtainable in no other way. The family itself would pretend to shrug off the uncle's presence as nothing of note, but the guests would immediately intensify their participation in the event, convinced of attributes in themselves newly revealed, since they'd been invited along with the uncle from Rome. They would consider themselves wittier, taller, more profound; some would become outright giddy from the sudden ascent up the social ladder. Others would become insufferable snobs for the duration of the gathering.

The idea intrigued Michael. He was, after all, an actor as much as he was a singer, and he invariably reveled in any role that came his way. And to play an Italian, a Roman, *and* an uncle was an opportunity he couldn't expect to have tossed his way every week of the year. Then, too, he was especially eager these days to grab at identities other than his own. Being an uncle from Rome—like playing the other roles, the operatic characters he'd come to Naples to play—could be a welcome invitation to identity that might relieve the sense of absence and vacancy that pervaded his own psyche at the moment. He was more than usually receptive to possession; gladly would he assume another's attitudes, needs, and prerogatives, even if it was only for a few hours. Since he didn't particularly appreciate Michael Ruane these days, he might find at least temporary refuge from his confusion by cloaking himself in the robes of someone defined by circumstances other than those that had so recently altered his life, someone he could create and control within his imagination.

What gave him pause, however, was that in this instance he'd be dealing not with ordinary mortals but with Neapolitans, and to be honest, Neapolitans scared him. They were too unpredictable, too inscrutable. Several times during his student days in Rome he'd come to Naples for the usual release from responsibility and commandment, a needed exploration of the possible. More often than not, he'd return, a sated weariness murmuring along his bones. But there had been several experiences, none of which he was prepared to divulge to La Calefati, that had given him a certain unease as regards the Neapolitan disposition. Yet how could he tell the pleading, implacable soprano, herself *una figlia di Napoli*—a daughter of Naples—that he found Neapolitans too contradictory to allow for ordinary human transaction and exchange? To Michael, her fellow citizens could be completely open and friendly, but at the same time more closed and private than any people he'd ever known—accepting and welcoming, but ultimately tribal and exclusionary. They were a gentle people, but fierce as well, the one characteristic equal in intensity to the other. That they were cunning is well known, but they were also generous and genuinely caring. Joyful they could be, more joyful than most, but the melancholy, the sorrow, was always there, and for all their prayerful piety, they were completely and irremediably fatalistic. Even their sensual and sensuous lures were desperate yet, at the same time, indifferent. And all these contradictions, all these opposites, were kept in precarious balance by an energy not famous for its stability. Sudden shifts, inexplicable tilts of the scale, were forever possible, and the results could, to say the least, be unsettling.

The source of these native traits, of course, was geographical. There, spread out before all of Naples, serene and nourishing, was the bay, calm and peaceful, the waters themselves easy and yielding. And there on its eastern flank was a volcano. What else but contradiction in the extreme could be expected of people born within sight and sound of such primal and opposing forces? Here were older gods, and the Neapolitans perhaps were still made in their dual image, possessing a larger humanity that ranged beyond the usual restricting covenants and intimate redemptions.

That Michael should involve himself so closely with these people was daunting enough, but to claim a right to their respect, to pretend a social superiority, to *lie* to them, would be just plain stupid.

He wanted to tell Aganice—she'd asked him to call her that in anticipation of his acquiescence—that he was not a coward, but neither was he a fool (although there was sufficient evidence accumulated over his thirty-seven years to suggest that he was both), but he settled instead for listing his disqualifications for the part. One by one, Aganice knocked them down.

Michael said he wasn't Italian, to begin with. No, Aganice replied, but he was black Irish; he could pass without difficulty. And besides, she added, he'd lived and studied in Rome; his Italian was accurate and impeccable. Very *romano,* almost *toscano.* To that she swore, and Michael had to admit it was true. But he then protested that people would ask him questions about the family, questions he wouldn't be able to answer. No, Aganice told him, they wouldn't have that much of a chance to ask anything. All Michael had to do was attend the church service. Then, because he was from Rome, it could be assumed that he would have to hurry back.

The groom, Peppino, Calefati explained, was the son of a woman with whom she'd studied piano as a child, Assunta

Spacagna. The bride was Rosalia Attanese, and that was as much as Aganice could tell him about her. But why Signora Spacagna wanted to revive the old custom, she had no idea. It might have something to do with there being no father. He was dead, killed eight years ago in the 1980 earthquake. He had gone to Laviano, a village in the mountains, to search for a cousin thought to be trapped in the rubble. During the search, a wall of stones fell on him. Michael would be his long-lost baby brother, given at birth to a charity—which in turn had sent him to yet another charity, in Rome—because the family had no food. The story was too common to be questioned. If anyone should require further details, Michael had only to say they were too painful to be recalled.

Michael stated flatly that black Irish or no black Irish, Roman Italian or Tuscan Italian, he'd never be convincing. No one would believe him in a million years.

It was here that La Calefati got him.

"I have seen you in rehearsals. You are such a superb actor. I have sung in opera houses throughout Europe, in South America, even, and nowhere—*nowhere*—have I seen such acting. Your Spoletta, especially in Act Two, sends chills, I will not tell you where. The way you've conceived the part, the way you act it, with that complete conviction, I am almost more repulsed by you than by Scarpia."

Michael had no choice but to accept this as true. He was, he knew, becoming an exceptional *comprimario*. He'd worked hard at it, and he had ambitions. He was a singing actor, an acting singer, in the great tradition, and whatever doubts and exasperations he may have concerning his life, his career, for the moment, wasn't one of them. He was a valued New York City Opera *comprimario*—and rumors had reached him that spies from the Met had seen his Basilio in *Figaro* and his Goro in *Butterfly*. No doubt he'd hear from them soon and be invited to make the short stroll across the Lincoln Center Plaza from the State Theater to the Met, a journey he had rehearsed in his mind with unflagging fidelity.

Michael's final objection to Calefati's proposal was—and even he had to admit it was rather weak—that he didn't really look the part. He was a bit too young, of only medium height, with no authoritative gray in his hair, and if one looked closely, there were freckles on his nose. He was not, in effect, distinguished-looking enough.

La Calefati took care of that. "Ah, Michele," she said, "how can you say those things? I look at you and I begin to see another Toscanini. Taller, of course. Younger than in most pictures that come down to us these days. Be honest. You are a very handsome man. And if I didn't have so many distractions, I might show a little more interest myself." With that, she chucked him under the chin, puckered her lips, and made a kissing sound.

Michael could hardly voice the real reasons for his reluctance—his fears and his susceptibilities—and so he agreed to do all that she asked, but only as a favor to her, and please, no money. She took his head in both hands, kissed both cheeks, then, to complete her condescension, gave the left one a light slap. But when, as he was leaving, she said, *"Grazie, caro Michele,"* it was obvious that she really meant it.

WHEN Michael got to Santa Chiara, the wedding party was nowhere to be seen, and nothing was as he'd expected it to be. Since this was in Naples, and in a basilica, no less, he'd prepared himself for an extravagant exaggeration of the Italian weddings he'd seen at Our Lady of Pompeii in Indianapolis when he was a boy. There would be three to six bridesmaids, with the groom attended by the equivalent of, if not a brigade, at least a hockey team. The bridesmaids would wear enough tulle to scrim an entire *Ring* cycle, and the groom's crew would be costumed in cutaways with striped pants, yet manage to look confident no matter how foolish they might feel.

A soprano would sing *"Ave Maria"* at the Offertory and *"Panis Angelicus"* at Communion. The church would be filled, with an overflow in the choir loft. The littlest children, *i bambini,* would test to see how far they could go in disobedience and sacrilege, chasing each other into forbidden side altars, playing hide-and-seek behind statues and candle racks. Gossip would occupy the wives, indulgence the husbands, who didn't exactly like to be seen at what was, after all, a women's affair. The young people, *la gioventù,* friends and cousins of the bride and groom, would be, by turns, grave and silly, more nervous in their way than the couple themselves.

Flowers and candles and perfume would compete as to which would be responsible for the imminent asphyxiation of everyone present. The colors of the women's dresses would suggest a garden that one would never want to tame—chaotic, tipsy on its own nectars, indifferent to its own gaudy excess. Everything would be bright and warmly glowing, excited and content, expectant and resigned. Then the organ would sound out, descending, rising in majesty, announcing the first step of the first timorous bridesmaid as she would begin the long, inexorable approach to the altar.

Michael had walked halfway down a side aisle of Santa Chiara, past the columned arches that opened onto the small side chapels, then stopped. He'd obviously come at the wrong time. Right in front of him was a small congregation of elderly and, it seemed, underfed women, scattered among a dozen pews that faced a chapel on his right. They were droning in Italian the *Sanctus* of the Mass being celebrated by a gnome of a priest, who, without waiting for them to finish, had gone on to the words of the Consecration.

Ahead of him, far down at the end of the nave, he could see the first five or six pews randomly occupied by worshipers bundled up against the chill that had obviously been given sanctuary in the church—as if the winter cold, now that it was March, was a threatened species and Santa Chiara herself had made its preservation her very own cause. There were two sprays of white flowers near the main altar. Gardenias? He couldn't tell. Candles had been lit, but no more than for the least celebratory

Mass of a common Sunday. The only indication that something
unusual might possibly take place was the red plush kneeler
placed in front of the altar and the two spindly gilded chairs
placed a few feet behind. Also, as he'd entered, he'd seen two
workmen unrolling a red carpet that would have to go all the
way from the main portal to the steps of the altar. The rug, he
was certain, could never make it. The basilica was almost a city
block long. Surely it would run out a little past halfway. But no,
its final curl now lapped the sanctuary step, and the two workmen, to put an immediate stop to such familiar behavior, were
busy tamping it down onto the aisle stones.

Michael wondered if he should wait at the side chapel until
after the Consecration of the Mass now in progress or if he
should just skirt the worshipers and continue on to the front
pew, where, he'd been instructed, he'd find a spare but handsome woman with gray-streaked black hair, wearing a fur coat
with a white flower at the neck. He was to go to her, open his
arms, say, "Assunta! *Cara!*" embrace her, kiss her on both
cheeks, then allow her to pin a white flower similar to her own
on his lapel, indicating that as the uncle from Rome he was an
important part of the celebration.

Michael decided to move down the aisle and get the first part
of his act over with, but before he could make his way around
the pews facing the chapel, a bell rang as if to warn him to go
no farther. He reverently bowed his head as the host was raised,
then the chalice. The priest, his slightly lopsided head coming to
no more than a foot above the altar table, invited the assembled
to proclaim *"il mistero della fede,"* the mystery of faith. Not sure
which of the several possible prayers had been prescribed for this
particular day, Michael waited for someone else to say the first
word. The priest began.

"Annunziamo . . ." was enough. The others joined in. *". . . la
tua morte, Signore, proclaimiamo la tua risurrezione, nell' attesa della
tua venuta."* When we tell of your death, Lord, we proclaim
your resurrection, in expectation of your coming.

The reference to death and resurrection made Michael wonder
if now might be the time to say a prayer for his friend, his once-

upon-a-time lover, Damian, now three months dead. Michael thought he should at least try.

His first thought was a familiar one: Damian is dead, and I feel no sorrow, no loss; I have no pity, no tears. One of the women, better fed than the others, with a face like a brown moon, turned and glared at him as if she'd heard his admission and had been scandalized. She got up and, without genuflection, headed for the back of the church. Michael took her departure as something of a rebuke and did what he could to prove himself a minimally decent human being.

Down on one knee he went. He begged that Damian be given eternal rest, eternal love, eternal joy. Then he waited, his head bowed, his knee still poking against the stone beneath it. But his patience was prompted not by piety or even by the wish for some assurance that his petition had been heard. He was waiting to see what feelings his prayer might awaken not in the Almighty but in himself. He wanted to see what this nearness to Damian might do, what response he might have at this joining of the two of them—himself and Damian—in the intimate presence of the author of love, a spiritual coupling before the divine witness.

Nothing happened except that his knee began to hurt. He considered lowering the other knee to relieve the pressure, but he didn't want to move, as if some shift in posture might put him at a remove from the sensations that could, at this moment, be headed his way, not exactly a thunderbolt but at least a tightening in his chest, a gasp of breath, a twitch in his cheek, the coming of grief.

As others in bereavement ask for comfort and release, he had prayed instead for sorrow and for desolation. He begged to be allowed to feel again the aching loss of his friend, the loss he'd felt for four years, from the time of their separation. He asked that at least the sorrow he'd known then be returned to him now. Absurd as it seemed, he was suffering from the loss of loss. It was as if he'd never loved his friend, had never during all those four years desperately wanted him back.

Kneeling on the aisle stones, Michael thought he might pray

just one time more, but he knew it would be useless. Perhaps, like wisdom and fortitude, sorrow and grief were gifts of the Holy Spirit and not to be had just for the asking. Like the assurances of faith, the desolations of loss could be given or withheld according to the divine will. If emptiness was to be his burden, he must accept it and not complain.

A distant organ made a somewhat feeble foray into the reaches of the great Gothic church. The wedding had begun, and Michael had yet to present himself to his *cognata,* his sister-in-law, Signora Assunta Spacagna (born, Aganice had told him, Gallifuoco), and prepare himself for the uncertainties that lay ahead.

He turned to see the first bridesmaid place her slippered foot on the red carpet. Instead he saw what must be the bride herself, since she was striding forward on the arm of a man who seemed a little old to be her father. Where were the bridesmaids? He looked again toward the altar, expecting to see the waiting groom, his best man, and a respectable complement of ushers. To one side of the step leading up into the sanctuary stood a pale and fair-haired boy, or, to be more exact, a young man. He was wearing a double-breasted black jacket, its only button down near his waist, giving it a low-slung appearance and making it look outsized, as if he had yet to grow into it. A very small black bow tie seemed to be clipped not to his shirt collar but to his Adam's apple. There was a white flower in his lapel, and he stood looking straight ahead at a stone on the far wall.

Michael had seen him before, in the portico, talking to three small boys, one of whom had held a soccer ball. The boys, as far as Michael could make out from the dialect, had been asking him questions about the wedding, and he had been asking them questions about soccer. Michael had made it a point not to look too long at the young man; it would be distracting when he should be concentrating on other matters. But he did remember feeling sorry for the groom, who couldn't possibly equal, much less surpass, the beauty of this presumed usher or best man. The bride would, at the sight of him, repent her decision or at least realize at a very crucial moment that she was settling for decidedly inferior goods. It wasn't just the soft fair hair and the soft fair skin, nor was it his soft brown eyes or soft fair lips; it was the quiet way he had been talking to the younger boys. There had been a tender patience in his voice, and on his face an eager sweetness. Michael had quickly paid the tribute that is beauty's due, an amalgam of awe, envy, exhilaration, and lust—with a strong dash of covetousness thrown in—and continued on into the basilica.

But this was not one of the ushers. This was the groom. He was Peppino Spacagna, Michael's presumptive nephew. And there were no ushers, any more than there were any brides-maids. This was not what he'd expected.

Rosalia Attanese, the bride, was now almost halfway to the altar, the ceremony was about to begin, and the "uncle from Rome" had not yet made his appearance. But Michael waited another moment so he could look more closely at the bride. He was hoping she'd be very beautiful, dark and luminous, with, perhaps, a proud modesty. She would wear the near-sorrowful smile of the conqueror, reflective and anticipatory. Yet she would glow with consent; she would advance with stately grace to the man she was destined to raise from the dust with all her cherishing and all her sly intelligence. If Michael was to play a supporting role, he at least hoped for the main characters to be worthy of the artistry he was prepared to bring to his *comprimario* part. The groom was acceptable indeed, but the event in gen-eral, with the drab congregation, the dusty, mustard-colored walls, the ancient sarcophagi as the only offered decoration, re-quired an equally superb bride, an added assertion of the glories of the flesh to bring into perspective the supreme austerity of the surrounding stones.

Now Michael could see her, one arm looped into that of her father—or grandfather. Her bearing was stately yet easy. She was indeed beautiful, more beautiful than even he had required. She was indeed dark and luminous, with, no doubt about it, a proud modesty. Everything his imagination had demanded had been granted, and more besides. There was an impishness, suggested probably by the nose, which nature had turned up slightly just before it could become too long. And a sympathy, obvious from the way she was adjusting her pace to that of the elderly man at her side. It was as if she were leading him, helping him to a place where he might find, if not rejuvenation, at least rest and quiet. She was making no apologies for his infirmity. She was doing honorable service, and it was giving her a great and mischievous joy.

Only when Michael began his own swift stride toward the front pew did he recognize what the organist was playing. Surely it had been chosen at random, without thought, without knowledge. Maybe it had been there on the music stand, left behind by some master of the organ who'd forgotten to pack it up and take it with him. But then, it could be right after all. It could be absolutely right. It was Handel, which made it somewhat appropriate, and it was from an oratorio, another point in its favor. But the oratorio was *Judas Maccabeus*—a celebration of release from oppression—and the music was the great choral march "See the Conquering Hero Comes."

Before Michael had taken six more steps, he thought the music completely appropriate. It was being played for him, for Michael Ruane, to give him courage, to buttress his faltering determination, to summon up a dignity, a conviction, suitable to his role. For the moment, he must transcend the *comprimario;* he must be Rhadames, he must be Chenier, he must be Rodolfo and, come to think of it, Judas Maccabeus as well.

He presented himself to the woman in the front pew. In fulfillment of what La Calefati had said, she was wearing the fur coat, the white flower. "Assunta! *Cara!*" he cried in a stage whisper intended for everyone unto the tenth pew behind them. He embraced her, kissed her on both cheeks, then held her slightly away from himself, the better to drink in the sight of her, watering to full flower a kinship that had lain too long in the dust.

The woman looked at him, startled. Michael felt the first twinge of horror; it tweaked the right edge of his upper lip and was preparing to give instruction to his eyelids, whether they should widen in aghast awareness or close, never to open again.

He'd made a mistake. This was not Assunta Spacagna, not the mother of the groom, not the long-ago piano teacher of the about-to-be-acclaimed *diva,* Aganice Calefati.

And he was not the uncle from Rome. He was a known madman given to assaulting important personages at sacred functions. This was probably not the first time he'd done it; he'd been known to strike before, at funerals, at ground-breakings, at the blessing of the fleet. In Rome, the prison was Regina Coeli, Queen of Heaven. To what saint of Naples would he be thrown in sacrifice for this latest transgression? Michael then remembered the massive hilltop fortress dominating the city, Castel Sant'Elmo. He would be sacrificed before nightfall to the greater honor and glory of Sant'Elmo.

Just as Michael began to rehearse in his mind the part of Florestan in *Fidelio,* just as he was beginning to see himself emerge out of the dungeon dark, the woman began reaching toward him, either to wring his neck or to pluck out his eyes, or some other response appropriate to his criminal gesture.

"Caro! Zio! All the way from Rome! *Bravo! Grazie, Zio, grazie."* She, too, took care that her words reach at least a dozen pews back. The outstretched arms gathered him into the cool animal fur; his cheeks were to be kissed, not clawed. Then it was she who held him at a slight distance, not just to radiate gratitude but to acquaint herself as quickly as possible with this fraud she'd just embraced.

The organ, satisfied that the conquering hero had arrived, ceased its exhortations as both Assunta and Michael turned to watch the groom step out toward his bride. Michael saw mostly the back of Peppino's head, the light-brown hair reaching gently to his white collar, the drape of the jacket still loose even as it stretched along the wide shoulders underneath.

Peppino was kissing Rosalia's father on both cheeks, then accepting Rosalia's hand, offered by her father. He bent down, but before he touched his lips to the flesh of his bride, Michael was being introduced to the people in the pew behind him.

"Lo zio," Signora Spacagna was saying with an almost defiant satisfaction. *"Lo zio, da Roma."* The uncle, from Rome.

JOHN CIARDI

(1916–1985)

In his classic book How Does a Poem Mean? *poet and critic John Ciardi wrote, "Americans generally need to be taught in school how to experience both poetry and opera. In Milan, on the other hand, no one need go to school in order to learn how to experience an opera: The Milanese do not study opera, they* inhale *it." Ciardi approached poetry with wit and common sense. He decried the "analysis" of poetry and exhorted his readers to experience it, inhale it.*

Ciardi taught at both Harvard and Rutgers and was the poetry editor of the Saturday Review *during the 1950s. He translated Dante's* Inferno, Purgatorio, *and* Paradiso *into idiomatic English. "Poems from Italy" was included in Ciardi's* Selected Poems, *published in 1984, the year before his death. This collection of six short poems celebrates Italy's physical beauty and the lives of ordinary people—a Calabrian nonna, a child of the alleys, a man peeling an apple.*

Poems from Italy

I

Nona Domenica Garnaro sits in the sun
    on the step of her house in Calabria.
      There are seven men and four women in the village
    who call her *Mama*, and the orange trees

fountain their blooms down all the hill and valley.
No one can see more memory from this step

than Nona Domenica. When she folds her hands
in her lap they fall together
like two Christs fallen from a driftwood shrine.
All their weathers are twisted into them.
There is that art in them that will not be carved
but can only be waited for. These hands are not

sad nor happy nor tired nor strong. They are simply
complete. They lie still in her lap
and she sits waiting quietly in the sun
for what will happen, as for example, a petal
may blow down on the wind and lie across
both of her thumbs, and she look down at it.

II

One day I went to look at the Mediterranean
and I found myself on an infected hill.
The waves under the sky and the sky over the waves
perfected themselves in endless repetition,
but the hill stumbled and twitched. A desert ate
into its sea front and a gully cankered
its piney back, or what had been
its piney back before that eczema
of stumps and stones and landslides. At its top
like a trollop's hat knocked cockeyed in a brawl
there leaned a tattered strawwork of gray grasses
that fizzed and popped with a plague of grasshoppers.
The grass was salt-burned and seemed wiry enough
to cut the hand that pulled it. And at its roots,
under the leaping gas of the live grasshoppers,
I saw a paste of the dead. There were so many
I thought at first it was the clay-sand soil
from which the wiregrass grew. I could not see

any of the living fall from their leaping
but the dead lay under them, a plague they made
invisibly of themselves who had come to feed
where the grass ate them on an infected hill.

And I saw there was no practice in the sea.

III

A man-face gathered on the eyes of a child
        measures me from an alleyway. The child
        stirs, but the face has lost its motion:
        the face stares at the traffic and the child
        picks with one finger at a scab on his knee.
        Not looking at it. Not knowing it is there.

He stares at me. I am part of what he knows.
        I am the traffic forever in his eyes
        and damnation, the way all worlds go
        leaving him neither admission nor understanding,
        as, somewhere in a thicket like the mind,
        a gargoyle might stare down at running water.

IV

You would never believe to watch this man
        open his pocket knife to cut his cheese
        (his bread he tears with his hands)
        and lay it down precisely on a leaf
        and tip his bottle off against his mouth
        (which he wipes with the back of his hand)
        and lift the knife again to peel an apple
        so carefully from stem to bud it is all
        one red spiral, and toss it on a bush
        to see it against green and color of loam
        and slap the crumbs from his lap for the birds to have
        before he sleeps with his hat over his eyes

(for a pillow he joins his hands behind his head)

that all the guns and lances looked to him
    all the maps and marches centered here
    and all the charges climbed this same small hill

that it was always this man in this field
    through all of Europe and the island–South
    the kingdoms and their kings were told about.

V

What the Roman sun says to the Romans
    (a boy fishing the Tiber with a seine
    while two old men and a tourist watch from the bridge
    that leads to Castel Sant' Angelo, where once
    a cypress forest mourned across the roof
    for a faded emperor gone like his forest
    into the stoneworks)
                    what the Roman sun
    (a species of tumulus or burial mound
    as for example pyramids cairns barrows
    and similar monuments common to many cultures)
    says to the Romans (the present structure
    visible on the Tiber being simply the base)
    I have said to you in all the tongues of sleep.

VI

The mountains quiver like a low flame
    on the horizon. They flicker and reappear,
    flicker and reappear. Sometimes
    there are no mountains and sometimes
    they are always there.
                    Mountains
    have no need of being seen. They can outwait
    all but these repetitions of the air.

ELEANOR CLARK
(1913–1996)

In 1945, Eleanor Clark went to Italy on a creative writing grant. Living in a sixteenth-century fortress, her intentions to write fiction were diverted by Rome—its piazzas, fountains, statues, and people. She wrote her impressions in a series of sketches and essays that evolved into her book Rome and a Villa, *which was published in 1952. In her review in* The New York Times, *Katharine Anne Porter wrote, "The whole book is a distillation of a deep personal experience; it is autobiographical in the truest sense." Although Clark wrote other books and contributed articles to* The New Republic *and* Partisan Review, *she is best known for* Rome and a Villa. *Revised and reprinted in 1975, it was received as a minor classic. Anatole Broyard wrote of the new edition that it is "perhaps the finest book ever to be written about a city."*

Fountains

You walk close to your dreams. Sometimes it seems that these pulsing crowds, with their daily and yearly rhythms established so long ago none of it has to be decided any more, with their elbows and knees and souls and buttocks touching and rubbing and everybody most pleased and agreeable when it is like that, in a bus for instance, will in another minute all be naked, or will have fish tails or horses' behinds like the characters of the fountains. For the Anglo-Saxon mind, ruled by conscience and the romantic, rigid in its privacies, everything here is shocking—an endless revelation and immersion; this is the vocabulary of our sleep; and the key image is always water.

That is the great assault of Rome, and it is total and terrible. It is really strange that foreigners of the polite centuries always used to wax so romantic about the fountains of Rome, and the music supposed to represent them was such as any young girl could listen to. The truth is, they are extremely indecent, in various ways. Their number is indecent, much as the lives of the Caesars were; common reason expires here; it is of their nature too to make those lives quite ordinary, nothing surprises you beside them. Their settings are apt to be extravagant; they can have sprung up anywhere, be tacked anywhere on the sides of buildings or are themselves a whole house wall; and their details have the candid, smiling sadism of dreams. But the worst is the life around them, and their part in it. They are not only memory, or the living singleness of time, though they are that too and the city would have fallen apart under the weight of its past a long time ago without them; this is easy to see; you notice at once when there is a drought and the fountains become quiet and stale, or empty, how old everything begins to look. But there is another unity or community within every single moment to which they are essential, and that is where the real outrage comes.

The romantic, the idealist, the tender-minded of any vein dies a thousand deaths in these fountains; their every dolphin is his nemesis.

The very genius spent on them makes them shocking. They are not *objets d'art* held off from life and treated with respect as they would be anywhere else; there is a closeness, an imminence of touch around them that nothing in our life has except dreams and sex, whence the awful burden on those. They are always being drunk from and splashed in and sat on, everybody dips into them as into his own private memory and quite often they have all kinds of rubbish in their lovely basins, because although the street cleaners of Rome are many and hard-working they cannot be everywhere at once.

The churches likewise; it is all physical and close; God is not up in any Gothic shadows but to be touched and smelled and fondled, reached into up to the armpit. The Anglo-Saxon, hunting everywhere for French cathedrals, feels his mind threatened like a lump of sugar in a cup of tea.

The spaces are shocking. They are close, too, and give no warnings, so that suddenly the Pantheon or the huge volutes of Sant' Ignazio are crowding right over you; you are not allowed to stand off, it seems you are not allowed to admire at all; it is as though a giant mother were squashing you to her breast. Besides those freakish squares and the narrow streets around them, most vividly in the old quarters, Trastevere and all the part between the Corso and the Tiber, do not constitute an *outside* in our sense, but a great rich withinness, an interior, and running water is its open fire. Even a tourist can tell in a Roman street that he is in something and not outside of something as he would be in most cities. In Rome to go out is to go home.

There are no sidewalks in these sections. The walls rise from the cobbles as from lagoons, only people are out all along them, under the laundry which is a drastic exposure in itself, more than for any Kinsey or Gallup, and unless they are playing football they are most often mending something. That is one of three occupations you see anywhere in Europe that are no longer known in America: people walk, they carry, and they mend. Not only women; men are mending too, in thousands of dark bicycle and mattress shops and tiny individual foundries opening on to the same streets, and which may be the family's windowless kitchen and bedroom as well. What makes these streets Roman, and not those of any old European city, is the demonic energy that goes into everything, and the divine disregard for any other form of life, especially in the football players; also an element of miracle in the way the motorcycles and other traffic get through, shooting straight from hell, without anyone's changing his expression or pace or direction at all. If a Roman does have to move an inch for your car he looks at you like an affronted emperor; but on the whole American cars are objects of as pure a passion as Romans are capable of. "Oh, what a fine machine!" a woman calls out. "When Baffoni comes that'll be for me!" Baffoni is Big Whiskers or Stalin—but it was only a gaiety this time, at the sight of a Buick in her living room.

The big spaces are distressing too. There is nothing French about them, none of that spacious public elegance of the Place de la Concorde or the views up past the Tuileries. Big Piazza del Popolo, where the great political mass meetings are held among trees and flowing streams and Egyptian tigers, was even designed by a Frenchman, but the Roman look soon grew over it, like the weeds and wild flowers in the crevices of its twin churches.

Piazza San Pietro, so splendidly reasonable as architecture, if you forget the Via della Conciliazione, is not a place for reasonable individuals to stroll with a happy sense of partaking in the achievement and somehow corresponding to it, as they would in such a square in Paris. It is a place for people to congregate in the terrific force of their gregariousness, their mass cravings, like cattle around a water-hole; and when it is empty, when there is no saint being made or other spectacle, it is lifeless: very admirable in its lines but cold, with a hollow look, like the scene of a dream in which after standing with a great crowd one has suddenly been left alone. But then as suddenly you find it filled another way; another sequence has begun. It is a sunny winter afternoon, and now even this enormous space has become a living room, or public nursery. The Dome, announcing itself for miles around as the center of the world, is actually presiding like a hen over thousands of babies and mothers and lovers and very ancient people strewn all over the steps of Bernini's colonnade and the awesome area it encloses, not as if they owned it but really owning it. It is where they live. The fountains, those two high waving flags of world Catholicism, are as local as a barnyard pump. There is no distance; there is no awe of anything.

It is like a party all the time; nobody has to worry about giving one or being invited; it is going on every day in the street and you can go down or be part of it from your window; nobody eats alone in the cafeteria, reading a book. A sickbed is another public gathering; there is a ritual of moaning, question and response; everybody must crowd in.

Then there are the periodic Big Parties, a great deal older

than their present ostensible occasions, dogmas and the names of
saints, so old that the tumescence of life they cause seems of an
order with the habits of bees and the motions of tides. Everybody knows what to do, none of it is to be decided any more,
there is no question of having a good time or not; if that is what
you are supposed to be having that day then you are having it.
The strolling places are all big with motion; the main sounds are
of laughter, easy as waterfalls, and motors, but the machines are
not going out of the city unless to the beaches in summer; they
are just expressing themselves. The little iron tables or big wooden
ones with their scars and rubbings of so many other such days,
or in some arbor restaurants the hideous cement ones like cut-
rate tombstones, are each a domestic fragment of the one sprawl-
ing family affair—the material of the public table is of intimate
importance in this form of life, more than a person's own last
name; the children are in and out of everything, no distance
there; other families, of four, five, six, rumble by packaged into
one bulbous organism astride the family Vespa; and at the proper
hour it is all one mass exodus, to bed.

The honored personage, in any gathering, is the pregnant
woman. She is exhibited, she exhibits herself, everyone feels
happier and more important if there is someone in that condition at the table; and nothing can be refused her. If you refuse a
pregnant woman something she wants you will get a sty in your
eye, and her frustrated wishes will appear as blemishes in the
child.

It is a deluge. You are in life way over your head, there is no
getting out of it, except in the *beaux quartiers* which are not
beaux at all but only pretentious; taste never functioned here on
anything between the hovel and the grand palazzo. There are
distances there but they are the result of a failure, not a natural
way of being. Those sections are always sad and on the big party
days, about a dozen a year though some percolate into a season
of two or three weeks, seem marked more than ever with the
black sign of the sickness of the middle class. The health of the
city is elsewhere, around the fountains, where the private soul is

in ceaseless disintegration; nothing is held back; the only secrecy is of the city itself.

Of course the fountains are not all for every purpose and time of day; it depends on the space. Piazza del Popolo is a fascinating crossroads, a place to sit a while, but far too big and unprotective really to live in; the little square around the lovely Tortoise Fountain is more like a back stoop. For general all-day use, but especially at l'ora della passeggiata and in the evening, two of the best are beautiful Piazza Navona with its three fountains—"godless Navona" the angry reformers of the Middle Ages called it—and the cobbled square of Santa Maria in Trastevere, which is not much less beautiful although only one of its buildings is a true palazzo. But the others are massive and handsome, too, of a comfortable height, and have the weathered stucco colors of embers, ochre to rose, darker under the ledges, that are the characteristic ones of the city and help to give the walls their mysterious organic relation to people, nothing one could think of clearing away in a hurry. The main beauty of the piazza, as of most of the others, is that in spite of its superb proportions it seems not to have been planned but to have come about as a widening in a cow path does, so that nobody has that unpleasant feeling of doing what is expected of him, though in fact they are doing in nearly every detail what has been done in the same place for a great many generations. The fountain here is large and central, as it needs to be. It is not a sculptured one but a high impersonal form, a real flowing goblet, chattery but serene, which both fosters and absolves all the immense amount of *being*, being then and there, not waiting, not conceiving or imagining, that goes on around it. All water has an aspect of holy water; you feel it most strongly in these unfigured basins, not shooting up great rousing banners of liquid light as at Saint Peter's but the stiller ones, especially where life is so thick around them. The main feeling around this one is of a perpetual wiping out of experience; continuity is all in the water.

The church is essential in the same way. It was the first one dedicated to Mary and has kept the modest, authentic dignity of its great age beneath its tatters and strange accretions—or not so strange: there has been no serious change since the Twelfth Century square tower and mosaic across the façade. It gives the square its deep subtlety of color and line, and is part of its other spaciousness, too, along with the moving water, and as a view of the mountains would be.

The place itself is voyage; that is why there is no restlessness. Neither is there anything for the tender heart, neither pity nor self-pity; for the delicate sensibility it is all scandal and continual death.

The most startling people are the children; no other Italians have quite that look. These are the boys painted by Caravaggio, with all the tough seductive wisdom of the city, the toying challenge miles beyond any illusion, in their eyes; painted sometimes, in their careless open shirts, as child saints, when all their sublimity is of the rock bottom. They have been spared nothing, nobody ever changed the subject when they came into the room; by the age of seven it seems there is no human temptation or degradation they have not walked through the boiling center of, no vice they have not made up their own minds about, and they can have the manners of mule drivers or of cardinals as they happen to choose; only they cannot dissemble; they have the appalling candor of all Rome, and when you see it in a child's face you do not know if you are looking at fish or at angels. You see something else in their eyes; it is themselves as very old men, then their children and great-grandchildren standing before you at the age of seven and of seventy or a hundred, all with the same two huge eyeballs looking at you in what might be a smile.

The wonder, you might think, is that their fathers can be so childish. The rages of these men are marvelous. A Vespa brushes with a Filobus and immediately the two drivers are at each other as if there had been a feud between their families for years. "HOO! LA! HO!" "Ignorante!" "Fesso!" "Coglione!" They gesticulate, point to their steering wheels and fenders, bring the city to witness; the buses run from overhead wires so soon twenty are held up. The owner of the Vespa in his fury gets his front wheel stuck sideways and the motor going full speed makes the machine buck like a wild horse; so the bus moves on but he catches up with it a block later, plants himself square in front of it and begins shouting again. The scene is mandatory, if you were in the wrong it is even more necessary to make out that you were not; and inside the bus everyone is pleased, more than they were already at being transported like a shipment of eels; they would have been cheated if one of the drivers had not played his part. The most relaxed-looking people in Rome are the bus conductors, patrons all day of a kind of party that puts the public at its best and wittiest, because the lack is not of sensibility, only of nerves. The Roman form of serenade is to race a motorcycle motor under the girl's window, but mufflers are not common in any situation; the only things as dearly loved as a good noise are breakneck speed and eye-splitting lights, preferably neon—all expressions of well-being, like a huge belly laugh.

The women are of the species. Foreign men who take up with them or try to are nearly dashed to pieces, which in these days is a common attraction. With their dumpy graceless bodies and an air of the Empire about their beautiful heads and shoulders, their faces not marred but somehow made more personal and approachable by the extraordinary frequency of wens on them, these Roman women move in the blazing noon of a terrible cold sensuality, that can kill because it is so truly gay. They are said to be the coldest women in Europe but they are probably also the most candid; they are no more nebulous than the sky above them, and seem incapable of the least affectation; and they lose not an atom of their tremendous inner conviction because their calculations have brought them to a prospect of doing the washing for the next fifty years under an image of the Madonna. Their power even takes on another depth of joyousness once that is settled. The drive of femininity, which is of the whole being and so just the opposite of nymphomania, never gives out; neither does the lung power; their voices carry like rockets across the square and in all the streets around, in a frenzy of anger you would suppose but it may be only to ask the time and in a moment will be as loud with laughter. With their children it is a torrent treatment that may go on for thirty years, or never stop, of huggings and slappings and spoiling and tyrannical ordering about. The American, reflecting on his own childhood, feels exposed as to a break in Boulder Dam.

The guitar player at one of the two restaurants there on the square, in the aura of the venerable church, is something worse than shocking; it is because of the church, and the fountain, that he can be.

The restaurant has become rather fancy lately and the two musicians, who are the most talented of the kind in the city, size up their little audiences with a brutal shrewdness that could be mistaken for ridicule. Those knowledgeable children, after all, have not lost anything in growing up; these men know what they are doing, and for tourists they will play the worst of the Neapolitan repertoire as soulfully as anybody else. The guitar player, who sings, brings a look of longing into his big dark eyes, set in a leathery egg-shaped face, broadest at the bottom of the cheeks, which for those five minutes is all wistfully racked by the incapacity of any human art to express such beauty as the heart perceives; the beauty of the lady at the table is also too much; if he rested his eyes on hers for more than the duration of one yearning middle G he would have to stop singing entirely; when business is brisk he may have to be overcome by such sorrow twenty or thirty times in an evening, while the violinist, who is taller and wears glasses, keeps expressionless and a little in the rear, knowing that his face—this is *his* sorrow—is more suited to a comedian, and not wanting it to intrude on so touching a performance. The only thing is that their little routine bow at the end, acknowledgment of the guest's superior station and extreme kindness in listening to them, never gets quite finished; they had already moved on when they started it.

Their real songs, and any Roman's, are the long obscene *stornelli,* ballads with a Moorish twist and many verses rising in detail as they go on. One is about the prison of Regina Coeli—nobody is a true Roman who has not been there, the song says, but that is only the beginning. One is about the fountain at Piazza Esedra where the bronze naked ladies are kicking up their heels while the man at the center wrestles with a dolphin: *"Oh what is he doing with that big fish . . ."* A Holy Year one may have come out of mothballs: *"I sin all the year round, now I am making up my accounts for l'anno santo . . ."* Santo goes into a dozen or fifteen syllables, a long spiraling, leering, eye-rolling cadenza as coarse as any of the items that follow; the violinist is not retiring at all now; his big comedian's face is crackling with obscene sugges-tion and the moaning of the strings has turned to a sly slithering and biting more skillfully dirty than any of the verses; and after this song the singer will have to get out his handkerchief though his forehead was dry enough after the sad ones, at which he seemed to be working so. But this is an act, too, and will not make you friends with them, though sporadically, depending on business and the sirocco, they may pretend so; friendship is an alien idea; sooner or later your feelings are going to get hurt, and then suddenly it appears that all this time you had not been where you thought at all, among the roots of your own mem-ory, but in China. It is an oriental city.

The spaghetti and the beads hanging in the doors to keep the flies out, the guttural singing notes and sudden rests of Roman speech are Chinese; the reverence for parents, the bright-colored swarming streets, the easy talk of death; there is nothing here that you will ever understand.

ANN CORNELISEN

(1926–   )

In 1954, Cleveland-born Ann Cornelisen went to Florence to study archaeology. Instead, she spent ten years with the British Save the Children Fund, setting up nurseries in an impoverished village in southern Italy. Her experience in social work shaped most of her writing, including Women of the Shadows, *from which this excerpt is taken.*

Cornelisen is a sharp observer of southern Italy, especially its women. She writes of them as heroes and survivors, rather than victims. Although Women of the Shadows *is a nonfiction account, Cornelisen imbues it with the literary techniques of fiction. Peter Nichols wrote in* The New York Times *that Cornelisen is a "great recorder . . . she avoids any resemblance to a sociological report, although she is handling a serious sociological problem."*

Cornelisen's other nonfiction includes Torregreca: Life, Death, Miracles; Vendetta of Silence; *and* Strangers and Pilgrims: The Last Italian Migration. *In 1983, she published a novel,* Any Four Women Could Rob the Bank of Italy. *A review in the* Los Angeles Times *concluded, "Although this [novel] is proof of Cornelisen's versatility, her heart clearly remains with the unsung, forgotten heroines of the Southern provinces."*

Cornelisen lives in Italy.

from WOMEN OF THE SHADOWS

The South's is *not* the gentle, terraced landscape of Renaissance painting. It is a bare, sepia world, a cruel world of jagged, parched hills, dry river beds and distant villages where clumps of low houses cling together on the edges of cut-banks. These villages have a certain pattern about them. At one end a long gray barracks, the elementary school, seems to teeter precariously on columns of spongy soil, all that is left between the flumes of erosion. One more winter of rain and the wall must sag, then crumble slowly down toward the valley. At the other end of town a four story "skyscraper," straight and arrogant in its finery of mosaic tiles and plastic panels, serves as an exclamation point: this is the end. In between the bureaucrats reign—government clerks, teachers, priests, police—and those aspiring to such nobility. They live as near the Piazza as they can afford in buildings which, locally, are called palaces, but are of uniform discomfort and disrepair. Peasants live in the lower world, a maze of narrow cobbled streets and dank two-room houses. They are not really part of life here; they merely pause for the dark hours of the night. In the cemetery, away from the town and below it, are the only trees, a few cypress, black scars on the clay. Trees are despised in the South, but cypress may guard the dead.

Twenty years ago (when I first came there) the living seemed in constant motion. The men and their women plied the paths between the villages and the minuscule fields, hauling grain or grapes or fodder, olives and wood, like chains of ants patiently stumbling after each other, determined to transport thousands of crumbs to an invisible lair behind a stone. Now, in the '70s, there are fewer people and fewer donkeys to click the rhythm of their perpetual march. Some of the men no longer go out to the fields but are content to roost on the low stone walls in front of the church or opposite the market. Bad weather drives them into the back rooms of cafés and wine shops, where they pull their caps a little lower to avoid the glare from a neon tube and slouch in chairs, listening half asleep to the monotonous grunts and boasts of other men playing cards. Those who still go to the fields are older. They are the ones who stayed at home. To them the factories of Milan and Germany were more frightening than the stingy land of Lucania. The women have had no such choice, nor even the luxury of fear. As they have for centuries, young and old alike, they leave for the fields in the false light of dawn and return at dusk, plodding slowly, heavily, stopping occasionally to shift their loads.

They are provident by nature, these women of the South, unable to let even ten square meters of land lie fallow. The land is their insurance against the caprices of an industrialized world they do not understand or trust. Their pessimism has been justified, it seems, for, as the factories of the North adjust to economic recession, their men are coming back and trying once more to buy land, not out of love, but out of fear, and so perhaps the cycle begins again.

IN SUCH places land holds a mysterious sway over life. It is food—or money: in the past it was the symbol of power. Even the poorest clay is everything or nothing, depending on man's ability to exploit it. Small wonder peasants watch it with cold, suspicious eyes and talk of disaster in the spring when the wheat shoots are tender and green and the barren slopes that are their only pastures are tufted with wiry bunchgrass. Spring can masquerade in the gay yellow of broom and the lacy blue blossoms of rosemary and wild flowers, scattered like confetti along the verges of the road, but these are only trappings to fool the innocent. The peasants' distrust is contagious. Now, after so many seasons, I realize that for me the southern landscape is most beautiful when it is scorched, when the smoke from burning stubble drifts heavily upward into a violet-red twilight sky which will slowly, almost imperceptibly darken to purple. Then when it promises nothing, we must make our peace with the land.

LIFE IN a Southern Italian village is exclusive of all other life. Distances are great, transportation expensive and difficult. No one seems to have friends in other villages, and cities are places you go to when you need a permit or special medical examinations. In time some subliminal influence relates austerity to good and frivolity to evil. (I remember driving once to the nearest city just to take a bath and see a film and on my return feeling so guilty that I invented "official" errands to explain my absence to neighbors who would never have thought of questioning me.) That I was there by choice and Southern Italians are not, that I could leave at any time, they could not, is incidental. As long as I stayed I was committed to a very particular, circumscribed life. There was no other choice, or so it seemed. I shared what there was, including food of poor quality at high prices, capricious utilities, a wretched climate and the disdain of every outsider. Money could not buy comfort, much less delicacies or amusements.

The town hall, post office and school had wood-burning stoves, water two hours a day, and enough electricity to make a bulb glow dimly in the darkest hours of the night, when there was no one to use it. Modern public housing supplied a stove flue for each apartment, but no heat, and when the pressure was low, no water even for the few precious hours we could expect. The old stone one- or two-room houses each had a chimney, rather like a snorkel, that poked its way to the surface at the front door or bedroom window of the house just above. Women waited in long lines at fountains, if their need for water happened to coincide with the erratic schedule of the aqueduct, and they dumped their slops down street drains from hip-high ceramic jars, called "Zio Pepes," which served them as toilets, but which had a brief and for me disconcerting vogue in the cities as umbrella stands.

My life could not be very different. I rented an apartment in one of the barracks-like buildings that the first post-war governments had thought appropriate housing for peasants. There were no stalls, no storerooms. Chickens, even piglets, roamed the stairways, and bicycles, push-carts and scooters which had, perforce, replaced the donkeys, clogged the entrances. One of the few benefits of these modern units was a Sitz bath where I could store water. I bailed it into the toilet, into the basin for the patchy sponge baths that I could manage, and I boiled it for my pasta. I, too, had a wood-burning stove that I lighted on those evenings when the wind was not gusting down the flue. If in the winter at lunchtime I wanted to read for a few minutes, I went to my car (in that I was unique) and ran the motor until the heater worked. My only other choice would have been to sit at the local baker's, but no one would have allowed me to read: that is the place to meet your friends for a good gossip. Since on Sundays we had water from early morning until midafternoon, I decided there must be some way to put in a water heater. There was not enough current for an electric heater. One that burned wood required not only a second flue, but a breather safety vent on the roof for which I could not get permission. Then finally I found a butane gas heater, which the tobacconist who doubled as plumber assured me would work beautifully. There was one drawback. To be safe, to insure ventilation the glass must be removed from the bathroom window! At 2,500 feet where a normal winter offers eight months of cold and fog and snow, I thought not and so admitted defeat. After lunch on Sundays, the only time I was not apt to have callers, I "bathed" in the kitchen sink, lifting my feet up over the edge and sponging my legs as best I could with water I boiled in caldrons on the wood-burning cookstove.

Delicacies were out of the question: the procurement of the banal minimum to sustain human life required some ingenuity and a great deal of time. Butter could be purchased but long before it reached us had gone rancid in a warehouse in Bari. Salty *pecorino* cheese with an indefinable flavor of old drains and sour rags was available; *parmigiano* was not. Meat was for holidays and both tough and expensive. Fish arrived in a truck which had offered its wares to every village on its seventy-five mile route and reached us with the load reduced to a few scaley mid-sections of unknown origin and some very suspect clams which annually brought hepatitis, typhoid and most recently cholera. For an egg one made friends with a neighbor who kept chickens and then paid eight cents apiece (in 1959!). The entire stock of a grocery store could be arranged in a room the size of a closet: tinned tomatoes, tomato paste, tuna fish, anchovies, canned peas, olives, artichokes and such in oil, *pecorino*, local *salame* with intimidating cubes of fat, pasta in an amazing number of shapes and sizes, though the larger it was, the better it was liked, and a bin of bread. If you were determined, somewhere behind a counter, in a dark corner, you could find minute boxes of soap powder (though it was not in demand because dishes were still washed with sand and cinders, clothes with yellow bar soap), bottles of muriatic acid, bleach and a few tattered floor rags. All the prices were high, the quality inferior, but there was no choice. More money or less cannot improve a diet based on pasta with oil and bread with oil. Oil, which is always very important, was not a bottled, commercial product, but the local opaque syrup that both tasted good and set your teeth on edge. There was, of course, the fruit and vegetable market where greens in season were sold and fruit from Naples: three months of cauliflower and broccoli, six, it seemed, of chicory; salad in the hot months when it was most dangerous to eat. The only local fruits were cherries and figs; each has a very short season. Anything else came from outside, was pockmarked, bruised and exorbitant, the rejects of more prosperous markets sent inland.

Amusements were even more elusive. The cinema, a concrete trough like a sheep dip, was reserved to the men, as were wine shops and cafés, one of which had in its back room the only television set in town. Radio was small consolation. All stations, except those from Yugoslavia across the Adriatic, seemed to be transmitting on pendulums that bounced sounds—now clear, now faint, now clear again—off the stone cliffs of the mountains that surrounded us. One of the three Italian stations never reached us at all, not even an echo. It transmitted classical music, and we were probably considered unworthy. Few read, even those who knew how and could afford to, so the stationery and electric shop which theoretically supplied us with what we wanted, specialized in crochet instructions, and *fumetti*, the Italian adult comic books which use photographs to tell stories somewhere between soap operas and *True Confessions*.

In the evening the women had few choices. They sat, relieved if they had nothing more to do, in a vacuum between one day and the next. Sometimes they knitted coarse, heavy undershirts, sometimes they mended, badly. Those same women who used weeding hoes with infinite care and patience, lunged at their buttons and darns as though seeking revenge for the day's frustrations. All over town small groups of women, usually related one to the other by the tenuous web of their great-grandfathers' and grandmothers' marriages, sat with their feet on the half-step up to the fireplace, their shawls still around their shoulders, elbows on their knees and chins almost in the fire, murmuring the latest bits of information. They needed no newspaper. What interested them would arrive by word of mouth. They sorted the bits as they would in their season sort beans, discarding shriveled ones, putting aside the best for later consideration, spreading those to be used at the moment into a uniform mass before them. It was all done with surprising accuracy. Their elliptical comments, rooted as they were in a common past, sounded almost biblical to the outsider. When they were bored or warm enough, they went to bed. In summer the work day is longer, but the evenings are cool and soft. The caucus meets as usual, now at one's front door or on another's balcony, not out of friendship really, nor even loneliness. To them loneliness is nothing more than an arbitrary factor of life. They meet, as all cliques do, to exchange useful gossip, to laugh at the expense of others and to avoid the danger of being themselves the victims. They know that somewhere else in town they *are* the victims.

Day after day I saw these same women. At first we exchanged the usual grumblings about the weather and prices, then slowly—simply because I was always there—we began to talk of the feuds and gossip and illnesses that make up daily life, and the misery, and the frustration of change that is forever promised but never materializes. I stayed and so I shared what there was—the physical discomforts, which in time are merely irritating, and the less tangible discomforts of intuition. There is no gay cameraderie in this poverty. These are people born knowing they have no expectations. They live alone, flailing about them for some escape from impending failure, knowing that no one, not even their kin, will help them. They do not expect it. They have never had enough for themselves and cannot stop their own flailing long enough to help someone else, nor do they recognize any rule—civil, religious or emotional—that says they should. Success, should it come, will be fleeting and bring with it a few physical necessities, some envy and a spate of anonymous letters of accusation to the provincial authorities. So much depends on luck which to a peasant is an elusive power, inextricably bound up with God's will. Somehow He is not to be placated in this lifetime.

More than ten years have passed since I lived year in, year out in a southern village, anchored there, aware each day of the disasters that plagued life and aware each day that nothing I could do was more than temporary relief. The slow repetition of those days created a sense of inner isolation that I have never entirely lost. It had nothing to do with physical distance from a more familiar world. When I went to Rome for Christmas or Easter I felt a secret joy as though I were off to an illicit love affair, not with a man, but with the comforts of a city, and like some love affairs, once I was there, I felt strangely let down. Nothing quite lived up to expectations. There was heat and light and water— all day—and rugs so deep they coddled my ankles. There were friends and parties, too, at which I was driven to talk about "conditions" and petty tragedies of interest to no one, and I would suddenly realize that I had not escaped from my own isolation. I had brought it with me.

I have returned to the village frequently, but always at longer and longer intervals. When I am first there my sense of inner isolation turns outward. I am isolated from the women, they from me, though perhaps I am more aware of it because I knew them well. They never questioned my other life. For however long I stayed I was to share theirs. I came from that other world: automatically I was like the people they saw on television. They were the alienated who had nothing in common with me but their fields, their children, their troubles and finally even their jokes. Each time I go back we start again from the beginning. I

must have changed. They fear that change. Some strange rever-
sal of character may make me sneer when before I sympathized.
We circle each other like stray dogs. Their features are carefully
ordered to blankness. We go through the ritual of kissing on
each cheek, the limp handshake and I see only a distant dull look
in their eyes and deep new lines around their mouths and I think
of aging. They make a careful, entirely frank inventory of me
and are reassured. By comparison I have discovered the secret of
eternal youth. Look at their gray hairs, their teeth falling out
(which begins when they are barely children anyway), their pro-
lapsed bellies. Why hasn't that happened to you, signora? And
then their ailments. So and so has been operated on for *un male
brutto,* which means cancer. *Maria u verdulaiu* died—and so we
chew on the months that have passed, slowly working our way
back to the present. We have begun again.

When I lived there I did not have to think each day, This is
all of life, there is nothing more. I doubt that I could fight as
they fight in enduring their days, or that whatever is human in
me, that sets me apart from an animal, could survive their lives.
They say "life brutalizes." That they recognize it explains why,
for all that has been said to the contrary, they remain painfully
human. They are women of tremendous strengths, these women
of the shadows.

CHARLES DICKENS
(1812–1870)

*Fresh from a triumphant trip to the United States and Canada in 1842
and the publication of* American Notes, *Charles Dickens decided to
tackle the Continent. He claimed his motives were financial in part, as
it was too expensive to maintain his large family in England. Dickens,
his wife Catherine, and their children moved to Italy and settled in
Genoa. He found delight in the city's unexpected lanes, as he had in
London's alleys. "You can lose your way (what a comfort that is, when
you idle!) twenty times a day, if you like; and turn up again, under the
most unexpected and surprising difficulties. It abounds in the strangest
contrasts; things that are picturesque, ugly, mean, magnificent, delightful and offensive, break upon the view at every turn." With characteristic restlessness, Dickens was not content to stay in Genoa and toured
Vesuvius, Rome, Naples, Florence, and Venice before returning to England. His year is captured in* Pictures from Italy, *published in 1845,
from which this excerpt is taken.*

Genoa and Its Neighbourhood
from PICTURES FROM ITALY

The first impressions of such a place as Albaro, the suburb of
Genoa, where I am now, as my American friends would say, "located," can hardly fail, I should imagine, to be mournful and dis-
appointing. It requires a little time and use to overcome the

feeling of depression consequent, at first, on so much ruin and neglect. Novelty, pleasant to most people, is particularly delightful, I think, to me. I am not easily dispirited when I have the means of pursuing my own fancies and occupations; and I believe I have some natural aptitude for accommodating myself to circumstances. But, as yet, I stroll about here, in all the holes and corners of the neighbourhood, in a perpetual state of forlorn surprise; and returning to my villa: the Villa Bagnerello (it sounds romantic, but Signor Bagnerello is a butcher hard by); have sufficient occupation in pondering over my new experiences, and comparing them, very much to my own amusement, with my expectations, until I wander out again.

The Villa Bagnerello: or the Pink Jail, a far more expressive name for the mansion: is in one of the most splendid situations imaginable. The noble bay of Genoa, with the deep blue Mediterranean, lies stretched out near at hand; monstrous old desolate houses and palaces are dotted all about; lofty hills, with their tops often hidden in the clouds, and with strong forts perched high up on their craggy sides, are close upon the left; and in front, stretching from the walls of the house, down to a ruined chapel which stands upon the bold and picturesque rocks on the seashore, are green vineyards, where you may wander all day long in partial shade, through interminable vistas of grapes, trained on a rough trellis-work across the narrow paths.

This sequestered spot is approached by lanes so very narrow, that when we arrived at the Customhouse, we found the people here had *taken the measure* of the narrowest among them, and were waiting to apply it to the carriage; which ceremony was gravely performed in the street, while we all stood by in breathless suspense. It was found to be a very tight fit, but just a possibility, and no more—as I am reminded every day, by the sight of various large holes which it punched in the walls on either side as it came along. We are more fortunate, I am told, than an old lady, who took a house in these parts not long ago, and who stuck fast in *her* carriage in a lane; and as it was impossible to open one of the doors, she was obliged to submit to the indignity of being hauled through one of the little front windows, like a harlequin.

When you have got through these narrow lanes, you come to an archway, imperfectly stopped up by a rusty old gate—my gate. The rusty old gate has a bell to correspond, which you ring as long as you like, and which nobody answers, as it has no connection whatever with the house. But there is a rusty old knocker, too—very loose, so that it slides round when you touch it—and if you learn the trick of it, and knock long enough, somebody comes. The brave Courier comes, and gives you admittance. You walk into a seedy little garden, all wild and weedy, from which the vineyard opens; cross it, enter a square hall like a cellar, walk up a cracked marble staircase, and pass into a most enormous room with a vaulted roof and whitewashed walls: not unlike a great Methodist chapel. This is the *sala*. It has five windows and five doors, and is decorated with pictures which would gladden the heart of one of those picture-cleaners in London who hang up, as a sign, a picture divided, like death and the lady, at the top of the old ballad: which always leaves you in a state of uncertainty whether the ingenious professor has cleaned one half, or dirtied the other. The furniture of this *sala* is a sort of red brocade. All the chairs are immovable and the sofa weighs several tons.

On the same floor, and opening out of this same chamber, are dining-room, drawing-room, and divers bedrooms: each with a multiplicity of doors and windows. Upstairs are divers other gaunt chambers, and a kitchen; and downstairs is another kitchen, which, with all sorts of strange contrivances for burning charcoal, looks like an alchemical laboratory. There are also some half-dozen small sitting-rooms, where the servants in this hot July, may escape from the heat of the fire, and where the brave Courier plays all sorts of musical instruments of his own manufacture, all the evening long. A mighty old, wandering, ghostly, echoing, grim, bare house it is, as ever I beheld or thought of.

There is a little vine-covered terrace, opening from the drawing-room; and under this terrace, and forming one side of the little garden, is what used to be the stable. It is now a cow-house, and has three cows in it, so that we get new milk by the bucket-ful. There is no pasture near, and they never go out, but are constantly lying down, and surfeiting themselves with vine-leaves—perfect Italian cows enjoying the *dolce far' niente* all day long. They are presided over, and slept with, by an old man named Antonio, and his son; two burnt-sienna natives with naked legs and feet, who wear, each, a shirt, a pair of trousers, and a red sash, with a relic, or some sacred charm like the bon-bon off a twelfth-cake, hanging round the neck. The old man is very anxious to convert me to the Catholic faith; and exhorts me frequently. We sit upon a stone by the door, sometimes in the evening, like Robinson Crusoe and Friday reversed; and he generally relates, towards my conversion, an abridgment of the History of Saint Peter—chiefly, I believe, from the unspeakable delight he has in his imitation of the cock.

The view, as I have said, is charming; but in the day you must keep the lattice-blinds close shut, or the sun would drive you mad; and when the sun goes down you must shut up all the windows, or the mosquitoes would tempt you to commit sui-cide. So at this time of the year, you don't see much of the prospect within doors. As for the flies, you don't mind them. Nor the fleas, whose size is prodigious, and whose name is Le-gion, and who populate the coachhouse to that extent that I daily expect to see the carriage going off bodily, drawn by myr-iads of industrious fleas in harness. The rats are kept away, quite comfortably, by scores of lean cats, who roam about the garden for that purpose. The lizards, of course, nobody cares for; they play in the sun, and don't bite. The little scorpions are merely curious. The beetles are rather late, and have not appeared yet. The frogs are company. There is a preserve of them in the grounds of the next villa; and after nightfall, one would think that scores upon scores of women in pattens were going up and down a set stone pavement without a moment's cessation. That is exactly the noise they make.

The ruined chapel, on the picturesque and beautiful seashore, was dedicated, once upon a time, to Saint John the Baptist. I believe there is a legend that Saint John's bones were received there, with various solemnities, when they were first brought to Genoa; for Genoa possesses them to this day. When there is any uncommon tempest at sea, they are brought out and exhibited to the raging weather, which they never fail to calm. In consequence of this connection of St. John with the city, great numbers of the common people are christened Giovanni Baptista, which latter name is pronounced in the Genoese patois "Batcheetcha," like a sneeze. To hear everybody calling everybody else Batcheetcha, on a Sunday, or festa-day, when there are crowds in the streets, is not a little singular and amusing to a stranger.

The narrow lanes have great villas opening into them, whose walls (outside walls, I mean) are profusely painted with all sorts of subjects, grim and holy. But time and the sea-air have nearly obliterated them; and they look like the entrance to Vauxhall Gardens on a sunny day. The court-yards of these houses are overgrown with grass and weeds; all sorts of hideous patches cover the bases of the statues, as if they were afflicted with a cutaneous disorder; the outer gates are rusty; and the iron bars outside the lower windows are all tumbling down. Firewood is kept in halls where costly treasures might be heaped up, mountains high; waterfalls are dry and choked; fountains, too dull to play, and too lazy to work, have just enough recollection of their identity, in their sleep, to make the neighbourhood damp; and the sirocco wind is often blowing over all these things for days together, like a gigantic oven out for a holiday.

Not long ago, there was a festa-day, in honour of the *Virgin's mother,* when the young men of the neighbourhood, having worn green wreaths of the vine in some procession or other, bathed in them, by scores. It looked very odd and pretty. Though I am bound to confess (not knowing of the festa at that time), that I thought, and was quite satisfied, they wore them as horses do—to keep the flies off.

Soon afterwards, there was another festa-day, in honour of St. Nazaro. One of the Albaro young men brought two large bouquets soon after breakfast, and coming upstairs into the great *sala,* presented them himself. This was a polite way of begging for a contribution towards the expenses of some music in the Saint's honour, so we gave him whatever it may have been, and his messenger departed: well satisfied. At six o'clock in the evening we went to the church—close at hand—a very gaudy place, hung all over with festoons and bright draperies, and filled, from the altar to the main door, with women, all seated. They wear no bonnets here, simply a long white veil—the "mezzero"; and it was the most gauzy, ethereal-looking audience I ever saw. The young women are not generally pretty, but they walk remarkably well, and in their personal carriage and the management of their veils, display much innate grace and elegance. There were some men present: not very many: and a few of these were kneeling about the aisles, while everybody else tumbled over them. Innumerable tapers were burning in the church; the bits of silver and tin about the saints (especially in the Virgin's necklace) sparkled brilliantly; the priests were seated about the chief altar; the organ played away, lustily, and a full band did the like; while a conductor, in a little gallery opposite to the band, hammered away on the desk before him, with a scroll; and a tenor, without any voice, sang. The band played one way, the organ played another, the singer went a third, and the unfortunate conductor banged and banged, and flourished his scroll on some principle of his own: apparently well satisfied with the whole performance. I never did hear such a discordant din. The heat was intense all the time.

The men, in red caps, and with loose coats hanging on their shoulders (they never put them on), were playing bowls, and buying sweetmeats, immediately outside the church. When half a dozen of them finished a game, they came into the aisle, crossed themselves with the holy water, knelt on one knee for an instant, and walked off again to play another game of bowls. They are remarkably expert at this diversion, and will play in the stony lanes and streets, and on the most uneven and disastrous ground for such a purpose, with as much nicety as on a billiard-table. But the most favourite game is the national one of Mora, which they pursue with surprising ardour, and at which they will stake everything they possess. It is a destructive kind of gambling, requiring no accessaries but the ten fingers, which are always—I intend no pun—at hand. Two men play together. One calls a number—say the extreme one, ten. He marks what portion of it he pleases by throwing out three, or four, or five fingers; and his adversary has, in the same instant, at hazard, and without seeing his hand, to throw out as many fingers, as will make the exact balance. Their eyes and hands become so used to this, and act with such astonishing rapidity, that an uninitiated bystander would find it very difficult, if not impossible, to follow the progress of the game. The initiated, however, of whom there is always an eager group looking on, devour it with the most intense avidity; and as they are always ready to champion one side or the other in case of a dispute, and are frequently divided in their partisanship, it is often a very noisy proceeding. It is never the quietest game in the world; for the numbers are always called in a loud sharp voice, and follow as close upon each other as they can be counted. On a holiday evening, standing at a window, or walking in a garden, or passing through the streets, or sauntering in any quiet place about the town, you will hear this game in progress in a score of wine-shops at once; and looking over any vineyard walk, or turning almost any corner, will come upon a knot of players in full cry. It is observable that most men have a propensity to throw out some particular number oftener than another; and the vigilance with which two sharp-eyed players will mutually endeavour to detect this weakness, and adapt their game to it, is very curious and entertaining. The effect is greatly heightened by the universal suddenness and vehemence of gesture; two men playing for half a farthing with an intensity as all-absorbing as if the stake were life.

Hard by here is a large Palazzo, formerly belonging to some member of the Brignole family, but just now hired by a school

of Jesuits for their summer quarters. I walked into its dismantled
precincts the other evening about sunset, and couldn't help pac-
ing up and down for a little time drowsily taking in the aspect of
the place: which is repeated hereabouts in all directions.

I loitered to and fro, under a colonnade, forming two sides of
a weedy, grass-grown court-yard, whereof the house formed a
third side, and a low terrace-walk, overlooking the garden and
the neighbouring hills, the fourth. I don't believe there was an
uncracked stone in the whole pavement. In the centre was a
melancholy statue, so piebald in its decay, that it looked exactly
as if it had been covered with sticking-plaster, and afterwards
powdered. The stables, coach-houses, offices, were all empty, all
ruinous, all utterly deserted.

Doors had lost their hinges, and were holding on by their
latches; windows were broken, painted plaster had peeled off,
and was lying about in clods; fowls and cats had so taken possession of the out-buildings, that I couldn't help thinking of the
fairy tales, and eyeing them with suspicion, as transformed re-
tainers, waiting to be changed back again. One old Tom in particular: a scraggy brute, with a hungry green eye (a poor relation,
in reality, I am inclined to think): came prowling round and
round me, as if he half believed, for the moment, that I might
be the hero come to marry the lady, and set all to rights; but discovering his mistake, he suddenly gave a grim snarl, and walked
away with such a tremendous tail, that he couldn't get into the
little hole where he lived, but was obliged to wait outside, until
his indignation and his tail had gone down together.

In a sort of summer-house, or whatever it may be, in this
colonnade, some Englishmen had been living, like grubs in a
nut; but the Jesuits had given them notice to go, and they had
gone, and *that* was shut up too. The house: a wandering, echoing, thundering barrack of a place, with the lower windows
barred up, as usual, was wide open at the door: and I have no
doubt I might have gone in, and gone to bed, and gone dead,
and nobody a bit the wiser. Only one suite of rooms on an upper floor was tenanted; and from one of these, the voice of a

young-lady vocalist, practising bravura lustily, came flaunting
out upon the silent evening.

I went down into the garden, intended to be prim and
quaint, with avenues, and terraces, and orange-trees, and statues,
and water in stone basins; and everything was green, gaunt,
weedy, straggling, under grown or over grown, mildewy, damp,
redolent of all sorts of slabby, clammy, creeping, and uncom-
fortable life. There was nothing bright in the whole scene but a
firefly—one solitary firefly—showing against the dark bushes
like the last little speck of the departed Glory of the house; and
even it went flitting up and down at sudden angles, and leaving
a place with a jerk, and describing an irregular circle, and returning to the same place with a twitch that startled one: as if it
were looking for the rest of the Glory, and wondering (Heaven
knows it might!) what had become of it.

LAWRENCE DURRELL

(1912–1990)

Lawrence Durrell led twin lives. He was a novelist and an accomplished travel writer, drawing from a career spent mainly in the Mediterranean as a diplomat in the British foreign service. As a novelist he is best known for The Alexandria Quartet: Justine, Balthazar, Mountolive, *and* Clea. *His travel books include* Prospero's Cell *(Greece),* Bitter Lemons *(Cyprus), and* Sicilian Carousel *(Italy), from which this selection "Erice" is taken.*

Carousello Siciliano is the name of the tour bus that carries Durrell around Sicily, accompanied by a maddening group: Roberto the guide, Mario the bus driver, an American dentist, an Anglican Bishop "experiencing doubts," a French couple, and, always hovering over the trip, the ghost of Durrell's dead friend Martine, who encouraged him to see Sicily.

Erice

from SICILIAN CAROUSEL

At Erice one feels that all the options of ordinary life are reversed. I do not know how else to put it. We steer our lives by certain beliefs which are perhaps fables but which give us the courage to continue living. But what happens even before you reach the "sickle" of Trapani is that you lose your inner bearings, become insecure. It's as if the giant of the mountain up there, riding its mists, had kicked away your crutches. History begins to stammer; the most famous and most privileged temple to Aphrodite in the whole of the Mediterranean has vanished without leaving a trace. The one late head of Aphrodite is nothing to write home about. The holy shrine of Eryx has been blown out like a light, yet as at Delphi, one can still smell the sulphur in the air. You feel it in the burning sun like a cold touch on the back of the neck. But I am going too fast for we are still approaching Trapani, that deceptively happy and unremarkable town so beautifully perched upon its seagirt headland. The old part of the town, rather as in the case of Syracuse, occupies a firm promontory thrust out into the sea like a pier; the town has developed on the landward side. Salt-pans and windmills, yes, and the view from the so-called Ligny Tower is a fine one; but what is really fine is the fresh sea-wind, frisky as a fox-terrier, which patters the awnings and bends the trees and sends old sailors' caps scuttering along the cobbles of the port. Westward a fine expanse of the Tyrrhenian Sea, smouldering in the sinking sun; two of the Egadi Isles with the choice names of Levanzo and Favignana glow with a kind of mysterious malevolence.

We were tired, we were really in no mood for further sightseeing, and Roberto let us off easily with a short visit to an indifferent church and a glimpse of the stern battlements constructed by Charles V. But the main thing was the frolicking wind whose playfulness allayed somewhat the curious feeling of tension and misgiving which I felt when I gazed upwards towards the ramps of Monte Giuliano and saw the sharp butt of Erice buried in the mountain like a flint axehead which had broken off with the impact. There was a short administrative pause while Mario made some growling remarks to the world at large and some adjustments to his brakes. Somewhere in the town a small municipal band had slunk into a square and started to play fragments of old waltzes and tangos. The sudden gusts of wind offered the musicians a fortuitous nautical syncopation— the music fading and reviving, full of an old-world charm. The Petremands ate a vividly coloured ice-cream and bought one for Mario. The Bishop had broken a shoelace. The old pre-Adamic

couple were fast asleep in their seats, arm in arm, smile in smile,
so to speak. It is pleasant when sleeping people smile and obviously enjoy their dreaming; they looked like representations of
the smiling Buddha—though he is very far from asleep, sunk
rather in smiling meditation. At last we began the ascent.

The sun was over the border now, rapidly westering, apparently increasing speed in its long slide into the ocean. Our little
red bus swung itself clear of the crooked streets of Trapani and
then started its tough climb up the dark prow of Eryx. Adieu
Via Fardella, Via Pepoli! The road now began to mount in short
spans on a steepening gradient, swinging about first to the right,
then to the left; and there came a gradually increasing sobriety
of spirit, a premonition perhaps of the Erycinean Aphrodite
whose territory we were approaching. I am not romancing, for
several of my fellow-travellers expressed a sharpened sense of
excitement in their several ways. Mario varied his engine speeds
with great skill and the little motor had us valiantly swarming up
the steep cliffs in good order.

The vegetation gradually thinned away, or made room for
hardier and perhaps more ancient plants to cling to the crevices
and caves in the rock. The precipices hereabouts were bathed in
the condensations of cloud, as if a rich dew had settled on them;
or as if the whole of nature had burst into a cold sweat. Yes,
there were clouds above us, hanging lower and lower as we
climbed, but they seemed to part as we reached them to offer us
passage. At each turn—for we were still tacking up the cliffs like
a sailboat—the view increased in grandeur and scope until the
whole province of Trapani lay below us bathed in golden light
and bounded by the motionless sea. Far off twinkled the Egadi,
with Marettimo printed in black-letter—the island which
Samuel Butler so surprisingly decided must be the historical
Ithaca in his weird book about the supposed female author of
the *Odyssey*. I love wrong-headed books. But a short residence
in modern Greece would have made Butler somewhat uncertain
about the main theme of his book. Only a man, only a Greek
could have written the poem—at least so think I.

We worked our way with elephantine determination round the north-eastern flank of our two-thousand-metre odd mountain. There was only one little village to traverse, Parparella, perched up in solitude like a nest and empty of inhabitants at that hour. Bare rock now, with sudden ferns, cistus, caper and an occasional asphodel to surprise one. And the views below us went on steadily unwinding like a scroll. The air had become purer, colder, as if filtered by the passing clouds. Once or twice our engine sneezed and Mario cocked an alert ear; but there was no trouble and on one of the penultimate loops we called a halt designed to let the amateur photographers in the party record the scene below. But while they clicked happily away at Trapani I found myself craning upwards to gaze at the crest of Eryx, printed on the unfaltering blue of the evening sky, still touched by the sun's rays. You could see a dabble of ancient wall and some higgledy-piggledy towers and minarets just below the summit. They must mark the site of the now vanished temple of Aphrodite. From the rugged Cyclopean bases the walls mounted in a faltering and somewhat ramshackle fashion—improvised in layers, in tiers, in afterthoughts and false starts—Phoenician, Greek, Roman and Norman.

Once we had broken the back of the ascent the road spanned pleasant but lonely pinewoods which scented the still air and led us in mysterious hesitant fashion to the gates of the little town, the Porte Trapani, where Roberto got down for a long confabulation with a clerk from the Mairie while the rest of us set about digging into our luggage for pullovers. The dusk was about us now though the higher heavens were still lit by the sun, and up there the swifts darted and rolled, feasting on insects. A chill struck suddenly and the Bishop shivered.

There had been a hitch, said Roberto, and we had been switched to an older hotel; this was irritating. Like all guides he decried the old-fashioned and only respected modernity. But in this case there was no need for apologies; the hotel was a fine old-fashioned tumbledown sort of place but with all the right amenities. Mario turned the bus round and conducted us steeply downhill upon a forest road; but it was not far, for we emerged upon a sort of ledge like an amphitheatre above the sea. It was a spacious site and belonged to spacious times when they built hotels with comfortable billiard-rooms and lounges and terracotta swimming pools. It was fine to be thus perched over the sea in the middle of a pine forest. The wooden floors creaked under our feet in comfortable fashion. There were several dusty bars full of dusty half-full liqueur bottles. But at the back underneath the dining-room there came a short stretch of forest followed by an astonishing vertical drop—a sheer drop to the bottom of the world as represented now in diagrammatic fashion by a Trapani with its salt-pans and harbour picked out in lights. We were a bit below the castle here and the little town was not visible. A heavy mist from the precipice rose and dispersed, rose and dispersed. "It's all very well, but I have got cold feet and I want my money back," said Beddoes to the distress of Roberto who took everything he said seriously. Despite the season the mountain chill and the fatigue had chastened us and we were glad to settle for a drink and dinner and early bed.

The Count walked about in the dark for a while before turning in—I saw the glow of his cigar. Deeds found a crossword in an ancient paper while Miss Lobb replaced her book and appropriated another. I retired to my narrow wooden chamber which reminded me a bit of a ship's cabin, or a room in a ski-chalet. The wood smelt lovely and it was not too cold to step out upon the balcony with its great view. All along the horizon line there was a tremulous flickering of an electrical storm, soundless from this great distance. It reminded me of the only naval engagement I have ever witnessed—if that is the correct word; the ships were all out of sight and only this steady flicker (followed centuries later by the thunder of guns) was to be seen. It went back and forth regular as a scythe-stroke.

I watched, straining to hear the following thunder, but none came for ages. It was up here, perhaps in this very room that Martine had spent a night of "intense nervous expectation." It was so intense that she could not sleep, and it was at last with weary elation that she had watched the dawn break over the exhausted sea. She felt as if she had escaped whatever it was that had been haunting her subconscious in the form of vague premonitions of something doom-laden which she would encounter here at Erice. Nor was she completely wrong. Nor had she escaped, for months afterwards she realised that it was here, and more especially on that sleepless night, that she had felt the first twinges in the joints, the first stiffness of the neck and backbone which were only to declare their meaning long months afterwards. "I recognise now in retrospect just what I went to Erice to find. It was a rendezvous which would finally lead me towards death—one must not fuss too much since it is everyone's lot. Only now I know what I did not at Erice—I know roughly when. Yes, I am going into a decline in a year or two. Or so they say, the professors in Rome. I like the Victorian phrase, don't you? It has pride and reserve—though I was never a woman of ice, was I?"

But all this was at another season, and the hotel had been deserted, and the rock-levels of Venus's temple had been smothered in tiny spring flowers she could not identify. Now I had followed her, not with quite such an acute apprehension of momentous happenings, but with something nevertheless which troubled and disturbed me and made me expectant. During that first night (I could hear the desultory click of billiard balls, where Beddoes was still up. Floors creaked.), during the long vigil she had spent some time "scratching about among the bewildering debris of legend and conjecture which makes everything Greek in Sicily such a puzzle. It is as if everything has been smashed into dust by a giant trip-hammer; one can reach nothing coherent among these shattered shards; just the tantalising hints and glints of vanished people and their myths. So finally one says, to hell with Daedalus the engineer, and first labyrinth-maker—what did he find to do here in Sicily? Head of public works for old King Cocalos? Why did he assent to the murder of Minos his old patron? One becomes so weary of the oft-repeated tales which make up the historic pattern. It is hopeless!

And then what about the ultra-famous temple of Venus—Astarte-Aphrodite-Venus—the goddess had diverse roots and multiple attributes? Everything, woman, wife, nurse, mother, Muse, as well as ritual prostitute. . . . There was no aspect she did not rule over. In this grim temple there was ritual prostitution, as well as fertility rites—while for the sailor the place was a notable navigational seamark to guide him to Trapani; and just as today the sailor asks for weather reports, so his ancestor took the omens for the voyage from the temple and acted according to whether they were fair or foul.

"But how could it have disappeared so completely from sight, this world-famous place? Nothing but a tiny bit of stone ramp remains to mark the site of the temple. Nothing? Well, only this intangible feeling of dread, of something momentous preparing itself. And the empty sockets mock one in the one late banal head of Aphrodite."

Youth, beauty, death—the three co-ordinates of the ancient world. Martine wrote: "I told myself that in Sufism and Taoism (it would take too long to convince you that the original Astarte of Erice was much older than Greek) they do not have any truck with the notion of disease as we see it. They do not talk of getting cured but simply of modifying conduct. It is presumed that your wrong action has procured a disharmony with the universe which manifests itself in disease. I believe this with all my heart, but I also believe in destiny, as well as in just wearing out like a pot. Then there is another aspect of things—I hate the Christian notion of prayer as an act of propitiation. But I like the old Byzantine notion of turning it into a sort of heart-beat—each man his own prayer-wheel so to speak. Everything you feel in Erice goes way back beyond any notion which the monkey mind or tongue can formulate. Into the darkness where those great vegetable forms, tuberose creatures, wait in order to munch your flesh when you are once in the ground. The chthonic gods and goddesses as they are so strangely called. . . ."

The light went out—the hotel generator packed up at midnight. It was still very light—a white milky light as if of moonlight diffused through a silk screen. I was weary now and I set down my papers and slept—but it was a light, nervous sort of sleep without great density.

At about three I woke with a start and sat up to look at the forest. I thought at first what I had heard was muffled sobbing somewhere in the building. I am still not sure. But what had happened was that a powerful surge of wind had sailed upon the promontory and bent the pines. It made a sudden rich hum, like a sweep of strings long drawn out but slowly dying away. Then the quivering silence returned. But one felt excited, on the *qui vive*. It was exactly as if one woke in the middle of the night on the African veldt slowly to realise that the noise which had wakened one was the breathing of a lion. The forest stirred and shook and resettled itself. A kind of breath of music had passed over it—like breath passing over embers. No, there was nothing particularly disquieting or singular about it, but waking, I felt the need to get up and drink some water. It was icy. I went to the balcony and looked down at the necklace of lights etching in their diagram of Trapani. It was some time off dawn yet but I felt completely rested and wondered if I would get to sleep again. Hesitating there I suddenly caught sight of a figure advancing towards the hotel through the pines. It was the German girl and she was naked.

The light, though diffused, was extremely bright and I saw quite clearly that she had no clothes on. I wondered if she could be sleep-walking but it did not seem so for she looked about her, turning her head now this way and now that. She carried her hands before her, palms turned up, but lightly and without emphasis. And her walk was slow and calm.

Perhaps the sweep of the wind in the pines had woken her also, or else the forest had evoked in her her native Bavarian landscapes? Or more simply still, she felt the incoherent stirrings of a primeval inheritance—suppose she were, without realising it, some Nordic goddess who had come on an accidental visit to a remote cousin called Aphrodite of Eryx? She walked slowly and calmly under my balcony and disappeared round the corner of the house. And that was all. I dwelt a little while on the spectacle, wondering about it. Then I turned in again and at once fell into the profound sleep which up to now had been lacking. The sun was up when I awoke. And the disquiet had been replaced by a calm elation. Yet in a sort of way I felt that it was a relief to have traversed the night without incident.

Breakfast was very welcome on that fine sunny day; and we had been promised a look at the castle before being spirited away to Segesta and thence Palermo. Our trip was soon going to be at an end, and the consciousness of it provoked a new sense of friendliness. Conversations became warmer and more animated. A Microscope helped the Japanese girl change a film. I looked curiously at Renata the German girl when she came down but she seemed perfectly normal and assured, and of course one could not question her about her nudist escapade. I wondered if her boy friend knew of it. They were both very obviously much in love and went to no pains to hide it—which crucified poor Roberto as he watched, biting his nails.

It was necessary to set the red bus to rights this morning, for the little town of Erice was only going to be a brief stop on the road to Segesta whence we would face a long haul into Palermo.

I rather feared the ardours of this journey but in fact the calculations of Roberto were fairly exact and we arrived at night not too late and not too fatigued. But Erice in that bright blue morning was something for a glider-pilot's eye or an eagle's. The drops, the views, the melting sea. Light clouds frolicked way below us. The little town had tucked itself into the nape of the mountain while the successive fortresses had been squarely planked down on the site of the ancient temple, thus obliterating it. But the rock promontory, sticking out like a stone thumb, was a perfect emplacement for a place of worship. "It makes me wonder," said Deeds, "since all the ancient shrines have served as Christian foundations for our churches, whether there isn't always a little bit of the pagan devil leaking into the stonework of our Christian edifices. I would like to think there was; we seem such a rigid and unfunny lot. But I don't think I dare ask the parson."

The little town stumbled up and down its net of cobbled streets below the fortress garden. The architecture was all that one finds in the Aegean—houses built round a courtyard tessellated with coloured pebbles and decorated with old corned-beef tins full of sprouting basil and other sweet-smelling plants. It was Samos, it was Tinos all over again. We were warmly bidden to enter several courtyards to admire the arrangements of the house; these dark-eyed smiling people might have been Corfiots. The snug little courtyards bounded-in their lives, and one felt that here, when once night fell and the mists began to climb up from the valley below, people did not hesitate to lock their courtyard-gates. After midnight one could knock a long time on a door without getting an answer, for their world was both ancient and also one of contemporary goblins and fays. And with the temple site brooding up there. . . . But the domestic organisation of their houses was that of birds' nests, and they had all the human force which comes from living on top of one another in a small place; making room for children, for livestock, for everything important to life—and not less for the sacred icons which ensure that the dark spirits shall be kept at bay.

Roberto had a small chore to do and it was quite a compliment that he should ask Deeds and myself if we would like to accompany him. He had to visit the ancient grandmother of a friend and give her some messages of congratulation for her eighty-sixth birthday plus various assorted messages. We found the house without much difficulty and when the portals opened to us we saw that quite a number of people were there on the same errand. It was rather a spacious house on its own courtyard, and a short flight of steps led up to the upper room and gallery where the old lady lay in state to receive her visitors, in a great bed like a galleon with carved headboards. It looked, as Deeds said afterwards, as if one could have hitched a horse to it and just ridden off into the sky, there were so many cherubs and saints carved upon it, all *con furioso*. She wore an old-fashioned shawl of fine black lace with a white fichu and her long witch-like hands with their filbert nails were spread on the sheet before her, while her clever old eyes accepted the compliments of her visitors with grace and no weariness. Her fine room was furnished with graceful Sicilian earthenware plates beautifully painted, and flowers in bloom. Two small children played with a sailboat upon a handsome carved trunk under the window. She must have been a person of great consequence for several of her visitors were local dignitaries, as Roberto explained later—the barber, the chemist, the *podesta* and *medico condotto*. It all went off with great style and ease, but the appearance of Roberto was a thrilling surprise and his presence evoked questions and answers which took a good twenty minutes. She had questions to ask involving several generations and several families and I had the impression that nobody was passed over—she checked up on the whole lot of them, for who knows when she might have another chance? The peasant memory and the peasant sense of life is a tenacious and determined thing—it draws its strength from this sense of a corporate life, shared by all, and to which all contribute a share of their sap. Moreover I think the old lady felt that she was not long for this world and that she must make the most of things, such as this surprise visit which had brought her all the gossip of a far corner of the island.

Duty thus done, Roberto kissed the long patrician fingers of the old lady and we made our way back into the sunshine to negotiate the little curling streets back to the main square where by now the rest of the party must be sitting under awnings and writing postcards or drinking lemonade. The day was bright and hot, and it was quite a contrast to think back to the evening before with its mists and murmurs of another world, another order of life. Nothing could be more ordinary in its beauty than Erice by day, with all the little shops functioning—post office, bank, gendarmerie. The minute main square was built upon a slope—indeed such an acute tilt that everything tended to slide about and run down to the bottom. Tables at this angle were in danger of falling over, as were chairs; as one wrote one's postcards or drank one's beer, one found one was insensibly sliding downhill. People who came out of the café had to brake sharply in order not to find themselves rolling about like dice.

A very fat policeman made something of an act of this natural attribute of Erice's Piazza Nationale by allowing himself to slide helplessly downhill until he ended up on the lap of a friend who was trying to eat ice-cream at an angle of fifty degrees. Just how the poor café owner managed to dispose his tables and chairs was something of a mystery—it would have seemed necessary to wedge them in place. Over the lintel of the butcher's hung a peeled and dry little kid which bore a label reading "*Castrato*" and giving a price per pound. This intrigued Beddoes who said: "It's a rum word, I thought it meant something frightful that Monteverdi did to his choirboys to enable them to hit high C." The kid was so neatly cut in half that it looked rather like a violin hanging up there; the rest of the meat on display was pretty indifferent-looking stuff; of course, like all Mediterranean islands Sicily is a lamb country.

Our little visit had cost us a bit of time and by now the others had already done the cathedral and the Church of St. John as well as the public gardens, so full of yellow broom; but the real heart of the place was the restored towers and the old castle standing grimly on its sacred site, sweating with every gush of mists from the lowlands. What a farewell sweep the eye takes in up there—the whole sweep of western Sicily exposed in a single slice, as if from an aeroplane! Roberto was disposed to be knowledgeable about the *Aeneid* with its famous cruise along this coast which is described in poetic detail—but to my shame I have never read it, and I rather doubted whether anyone else had either. But the few lines he quoted from memory sounded sinewy and musical on that fine silent air and I made a mental note to repair this grave omission as soon as I could happen upon a version of the poem in parallel text. We were leaving and suddenly as we entered the bus I had a sudden reversion to the mood of the night before—a sudden atmosphere of unreality in which some momentous happening lay embedded, encysted, waiting to flower. But the faces of my fellow-travellers did not seem to express any untoward emotion and it was perhaps my own imagination. But whatever they were, these small preoccupations, they were swept away like cobwebs by the fine speed of our descent, for Mario was in a particularly expansive humour and swung the little bus about with a professional dexterity that was marvellous—in the sense that it caused us no alarm, so confident were we in his ability. And the land swept about with him on this turntable of a road, swinging like a cradle this way and that. At one corner he slowed for the Japanese girl and her camera and I caught a glimpse of a couple of appropriate eagles sitting motionless in the mid-heaven, staring down at the vanished altars of Erice.

GEORGE ELIOT

(1819–1880)

In March of 1860, just after finishing The Mill on the Floss, *George Eliot embarked on a five-month tour of Italy with her common-law husband, George Henry Lewes. Eliot intended Italy to "chase away Maggie and the Mill from my thoughts; I hope it will, for she and her sorrows have clung to me painfully." The trip was all she could have hoped. Despite the rigors of travel over snow-covered mountain passes, and despite her precarious health, Eliot was exhilarated by Italy and wrote to a friend of her astonishment that she had not suffered a single headache since setting out. Eliot and Lewes explored Genoa, Pisa, Rome, Naples, Florence, Bologna, Padua, Venice, and Milan with unusual energy and enthusiasm. Despite initial disappointment with her first views of modern Rome, visits to its ancient ruins led Eliot to feel "an intoxication of delight, making me long to stay here and study till I know Rome by heart all except those ugly modern streets which are enough to scare away every haunting spirit of the past." In Florence, the haunting spirits of the past inspired Eliot with the idea of setting a novel in fifteenth-century Florence. That impulse bore fruit two years later, with the publication of* Romola *in 1862. In Eliot's later masterpiece,* Middlemarch, *her heroine Dorothea retraces Eliot's steps as she goes sightseeing in Rome during her honeymoon, but unhappiness prevents Dorothea from feeling the sheer delight in her surroundings that we find recorded in the letters and journals Eliot wrote during her Italian journey.*

Journals from Italy

JOURNAL, ITALY, 1860

I had looked forward for years to the journey to Italy, rather with the hope of the new elements it would bring to my culture, than with the hope of immediate pleasure. Travelling can hardly be without a continual current of disappointment if the main object is not the enlargement of one's general life, so as to make even weariness and annoyances enter into the sum of benefit. One great deduction to me from the delight of seeing world-famous objects is the frequent double consciousness which tells me that I am not enjoying the actual vision enough, and that when higher enjoyment comes with the reproduction of the scenes in my imagination, I shall have lost some of the details, which impress me too feebly in the present because the faculties are not wrought up into energetic action.

Here follow some selected impressions of the journey:—
Perhaps the world can hardly offer a more interesting outlook than that from the tower of the Roman Capitol. The eye leaps first to the mountains that bound the Campagna—the Sabine and Alban hills and the solitary Soracte farther on to the left. Then wandering back across the Campagna, it searches for the Sister hills, hardly distinguishable now as hills. The Palatine is conspicuous enough, marked by the ruins of the Palace of the Cæsars, and rising up beyond the extremity of the Forum. And now, once resting on the Forum, the eye will not readily quit the long area that begins with the Clivus Capitolinus and extends to

the Coliseum—an area that was once the very focus of the world. The Campo Vaccino, the site probably of the Comitium, was this first morning covered with carts and animals, mingling a simple form of actual life with those signs of the highly artificial life that had been crowded here in ages gone by: the three Corinthian pillars at the extremity of the Forum, said to have belonged to the Temple of Jupiter Stator; the grand temple of Antoninus and Faustina; the white arch of Titus; the Basilica of Constantine; the temple built by Adrian, with its great broken granite columns scattered around on the green rising ground; the huge arc of the Coliseum and the arch of Constantine.

The scene of these great relics remained our favourite haunt during our stay at Rome; and one day near the end of it we entered the enclosure of the Clivus Capitolinus and the excavated space of the Forum. The ruins on the Clivus—the façade of massive columns on the right, called the temple of Vespasian; the two Corinthian columns, called the temple of Saturn, in the centre, and the arch of Septimius Severus on the left—have their rich colour set off by the luxuriant green, clothing the lower masonry, which formed the foundations of the crowded buildings on this narrow space, and as a background to them all, the rough solidity of the ancient wall forming the back of the central building on the Intermontium, and regarded as one of the few remains of Republican constructions. On either hand, at another angle from the arch, the ancient road forming the double ascent of the Clivus is seen firm and level with its great blocks of pavement. The arch of Septimius Severus is particularly rich in colour; and the poorly executed bas-reliefs of military groups still look out in grotesque completeness of attitude and expression, even on the sides exposed to the weather. From the Clivus, a passage, underneath the present road, leads into the Forum, whose immense, pinkish, granite columns lie on the weather-worn white marble pavement. The column of Phocas, with its base no longer "buried," stands at the extreme corner nearest the Clivus; and the three elegant columns of the temple (say some) of Jupiter Stator, mark the opposite extremity: between lie traces, utterly confused to all but erudite eyes, of marble steps and of pedestals stripped of their marble.

Let me see what I most delighted in, in Rome. Certainly this drive from the Clivus to the Coliseum was, from first to last, one of the chief things; but there are many objects and many impressions of various kinds which I can reckon up as of almost equal interest: the Coliseum itself, with the view from it; the drive along the Appian Way to the tomb of Cecilia Metella, and the view from thence of the Campagna bridged by the aqueduct: the baths of Titus, with the remnants of their arabesques, seen by the light of torches, in the now damp and gloomy spaces; the glimpse of the Tarpeian rock, with its growth of cactus and rough herbage; the grand bare arch brickwork of the Palace of the Cæsars rising in huge masses on the Palatine; the theatre of Marcellus bursting suddenly into view from among the crowded mean houses of the modern city, and still more the temple of Minerva and temple of Nerva, also set in the crowded city of the present; and that exterior of the Pantheon, if it were not marred by the Papal belfries,—these are the traces of ancient Rome that have left the strongest image of themselves in my mind. I ought not to leave out Trajan's column, and the forum in which it stands; though the severe cold tint of the grey granite columns, or fragments of columns, gave this forum rather a dreary effect to me. For vastness there is perhaps nothing more impressive in Rome than the Baths of Caracalla, except the Coliseum: and I remember that it was amongst them that I first noticed the lovely effect of the giant fennel, luxuriant among the crumbling brickwork.

We should have regretted entirely our efforts to get to Rome during the Holy Week, instead of making Florence our first resting-place, if we had not had the compensation for wearisome, empty ceremonies and closed museums in the wonderful spectacle of the illumination of St. Peter's. That, really, is a thing so wondrous, so magically beautiful, that one can't find in one's heart to say it is not worth doing. I remember well the first glimpse we had, as we drove out towards it, of the outline of the dome like a new constellation on the black sky. I thought *that* was the final illumination, and was regretting our tardy arrival, from the *détour* we had to make, when, as our carriage stopped in front of the cathedral, the great bell sounded, and in an instant the grand illumination flashed out and turned the outline of stars into a palace of gold. Venus looked on palely.

LETTER TO MRS. CONGREVE, 4TH APRIL

Oh, the beautiful men and women and children here! Such wonderful babies with wise eyes!—such grand-featured mothers nursing them! As one drives along the streets sometimes, one sees a madonna and child at every third or fourth upper window; and on Monday a little crippled girl seated at the door of a church looked up at us with a face full of such pathetic sweetness and beauty, that I think it can hardly leave me again. Yesterday we went to see dear Shelley's tomb, and it was like a personal consolation to me to see that simple outward sign that he is at rest, where no hatred can ever reach him again. Poor Keats's tombstone, with that despairing bitter inscription,* is almost as painful to think of as Swift's.

JOURNAL, JUNE

We left Florence on the evening of the first of June, by diligence, travelling all night and until eleven the next morning to get to Bologna. I wish we could have made that journey across the Apennines by daylight, though in that case I should have missed certain grand startling effects that came to me in my occasional wakings. Wonderful heights and depths I saw on each side of us by the fading light of the evening. Then in the middle of the night, while the lightning was flashing and the sky was heavy with threatening storm-clouds, I waked to find the six horses resolutely refusing or unable to move the diligence—till at last two meek oxen were tied to the axle, and their added strength dragged us up the hill. But one of the strangest effects I ever saw was just before dawn, when we seemed to be high up

* "Here lies one whose name was writ in water."

on mighty mountains, which fell precipitously and showed us the awful pale horizon far, far below.

We left Bologna in the afternoon, rested at Ferrara for the night, and passed the Euganean Mountains on our left hand as we approached Padua in the middle of the next day.

After dinner and rest from our dusty journeying, we took a carriage and went out to see the town, desiring most of all to see the Arena Chapel.

It stands apart, and is approached at present through a pretty garden. Here one is uninterruptedly with Giotto. The whole chapel was designed and painted by himself alone; and it is said that while he was at work on it, Dante lodged with him at Padua. The nave of the chapel is in tolerably good preservation, but the apsis has suffered severely from damp. It is in this apsis that the lovely Madonna, with the Infant at her breast, is painted in a niche, now quite hidden by some altar-piece or woodwork, which one has to push by in order to see the tenderest bit of Giotto's painting. This chapel must have been a blessed vision when it was fresh from Giotto's hand—the blue vaulted roof; the exquisite bands of which he was so fond, representing inlaid marble, uniting roof and walls and forming the divisions between the various frescoes which cover the upper part of the wall. The glory of Paradise at one end, and the histories of Mary and Jesus on the two sides; and the subdued effect of the series of monochromes representing the Virtues and Vices below.

From Padua to Venice.

We make the journey to Chioggia but with small pleasure, on account of my illness, which continued all day. Otherwise that long floating over the water, with the forts and mountains looking as if they were suspended in the air, would have been very enjoyable. Of all dreamy delights, that of floating in a gondola along the canals and out on the Lagoon is surely the greatest. We were out one night on the Lagoon when the sun was setting, and the wide waters were flushed with the reddened light. I should have liked it to last for hours: it is the sort of scene in which I could most readily forget my own existence, and feel melted into the general life.

Another charm of evening time was to walk up and down the Piazza of San Marco as the stars were brightening and look at the grand dim buildings, and the flocks of pigeons flitting about them; or to walk on to the Bridge of La Paglia and look along the dark canal that runs under the Bridge of Sighs—its blackness lit up by a gaslight here and there, and the plash of the oar of blackest gondola slowly advancing.

From Venice to Vernona and Milan.

We left Milan for Como on a fine Sunday morning, and arrived at beautiful Bellagio by steamer in the evening. Here we spent a delicious day—going to the Villa Somma Riva in the morning, and in the evening to the Serbellone Gardens, from the heights of which we saw the mountain-peaks reddened with the last rays of the sun. The next day we reached lovely Chiavenna, at the foot of the Splügen Pass, and spent the evening in company with a glorious mountain torrent, mountain peaks, huge boulders, with rippling miniature torrents and lovely young flowers among them, and grassy heights with rich Spanish chestnuts shadowing them. Then, the next morning, we set off by post and climbed the almost perpendicular heights of the pass—chiefly in heavy rain that would hardly let us discern the patches of snow when we reached the table-land of the summit. About five o'clock we reached grassy Splügen, and felt that we had left Italy behind us. Already our driver had been German for the last long post, and now we had come to an hotel where host and waiters were German. Swiss houses of dark wood, outside staircases and broad eaves, stood on the steep, green, and flowery slope that led up to the waterfall; and the hotel and other buildings of masonry were thoroughly German in their aspect. In the evening we enjoyed a walk between the mountains, whose lower sides down to the torrent bed were set with tall dark pines. But the climax of grand—nay, terrible—scenery came the next day as we traversed the Via Mala.

After this came open green valleys, with dotted white churches and homesteads. We were in Switzerland, and the mighty wall of the Valtelline Alps shut us out from Italy on the 21st of June.

E. M. FORSTER

(1879–1970)

E. M. Forster, London born and Cambridge educated, took his first trip to Italy after his graduation from Kings College. A Room with a View, *his third novel, was published in 1908 just before his thirtieth birthday.*

Under the guise of a predictable romantic novel, A Room with a View *is a social commentary on the British middle class. Its heroine, Lucy Honeychurch, is mired in her family's pedestrian values and strapped with an unrelenting chaperone, Charlotte Bartlett, who reins in Lucy's feeble rebellions during an Italian tour. Lucy, Charlotte, the Socialist Mr. Emerson, and his son George, a lady novelist, Miss Lavish, the Reverends Beebe and Eager, the spinster sisters, the Misses Alan, and several other English "characters" are residents of Pensione Bertolini in Florence. Lucy and Charlotte want a "room with a view" and are graciously offered a trade in accommodations by the Emersons. While sightseeing with the flighty Miss Lavish, Lucy encounters the Emersons in a cathedral, a meeting that will alter her life. Despite the vagaries of their romance, Forster makes it almost inevitable that Lucy and George will marry and honeymoon at Pensione Bertolini.*

In Santa Croce with No Baedeker

from A ROOM WITH A VIEW

It was pleasant to wake up in Florence, to open the eyes upon a bright bare room, with a floor of red tiles which look clean though they are not; with a painted ceiling whereon pink griffins and blue amorini sport in a forest of yellow violins and bassoons. It was pleasant, too, to fling wide the windows, pinching the fingers in unfamiliar fastenings, to lean out into sunshine with beautiful hills and trees and marble churches opposite, and close below, the Arno, gurgling against the embankment of the road.

Over the river men were at work with spades and sieves on the sandy foreshore, and on the river was a boat, also diligently employed for some mysterious end. An electric tram came rushing underneath the window. No one was inside it, except one tourist; but its platforms were overflowing with Italians, who preferred to stand. Children tried to hang on behind, and the conductor, with no malice, spat in their faces to make them let go. Then soldiers appeared—good-looking, undersized men—wearing each a knapsack covered with mangy fur, and a greatcoat which had been cut for some larger soldier. Beside them walked officers, looking foolish and fierce, and before them went little boys, turning somersaults in time with the band. The tramcar became entangled in their ranks, and moved on painfully, like a caterpillar in a swarm of ants. One of the little boys fell down, and some white bullocks came out of an archway. Indeed, if it had not been for the good advice of an old man who was selling button-hooks, the road might never have got clear.

Over such trivialities as these many a valuable hour may slip away, and the traveller who has gone to Italy to study the tactile values of Giotto, or the corruption of the Papacy, may return remembering nothing but the blue sky and the men and women who live under it. So it was as well that Miss Bartlett should tap and come in, and having commented on Lucy's leaving the door unlocked, and on her leaning out of the window before she was fully dressed, should urge her to hasten herself, or the best of the day would be gone. By the time Lucy was ready her cousin had done her breakfast, and was listening to the clever lady among the crumbs.

A conversation then ensued, on not unfamiliar lines. Miss Bartlett was, after all, a wee bit tired, and thought they had better spend the morning settling in; unless Lucy would at all like to go out? Lucy would rather like to go out, as it was her first day in Florence, but, of course, she could go alone. Miss Bartlett could not allow this. Of course she would accompany Lucy everywhere. Oh, certainly not; Lucy would stop with her cousin. Oh, no! that would never do. Oh, yes!

At this point the clever lady broke in.

"If it is Mrs. Grundy who is troubling you, I do assure you that you can neglect the good person. Being English, Miss Honeychurch will be perfectly safe. Italians understand. A dear friend of mine, Contessa Baroncelli, has two daughters, and when she cannot send a maid to school with them, she lets them go in sailor-hats instead. Every one takes them for English, you see, especially if their hair is strained tightly behind."

Miss Bartlett was unconvinced by the safety of Contessa Baroncelli's daughters. She was determined to take Lucy herself, her head not being so very bad. The clever lady then said that she was going to spend a long morning in Santa Croce, and if Lucy would come too, she would be delighted.

"I will take you by a dear dirty back way, Miss Honeychurch, and if you bring me luck, we shall have an adventure."

Lucy said that this was most kind, and at once opened the Baedeker, to see where Santa Croce was.

"Tut, tut! Miss Lucy! I hope we shall soon emancipate you from Baedeker. He does but touch the surface of things. As to the true Italy—he does not even dream of it. The true Italy is only to be found by patient observation."

This sounded very interesting, and Lucy hurried over her breakfast, and started with her new friend in high spirits. Italy was coming at last. The Cockney Signora and her works had vanished like a bad dream.

Miss Lavish—for that was the clever lady's name—turned to the right along the sunny Lung' Arno. How delightfully warm! But a wind down the side streets cut like a knife, didn't it? Ponte alle Grazie—particularly interesting, mentioned by Dante. San Miniato—beautiful as well as interesting; the crucifix that kissed a murderer—Miss Honeychurch would remember the story. The men on the river were fishing. (Untrue; but then, so is most information.) Then Miss Lavish darted under the archway of the white bullocks, and she stopped, and she cried:

"A smell! a true Florentine smell! Every city, let me teach you, has its own smell."

"Is it a very nice smell?" said Lucy, who had inherited from her mother a distaste to dirt.

"One doesn't come to Italy for niceness," was the retort; "one comes for life. Buon giorno! Buon giorno!" bowing right and left. "Look at that adorable wine-cart! How the driver stares at us, dear, simple soul!"

So Miss Lavish proceeded through the streets of the city of Florence, short, fidgety, and playful as a kitten, though without a kitten's grace. It was a treat for the girl to be with any one so clever and so cheerful; and a blue military cloak, such as an Italian officer wears, only increased the sense of festivity.

"Buon giorno! Take the word of an old woman, Miss Lucy: you will never repent of a little civility to your inferiors. *That* is the true democracy. Though I am a real Radical as well. There, now you're shocked."

"Indeed, I'm not!" exclaimed Lucy. "We are Radicals, too, out and out. My father always voted for Mr. Gladstone, until he was so dreadful about Ireland."

"I see, I see. And now you have gone over to the enemy."

"Oh please—! If my father was alive, I am sure he would vote Radical again now that Ireland is all right. And as it is, the glass over our front-door was broken last election, and Freddy is sure it was the Tories; but mother says nonsense, a tramp."

"Shameful! A manufacturing district, I suppose?"

"No—in the Surrey hills. About five miles from Dorking, looking over the Weald."

Miss Lavish seemed interested, and slackened her trot.

"What a delightful part; I know it so well. It is full of the very nicest people. Do you know Sir Harry Otway—a Radical if ever there was?"

"Very well indeed."

"And old Mrs. Butterworth the philanthropist?"

"Why, she rents a field of us! How funny!"

Miss Lavish looked at the narrow ribbon of sky, and murmured:

"Oh, you have property in Surrey?"

"Hardly any," said Lucy, fearful of being thought a snob. "Only thirty acres—just the garden, all downhill, and some fields."

Miss Lavish was not disgusted, and said it was just the size of her aunt's Suffolk estate. Italy receded. They tried to remember the last name of Lady Louisa some one, who had taken a house near Summer Street the other year, but she had not liked it, which was odd of her. And just as Miss Lavish had got the name, she broke off and exclaimed:

"Bless us! Bless us and save us! We've lost the way."

Certainly they had seemed a long time in reaching Santa Croce, the tower of which had been plainly visible from the landing window. But Miss Lavish had said so much about knowing her Florence by heart, that Lucy had followed her with no misgivings.

"Lost! lost! My dear Lucy, during our political diatribes we have taken a wrong turning. How those horrid Conservatives would jeer us! What are we to do? Two lone females in an unknown town. Now, this is what *I* call an adventure."

Lucy, who wanted to see Santa Croce, suggested, as a possible solution, that they should ask the way there.

"Oh, but that is the word of a craven! And no, you are not, not, *not* to look at your Baedeker. Give it to me: I shan't let you carry it. We will simply drift."

Accordingly, they drifted through a series of those grey-brown streets, neither commodious nor picturesque, in which the eastern quarter of the city abounds. Lucy soon lost interest in the discontent of Lady Louisa, and became discontented herself. For one ravishing moment Italy appeared. She stood in the Square of the Annunziata and saw in the living terra-cotta those divine babies whom no cheap reproduction can ever stale. There they stood, with their shining limbs bursting from the garments of charity, and their strong white arms extended against circlets of heaven. Lucy thought she had never seen anything more beautiful; but Miss Lavish, with a shriek of dismay, dragged her forward, declaring that they were out of their path now by at least a mile.

The hour was approaching at which the continental breakfast begins, or rather ceases, to tell, and the ladies bought some hot chestnut paste out of a little shop, because it looked so typical. It tasted partly of the paper in which it was wrapped, partly of hair oil, partly of the great unknown. But it gave them strength to drift into another Piazza, large and dusty, on the farther side of which rose a black-and-white facade of surpassing ugliness. Miss Lavish spoke to it dramatically. It was Santa Croce. The adventure was over.

"Stop a minute; let those two people go on, or I shall have to speak to them. I do detest conventional intercourse. Nasty! they are going into the church, too. Oh, the Britisher abroad!"

"We sat opposite them at dinner last night. They have given us their rooms. They were so very kind."

"Look at their figures!" laughed Miss Lavish. "They walk through my Italy like a pair of cows. It's very naughty of me, but I would like to set an examination paper at Dover, and turn back every tourist who couldn't pass it."

"What would you ask us?"

Miss Lavish laid her hand pleasantly on Lucy's arm, as if to suggest that she, at all events, would get full marks. In this exalted mood they reached the steps of the great church, and were about to enter it when Miss Lavish stopped, squeaked, flung up her arms, and cried:

"There goes my local-colour box! I must have a word with him!"

And in a moment she was away over the Piazza, her military cloak flapping in the wind; nor did she slacken speed till she caught up an old man with white whiskers, and nipped him playfully upon the arm.

Lucy waited for nearly ten minutes. Then she began to get tired. The beggars worried her, the dust blew in her eyes, and she remembered that a young girl ought not to loiter in public places. She descended slowly into the Piazza with the intention of rejoining Miss Lavish, who was really almost too original. But at that moment Miss Lavish and her local-colour box moved also, and disappeared down a side street, both gesticulating largely.

Tears of indignation came to Lucy's eyes—partly because Miss Lavish had jilted her, partly because she had taken her Baedeker. How could she find her way home? How could she find her way about in Santa Croce? Her first morning was ruined, and she might never be in Florence again. A few minutes ago she had been all high spirits, talking as a woman of culture, and half persuading herself that she was full of originality. Now she entered the church depressed and humiliated, not even able to remember whether it was built by the Franciscans or the Dominicans.

Of course, it must be a wonderful building. But how like a barn! And how very cold! Of course, it contained frescoes by

Giotto, in the presence of whose tactile values she was capable of feeling what was proper. But who was to tell her which they were? She walked about disdainfully, unwilling to be enthusiastic over monuments of uncertain authorship or date. There was no one even to tell her which, of all the sepulchral slabs that paved the nave and transepts, was the one that was really beautiful, the one that had been most praised by Mr. Ruskin.

Then the pernicious charm of Italy worked on her, and, instead of acquiring information, she began to be happy. She puzzled out the Italian notices—the notices that forbade people to introduce dogs into the church—the notice that prayed people, in the interest of health and out of respect to the sacred edifice in which they found themselves, not to spit. She watched the tourists; their noses were as red as their Baedekers, so cold was Santa Croce. She beheld the horrible fate that overtook three Papists—two he-babies and a she-baby—who began their career by sousing each other with the Holy Water, and then proceeded to the Machiavelli memorial, dripped but hallowed. Advancing towards it very slowly and from immense distances, they touched the stone with their fingers, with their handkerchiefs, with their heads, and then retreated. What could this mean? They did it again and again. Then Lucy realized that they had mistaken Machiavelli for some saint, hoping to acquire virtue. Punishment followed quickly. The smallest he-baby stumbled over one of the sepulchral slabs so much admired by Mr. Ruskin, and entangled his feet in the features of a recumbent bishop. Protestant as she was, Lucy darted forward. She was too late. He fell heavily upon the prelate's upturned toes.

"Hateful bishop!" exclaimed the voice of old Mr. Emerson, who had darted forward also. "Hard in life, hard in death. Go out into the sunshine, little boy, and kiss your hand to the sun, for that is where you ought to be. Intolerable bishop!"

The child screamed frantically at these words, and at these dreadful people who picked him up, dusted him, rubbed his bruises, and told him not to be superstitious.

"Look at him!" said Mr. Emerson to Lucy. "Here's a mess: a

baby hurt, cold, and frightened! But what else can you expect from a church?"

The child's legs had become as melting wax. Each time that old Mr. Emerson and Lucy set it erect it collapsed with a roar. Fortunately an Italian lady, who ought to have been saying her prayers, came to the rescue. By some mysterious virtue, which mothers alone possess, she stiffened the little boy's back-bone and imparted strength to his knees. He stood. Still gibbering with agitation, he walked away.

"You are a clever woman," said Mr. Emerson. "You have done more than all the relics in the world. I am not of your creed, but I do believe in those who make their fellow-creatures happy. There is no scheme of the universe—"

He paused for a phrase.

"Niente," said the Italian lady, and returned to her prayers.

"I'm not sure she understands English," suggested Lucy.

In her chastened mood she no longer despised the Emersons. She was determined to be gracious to them, beautiful rather than delicate, and, if possible, to erase Miss Bartlett's civility by some gracious reference to the pleasant rooms.

"That woman understands everything," was Mr. Emerson's reply. "But what are you doing here? Are you doing the church? Are you through with the church?"

"No," cried Lucy, remembering her grievance. "I came here with Miss Lavish, who was to explain everything; and just by the door—it is too bad!—she simply ran away, and after waiting quite a time, I had to come in by myself."

"Why shouldn't you?" said Mr. Emerson.

"Yes, why shouldn't you come by yourself?" asked the son, addressing the young lady for the first time.

"But Miss Lavish had taken away Baedeker."

"Baedeker?" said Mr. Emerson. "I'm glad it's *that* you minded. It's worth minding, the loss of a Baedeker. *That's* worth minding."

Lucy was puzzled. She was again conscious of some new idea, and was not sure whither it would lead her.

"If you've no Baedeker," said the son, "you'd better join us."

Was this where the idea would lead? She took refuge in her dignity.

"Thank you very much, but I could not think of that. I hope you do not suppose that I came to join on to you. I really came to help with the child, and to thank you for so kindly giving us your rooms last night. I hope that you have not been put to any great inconvenience."

"My dear," said the old man gently, "I think that you are repeating what you have heard older people say. You are pretending to be touchy; but you are not really. Stop being so tiresome, and tell me instead what part of the church you want to see. To take you to it will be a real pleasure."

Now, this was abominably impertinent, and she ought to have been furious. But it is sometimes as difficult to lose one's temper as it is difficult at other times to keep it. Lucy could not get cross. Mr. Emerson was an old man, and surely a girl might humour him. On the other hand, his son was a young man, and she felt that a girl ought to be offended with him, or at all events be offended before him. It was at him that she gazed before replying.

"I am not touchy, I hope. It is the Giottos that I want to see, if you will kindly tell me which they are."

The son nodded. With a look of sombre satisfaction, he led the way to the Peruzzi Chapel. There was a hint of the teacher about him. She felt like a child in school who had answered a question rightly.

The chapel was already filled with an earnest congregation, and out of them rose the voice of a lecturer, directing them how to worship Giotto, not by tactful valuations, but by the standards of the spirit.

"Remember," he was saying, "the facts about this church of Santa Croce; how it was built by faith in the full fervour of mediævalism, before any taint of the Renaissance had appeared. Observe how Giotto in these frescoes—now, unhappily, ruined by restoration—is untroubled by the snares of anatomy and perspective. Could anything be more majestic, more pathetic, beautiful, true? How little, we feel, avails knowledge and technical cleverness against a man who truly feels!"

"No!" exclaimed Mr. Emerson, in much too loud a voice for church. "Remember nothing of the sort! Built by faith indeed! That simply means the workmen weren't paid properly. And as for the frescoes, I see no truth in them. Look at that fat man in blue! He must weigh as much as I do, and he is shooting into the sky like an air-balloon."

He was referring to the fresco of the "Ascension of St. John." Inside, the lecturer's voice faltered, as well it might. The audience shifted uneasily, and so did Lucy. She was sure that she ought not to be with these men; but they had cast a spell over her. They were so serious and so strange that she could not remember how to behave.

"Now, did this happen, or didn't it? Yes or no?"

George replied:

"It happened like this, if it happened at all. I would rather go up to heaven by myself than be pushed by cherubs; and if I got there I should like my friends to lean out of it, just as they do here."

"You will never go up," said his father. "You and *I,* dear boy, will lie at peace in the earth that bore us, and our names will disappear as surely as our work survives."

"Some of the people can only see the empty grave, not the saint, whoever he is, going up. It did happen like that, if it happened at all."

"Pardon me," said a frigid voice. "The chapel is somewhat small for two parties. We will incommode you no longer."

The lecturer was a clergyman, and his audience must be also his flock, for they held prayer-books as well as guide-books in their hands. They filed out of the chapel in silence. Among them were two little old ladies of the Pensione Bertolini—Miss Teresa and Miss Catharine Alan.

"Stop!" cried Mr. Emerson. "There's plenty of room for us all. Stop!"

The procession disappeared without a word. Soon the lecturer could be heard in the next chapel, describing the life of St. Francis.

"George, I do believe that clergyman is the Brixton curate."

George went into the next chapel and returned saying, "Perhaps he is. I don't remember."

"Then I had better speak to him and remind him who I am. It's that Mr. Eager. Why did he go? Did we talk too loud? How vexatious. I shall go and say we are sorry. Hadn't I better? Then perhaps he will come back."

"He will not come back," said George.

But Mr. Emerson, contrite and unhappy, hurried away to apologize to the Rev. Cuthbert Eager. Lucy, apparently absorbed in a lunette, could hear the lecture again interrupted, the anxious, aggressive voice of the old man, the curt, injured replies of his opponent. The son, who took every little contretemps as if it were a tragedy, was listening also.

"My father has that effect on nearly every one," he informed her. "He will try to be kind."

"I hope we all try," said she, smiling nervously.

"Because we think it improves our characters. But he is kind to people because he loves them; and they find him out, and are offended, or frightened."

"How silly of them!" said Lucy, though in her heart she sympathized; "I think that a kind action done tactfully—"

"Tact!"

He threw up his head in disdain. Apparently she had given the wrong answer. She watched the singular creature pace up and down the chapel. For a young man his face was rugged, and—until the shadows fell upon it—hard. Enshadowed, it sprang into tenderness. She saw him once again at Rome, on the ceiling of the Sistine Chapel, carrying a burden of acorns. Healthy and muscular, he yet gave her the feeling of greyness, of tragedy that might only find solution in the night. The feeling soon passed; it was unlike her to have entertained anything so subtle. Born of silence and of unknown emotion, it passed when Mr. Emerson returned, and she could re-enter the world of rapid talk, which was alone familiar to her.

"Were you snubbed?" asked his son tranquilly.

"But we have spoilt the pleasure of I don't know how many people. They won't come back."

". . . full of innate sympathy . . . quickness to perceive good in others . . . vision of the brotherhood of man . . ." Scraps of the lecture on St. Francis came floating round the partition wall.

"Don't let us spoil yours," he continued to Lucy. "Have you looked at those saints?"

"Yes," said Lucy. "They are lovely. Do you know which is the tombstone that is praised in Ruskin?"

He did not know, and suggested that they should try to guess it. George, rather to her relief, refused to move, and she and the old man wandered not unpleasantly about Santa Croce, which, though it is like a barn, has harvested many beautiful things inside its walls. There were also beggars to avoid, and guides to dodge round the pillars, and an old lady with her dog, and here and there a priest modestly edging to his Mass through the groups of tourists. But Mr. Emerson was only half interested. He watched the lecturer, whose success he believed he had impaired, and then he anxiously watched his son.

"Why will he look at the fresco?" he said uneasily. "I saw nothing in it."

"I like Giotto," she replied. "It is so wonderful what they say about his tactile values. Though I like things like the Della Robbia babies better."

"So you ought. A baby is worth a dozen saints. And my baby's worth the whole of Paradise, and as far as I can see he lives in Hell."

Lucy again felt that this did not do.

"In Hell," he repeated. "He's unhappy."

"Oh, dear!" said Lucy.

"How can he be unhappy when he is strong and alive? What more is one to give him? And think how he has been brought up—free from all the superstition and ignorance that lead men to hate one another in the name of God. With such an education as that, I thought he was bound to grow up happy."

She was no theologian, but she felt that here was a very foolish old man, as well as a very irreligious one. She also felt that her mother might not like her talking to that kind of person, and that Charlotte would object most strongly.

"What are we to do with him?" he asked. "He comes out for his holiday to Italy, and behaves—like that; like the little child who ought to have been playing, and who hurt himself upon the tombstone. Eh? What did you say?"

Lucy had made no suggestion. Suddenly he said:

"Now don't be stupid over this. I don't require you to fall in love with my boy, but I do think you might try and understand him. You are nearer his age, and if you let yourself go I am sure you are sensible. You might help me. He has known so few women, and you have the time. You stop here several weeks, I suppose? But let yourself go. You are inclined to get muddled, if I may judge from last night. Let yourself go. Pull out from the depths those thoughts that you do not understand, and spread them out in the sunlight and know the meaning of them. By understanding George you may learn to understand yourself. It will be good for both of you."

To this extraordinary speech Lucy found no answer.

"I only know what it is that's wrong with him; not why it is."

"And what is it?" asked Lucy fearfully, expecting some harrowing tale.

"The old trouble; things won't fit."

"What things?"

"The things of the universe. It is quite true. They don't."

"Oh, Mr. Emerson, whatever do you mean?"

In his ordinary voice, so that she scarcely realized he was quoting poetry, he said:

> " 'From far, from eve and morning,
>   And yon twelve-winded sky,
>   The stuff of life to knit me
>   Blew hither: here am I.'

George and I both know this, but why does it distress him? We know that we come from the winds, and that we shall return to them; that all life is perhaps a knot, a tangle, a blemish in the eternal smoothness. But why should this make us unhappy? Let us rather love one another, and work and rejoice. I don't believe in this world sorrow."

Miss Honeychurch assented.

"Then make my boy think like us. Make him realize that by the side of the everlasting Why there is a Yes—a transitory Yes if you like, but a Yes."

Suddenly she laughed; surely one ought to laugh. A young man melancholy because the universe wouldn't fit, because life was a tangle or a wind, or a Yes, or something!

"I'm very sorry," she cried. "You'll think me unfeeling, but— but—" Then she became matronly. "Oh, but your son wants employment. Has he no particular hobby? Why, I myself have worries, but I can generally forget them at the piano; and collecting stamps did no end of good for my brother. Perhaps Italy bores him; you ought to try the Alps or the Lakes."

The old man's face saddened, and he touched her gently with his hand. This did not alarm her; she thought that her advice had impressed him and that he was thanking her for it. Indeed, he no longer alarmed her at all; she regarded him as a kind thing, but quite silly. Her feelings were as inflated spiritually as they had been an hour ago æsthetically, before she lost Baedeker. The dear George, now striding towards them over the tombstones, seemed both pitiable and absurd. He approached, his face in the shadow. He said:

"Miss Bartlett."

"Oh, good gracious me!" said Lucy, suddenly collapsing and again seeing the whole of life in a new perspective. "Where? Where?"

"In the nave."

"I see. Those gossiping little Miss Alans must have—" She checked herself.

"Poor girl!" exploded Mr. Emerson. "Poor girl!"

She could not let this pass, for it was just what she was feeling herself.

"Poor girl? I fail to understand the point of that remark. I think myself a very fortunate girl, I assure you. I'm thoroughly happy, and having a splendid time. Pray don't waste time mourning over *me*. There's enough sorrow in the world, isn't there, without trying to invent it. Good-bye. Thank you both so much for all your kindness. Ah, yes! there does come my cousin. A delightful morning! Santa Croce is a wonderful church."

She joined her cousin.

BARBARA GRIZZUTI HARRISON
(1934–)

In the 1980s Brooklyn-born Barbara Grizzuti Harrison spent four years in Italy, in the places where her immigrant parents were born and raised. Her book Italian Days *included her encounters with distant relatives and an analysis of herself. She wrote in a prologue, "I did not know, when I went to Italy, the nature of my undertaking, nor did I anticipate the meaning of my journey. I lived every day as I found it. I now know—writing this book has taught me this—that it was a journey of reconciliation. . . . I discovered everything I feared and everything I loved. There was more to love than to fear." She followed* Italian Days *with* The Islands of Italy: Sicily, Sardinia and the Aeonian Islands, *from which this excerpt is taken.*

In both Italian Days *and* The Islands of Italy, *Barbara Grizzuti Harrison weaves autobiography and journalism. According to* The New York Times, *she "comes to her subjects with receptivity, energy and a critical awareness of human fallibility." Her most recent book,* An Accidental Autobiography, *was published in 1996.*

from THE ISLANDS OF ITALY

On the *autostrada* there is a roadblock sign. Not one driver pays it any mind. We think it is a way of foxing us (we have caught the Sicilian habit of distrusting all authority), to what end we can only guess. Eight cars play follow-the-blind-leader. We come, just as the road sign warned, to a dead end, and we must detour now for miles. We can read the thoughts of the driver ahead of us in a white van, his outstretched hand in eloquent gestures reveals his mind:

Why did they do this? Stupid, and where do we go now? Ah, well, life is like that. And look at the people behind us, fools like us.

Sheila's husband, Giuseppe, says that no man who drives wearing a hat is a good driver, and he is right.

On the way to Noto tongues of fire ignite spontaneously near dry walls that are incoherently placed, this in an arid landscape that has no logic. Everything that grows is gallant. The fire spins itself into a fury: dervishes of fire accompany us for miles.

In the spring, blankets of flowers are woven to cover the streets of Noto, a city of golden Sicilian baroque, brazenly theatrical . . . and, ravaged by earthquakes and time, falling to pieces, shored up, like those pictures one sees of Noah's Ark, on wooden supporting ramps—but not so likely to survive a deluge. Noto is a dream of what Noto once was . . . might have been . . . may be again—provisional, all netting and bulwarks and scaffolding, existing in limbo, in a kind of stasis that contradicts the restless spirit of the baroque. A city on the cusp between death and rebirth. Weeds sprout. Atlantis: a golden city dying before one's eyes. A city of jumped metaphors that mocks one's attempts to make sense of it: restoration and decay. At night one is almost able (intermittently) to believe that its gold is not false coin: the Duomo glimpsed through branches of a monkey-puzzle tree (three old men sitting on green plastic chairs in front of it).

I find the Noto I will remember on Via Duccezio: the concave, rococo, confectionary church of Santa Maria del Carmine, which embraces you, and a restaurant called Carmine, and the Pasticceria Mandolfiore, in which the confections are rococo and baroque, as exuberant as poor Noto is not.

Carmine's proprietor wears two wedding bands, his, and that of his wife, recently dead. He has three boys and three grown daughters and any mention of anything that remotely pertains to their mother sets the women crying. They cry as they serve

us dressed in black. One sees the daughters' futures clearly: sac-
rificial lives, forever black.

They do what they do in spite of all: we have an exquisite
rabbit casserole, the rabbit sautéed in olive oil and cooked in
white wine and the red wine vinegar that they make, a *soffritto* of
carrots and mint and olives and capers and white wine brought
together with the rabbit at the end of cooking (the surprise is in
the mint).

We look at many snapshots of the couple's fiftieth wedding
anniversary; Carmine offers us his ocean villa for the season; and
I wonder, as I have wondered often on this island: where is the
fabled Sicilian reserve?

(And I wonder as I have wondered before: if I could understand why Sicily is in love with its own grotesques and its dark
caves, would I have the key to Sicily?)

The Pasticceria Mandolfiore presents us with onerous choices:
cassata iced with lime ice cream; vanilla ice cream flecked with
chocolate and studded with citron and candied cherries (buried
treasure, jewels); strawberry *cassata* with chocolate pips; marzipan: corn, figs, mandarins (deliberately and artistically flawed),
marzipan cakes of Lux soap (it is a joke told against the Sicilians
that when Garibaldi gave them soap they thought it was cheese
and ate it; and this is their retaliatory joke, a nice last word); ricotta ice cream (ricotta, milk, and sugar) in conical bamboo-
and-straw containers, scaled-down versions of those the cheese
comes in (these are made by old people who might otherwise
have nothing with which to occupy their hands); marzipan sacred hearts and curly-haired white lambs; meringues and peach-
and-cream ice cream in pastry peaches (with sugar-fuzz—the
Sicilians take this business seriously; these confections are made
in a place that is called a laboratory). Ephemeral art.

Ex-votos made of bread: eyes of dough (for Santa Lucia, pa-
troness of sight); lungs and hands of dough; buns of San Biag-
gio, patron of the trachea.

Ciambelle i cudduri—giant doughnuts decorated with pasta
snakes, protection against snakebite.

On the Feast of the Dead, November 2, children are given grapes and suns and moons and thighbones made of sugar.

Conceptual art.

"If you ask, 'Why is . . . construction taking such a long time?' the inhabitants . . . answer, 'So that its destruction cannot begin.' And if asked whether they fear that, once the scaffoldings are removed, the city may begin to crumble and fall to pieces, they add hastily, in a whisper, 'Not only the city.'"—Italo Calvino, *Invisible Cities.*

After noon the fishing boats come in, fish is auctioned on white tile slabs, a private rite in a public place, incomprehensible words fluid and fast as rushing waters, foreign gestures, a cult, a temple of bloody fish. Cuttlefish and squid, lobster and swordfish and sea bass and *gamberoni*; fish with golden eyes; wrinkled, black-spotted coral fish with fanlike tails and gills, ugly and elegant, like Diana Vreeland. The eels are orphaned, nobody buys them, they are so fresh their eyes, amazed and alert, look as if they contain a live and lively intelligence. The fishermen are paunchy as, if tired of fish, they eat olives and bread and pasta and meat and cream. They eat sweet buns and drink sweet coffee in the trattoria on the docks.

For dinner I have smoked swordfish garnished with the orange pulp of sea urchins.

A Venetian of severe beauty is sitting with her lover on the terrace under an orange moon. She is drinking almond nectar from Avola, a drink like crushed pearls. Happiness has made him raucous; he is arguing that the fish auctioneers start with high prices and then go down, she that the auction works the other way around, from low prices to high; this is love play. Next they quarrel over whether the market has fresh buffalo mozzarella on Tuesday, this is serious business. She says that the reason there are no gardens in Portopalo is that it was for the grand *seigneur* to have gardens, not the *contadini,* this is a legacy from feudalism. Besides, she says, why bother, when left to itself the earth will sprout in its own time and way, trust it—and the Sicilians are clusters of flowers, she says, they live in the open. She comes to

Portopalo for "a little bit of Africa," she says . . . and because her first husband was Sicilian.

There is a poetry Italians tell. We say the names of towns we love. *Aaah, Luccignano!* the Venetian says. There is silence; and then we sigh. We are inwardly rehearsing all the reasons for our love; we are brought together by diverse memories unspoken.

Near Portopalo, unmarked on the map, is a nature and wildlife reserve, Vendicari. "We make love there," the Venetian's lover says, she kicks him gently with a long, elegantly shod foot (too practiced to blush).

The road ends a kilometer from the white sand beach. I walk past unworked salt flats, crystals oddly dull but palely magical under the morning sun. And then past a march and then a swamp which adds a not unpleasant undertone of overripe decaying vegetable matter to the frank sweet fragrance of ripe strawberries. White butterflies among raspberry canes; whispering papyrus. The air is delicious, this is a still delirium. There is no one making love on the beach. Far away there is a tableau: a fat baby, back to the sea, tearing up his picture book while fond parents look on. I walk another kilometer into the sea before my shoulders are immersed in water. Paradise enough to make one wish Eve hadn't eaten the apple. The Ionian meets the Mediterranean here, it is like a friendly turquoise pond. The warm safe waters are so clear; I see my friendly feet. A fisherman gives me a lift back to the main road. His car smells of sweat, tuna, and beer. On his bare chest are tattooed the words: VIVA LA MALAVITA!—Long Live the Mafia!

I AM in a restaurant on the waterfront and I am crying. I don't know why I am crying. Suddenly I do; memory has sprung a tender trap: Over twenty years ago I sat in this very place with my children, two and three. (How could I have forgotten. These days I don't set my mind the task of remembering my children's infancy, I am never sure whether the pain I feel when I peel back the years belongs to them or to me; one can understand one's

own pain and how one has earned it—one can trace the geneal-
ogy of one's pain; but the pain of others is unbearable because it
is obscure, each life is a mystery, dread accompanies the contemplation of it.) Twenty years ago we sailed from Bombay to
New York, stopping here in Siracusa . . . Stopping first in Suez,
where a black-robed magician put a coin in my daughter's hand
that changed into a yellow bird . . . I saw this happen. The
hooli-booli man he was called. So then in Siracusa, my daughter, Anna, pointed at every black-robed priest she saw: "Is he the
hooli-booli man?" she asked. Perhaps the reason Anna studies
theology is that a base coin turned into a golden bird in her hand
and when we lit candles in the cathedral of Siracusa she thanked
the hooli-booli man, believing him to be part of the same
magic. (Perhaps when I am a grandmother I will set my mind
the task of remembering my children's infancy. . . . Everyone in
Sicily my age is a grandmother!)

Those years ago, in this very port, a country woman dressed
all in black fell to her knees in horror and prayer when she spied
me, because I was wearing slacks . . . though one would have
thought, my arms being full of babies, she might have found me
acceptable—how things have changed. Not that Siracusa isn't
witchy anymore. . . .

In the vicinity of the port is the Fountain of Arethusa—a
kind of tank, a square enclosure of sweet water near the salt of
the sea. Pursued by the river god Alpheus in Arcadia, the nymph
Arethusa begged Artemis, the goddess of virginity, to save her;
Artemis obliged by turning her into a river, and as a river she
fled from Arcadia to Sicily and surfaced here, in this fountain,
where the waters of the pursued and the pursuer mingle. (We
are not told whether they were happy thus; happiness seems not
to be the point of Greek myths.) The fountain is surrounded by
papyrus, very elegant, and infested with swans (monogamous
and cruel); the graceful birds stand on their heads in the water;
they sit, like domestic cats, on haunches one didn't know they
had.

The cathedral is a five-minute walk from the port (which is

in the old city of Ortigia, joined to the modern mainland by two bridges; we eschew the nervous and ugly modern mainland). Kind women stop us: Watch your purse, your purse! they say; bad boys are here, they say. But I can't work up any fear. (After all, my children once were here.) The lanes of Ortigia are dark and narrow but they are unthreatening. We can see into the courtyards where the Ortigians (like the Milanesi) live; the life of courtyards dissipates fears, life is just beyond one's footfalls, all around me.

Grotesques sag under the weight of ruined baroque balconies. . . . We walk. . . .

And then—the bliss—cathedral square. *Granita!* Privacy achieved in public, the bliss! This square is handsome enough for cardinals. And accommodating: in the boat-shaped, oleander-lined piazza, black Moroccans in long white dresses walk hand in manly hand; cheeky boys in shorts manipulate remote controls—their toy Maseratis scoot under the feet of dogs who play a mating game; a couple quarrels unselfconsciously (she in a flowered dress and slippers): they have brought their quarrel out into this public living room to which *cortili,* courtyards, are an anteroom. Girls in golden sandals. *Froci* boys, their pinkies linked. A beribboned little girl in pajamas taking her first steps. Tourists. Lovers. *Carabinieri* in blinding white shirts. Vespas. "I have so missed a piazza," Calvino wrote when he was a long time without one, and so have I. I want to be a sedentary tourist, breakfast in the piazza, and lunch, and ices, dinner, newspapers, safely observing, safely observed.

Where does one go for solitude in a city? To a square.

Opposite the cathedral the square widens. The buildings facing the cathedral are almost imperceptibly concave, a discreet gesture of homage to the Duomo, which is an example of architectural Darwinism, it has evolved from the ruins of a temple of Athena; Doric columns remain (a lovely skeleton) in the Norman interior, their austerity enhanced by the baroque façade. A friendly church . . . a neighborhood church.

Somewhat guiltily I went to the Archeological Park on the

mainland to see the ruins of Greek altars and theaters; I had grown weary of antiquities, I longed for the life of the squares. I'd had enough of stone stoniness, blossoms in the dust, capers growing from the ruins, citrus groves heavy with the scent of fallen fruit decaying among decaying stone. I stayed to see the caverns and the caves; a cave, man's first home, and, perhaps, his last, promises both protection and obliteration, it is a dicey refuge from the living storm. There is an artificial grotto in the park, no one knows why it was built. Hundreds of doves make it their home (well; so long as bats do not). No guarantees: twenty-three meters high, the grotto reaches upward into darkness and stretches forward into darkness; its mouth is a series of sensual folds that Caravaggio, we are told, christened "the ear of Dionysius"—why? He must have seen in the forms of the grotto the lips of a vagina, and a womb, he was a sensualist, he loved women. Ah, but love of women coexists with terror of the womb, the catacomb from which we reach out and into our little lives.

The Grotta dei Cordari, nearby, is another matter: one sees the end from the beginning, the sunlight reaches the magnolia leaves at this cave's entrance from the other side. And that lessens the terror . . . also the thrill.

ERNEST HEMINGWAY
(1898–1961)

Ernest Hemingway immortalized his wartime affair with a young American nurse in A Farewell to Arms. *In it, Frederic Henry and Catherine Barkley mirror Hemingway and Agnes von Kurowsky, who tended him after he was wounded on the Italian front during World War I. In* A Farewell to Arms *Henry and Barkley's relationship ends tragically with Catherine's death in childbirth. In life, von Kurowsky returned to America and became a literary postscript to a poignant novel of war and romance. After World War I Hemingway briefly returned to the United States, but came back to Europe to settle in the famous postwar expatriate community that included the Fitzgeralds, Gertrude Stein, Ezra Pound, and Gerald and Sarah Murphy.*

A Farewell to Arms *is set in northern Italy and juxtaposes an intense romance with a powerful portrait of the inhumanity of war. Frederic Henry meets nurse Catherine Barkley; they are separated, and then reunited after Henry is wounded. Catherine nurses him in Milan, and he is about to return to active duty when she tells him that she is pregnant. Although he briefly returns to fight, Henry eventually deserts and he and Catherine flee Italy, rowing across Lago Maggiore to the Swiss border and safety in a neutral country. There they await the birth of their child.*

from A FAREWELL TO ARMS

I rowed in the dark keeping the wind in my face. The rain had stopped and only came occasionally in gusts. It was very dark, and the wind was cold. I could see Catherine in the stern but I could not see the water where the blades of the oars dipped. The oars were long and there were no leathers to keep them from slipping out. I pulled, raised, leaned forward, found the water, dipped and pulled, rowing as easily as I could. I did not feather the oars because the wind was with us. I knew my hands would blister and I wanted to delay it as long as I could. The boat was light and rowed easily. I pulled it along in the dark water. I could not see, and hoped we would soon come opposite Pallanza.

We never saw Pallanza. The wind was blowing up the lake and we passed the point that hides Pallanza in the dark and never saw the lights. When we finally saw some lights much further up the lake and close to the shore it was Intra. But for a long time we did not see any lights, nor did we see the shore but rowed steadily in the dark riding with the waves. Sometimes I missed the water with the oars in the dark as a wave lifted the boat. It was quite rough; but I kept on rowing, until suddenly we were close ashore against a point of rock that rose beside us; the waves striking against it, rushing high up, then falling back. I pulled hard on the right oar and backed water with the other and we went out into the lake again; the point was out of sight and we were going on up the lake.

"We're across the lake," I said to Catherine.

"Weren't we going to see Pallanza?"

"We've missed it."

"How are you, darling?"

"I'm fine."

"I could take the oars awhile?"

"No, I'm fine."

"Poor Ferguson," Catherine said. "In the morning she'll come to the hotel and find we're gone."

"I'm not worrying so much about that," I said, "as about getting into the Swiss part of the lake before it's daylight and the custom guards see us."

"Is it a long way?"

"It's some thirty kilometres from here."

I ROWED all night. Finally my hands were so sore I could hardly close them over the oars. We were nearly smashed up on the shore several times. I kept fairly close to the shore because I was afraid of getting lost on the lake and losing time. Sometimes we were so close we could see a row of trees and the road along the shore with the mountains behind. The rain stopped and the wind drove the clouds so that the moon shone through and looking back I could see the long dark point of Castagnola and the lake with white-caps and beyond, the moon on the high snow mountains. Then the clouds came over the moon again and the mountains and the lake were gone, but it was much lighter than it had been before and we could see the shore. I could see it too clearly and pulled out where they would not see the boat if there were custom guards along the Pallanza road. When the moon came out again we could see white villas on the shore on the slopes of the mountain and the white road where it showed through the trees. All the time I was rowing.

The lake widened and across it on the shore at the foot of the mountains on the other side we saw a few lights that should be Luino. I saw a wedgelike gap between the mountains on the other shore and I thought that must be Luino. If it was we were making good time. I pulled in the oars and lay back on the seat. I was very, very tired of rowing. My arms and shoulders and back ached and my hands were sore.

"I could hold the umbrella," Catherine said. "We could sail with that with the wind."

"Can you steer?"

"I think so."

"You take this oar and hold it under your arm close to the side of the boat and steer and I'll hold the umbrella." I went back to the stern and showed her how to hold the oar. I took the big umbrella the porter had given me and sat facing the bow and opened it. It opened with a clap. I held it on both sides, sitting astride the handle hooked over the seat. The wind was full in it and I felt the boat suck forward while I held as hard as I could to the two edges. It pulled hard. The boat was moving fast.

"We're going beautifully," Catherine said. All I could see was umbrella ribs. The umbrella strained and pulled and I felt us driving along with it. I braced my feet and held back on it, then suddenly, it buckled; I felt a rib snap on my forehead, I tried to grab the top that was bending with the wind and the whole thing buckled and went inside out and I was astride the handle of an inside-out, ripped umbrella, where I had been holding a wind-filled pulling sail. I unhooked the handle from the seat, laid the umbrella in the bow and went back to Catherine for the oar. She was laughing. She took my hand and kept on laughing.

"What's the matter?" I took the oar.

"You looked so funny holding that thing."

"I suppose so."

"Don't be cross, darling. It was awfully funny. You looked about twenty feet broad and very affectionate holding the umbrella by the edges—" she choked.

"I'll row."

"Take a rest and a drink. It's a grand night and we've come a long way."

"I'll have to keep the boat out of the trough of the waves."

"I'll get you a drink. Then rest a little while, darling."

I held the oars up and we sailed with them. Catherine was opening the bag. She handed me the brandy bottle. I pulled the cork with my pocket-knife and took a long drink. It was smooth and hot and the heat went all through me and I felt warmed and cheerful. "It's lovely brandy," I said. The moon was under again but I could see the shore. There seemed to be another point going out a long way ahead into the lake.

"Are you warm enough, Cat?"

"I'm splendid. I'm a little stiff."

"Bail out that water and you can put your feet down."

Then I rowed and listened to the oarlocks and the dip and scrape of the bailing tin under the stern seat.

"Would you give me the bailer?" I said. "I want a drink."

"It's awful dirty."

"That's all right. I'll rinse it."

I heard Catherine rinsing it over the side. Then she handed it to me dipped full of water. I was thirsty after the brandy and the water was icy cold, so cold it made my teeth ache. I looked toward the shore. We were closer to the long point. There were lights in the bay ahead.

"Thanks," I said and handed back the tin pail.

"You're ever so welcome," Catherine said. "There's much more if you want it."

"Don't you want to eat something?"

"No. I'll be hungry in a little while. We'll save it till then."

"All right."

What looked like a point ahead was a long high headland. I went further out in the lake to pass it. The lake was much narrower now. The moon was out again and the *guardia di finanza* could have seen our boat black on the water if they had been watching.

"How are you, Cat?" I asked.

"I'm all right. Where are we?"

"I don't think we have more than about eight miles more."

"That's a long way to row, you poor sweet. Aren't you dead?"

"No. I'm all right. My hands are sore is all."

We went on up the lake. There was a break in the mountains on the right bank, a flattening-out with a low shore line that I thought must be Cannobio. I stayed a long way out because it was from now on that we ran the most danger of meeting *guardia*. There was a high dome-capped mountain on the other shore a way ahead. I was tired. It was no great distance to row but when you were out of condition it had been a long way. I knew I had to pass that mountain and go up the lake at least five miles further before we would be in Swiss water. The moon was almost down now but before it went down the sky clouded over again and it was very dark. I stayed well out in the lake, rowing awhile, then resting and holding the oars so that the wind struck the blades.

"Let me row awhile," Catherine said.

"I don't think you ought to."

"Nonsense. It would be good for me. It would keep me from being too stiff."

"I don't think you should, Cat."

"Nonsense. Rowing in moderation is very good for the pregnant lady."

"All right, you row a little moderately. I'll go back, then you come up. Hold on to both gunwales when you come up."

I sat in the stern with my coat on and the collar turned up and watched Catherine row. She rowed very well but the oars were too long and bothered her. I opened the bag and ate a couple of sandwiches and took a drink of the brandy. It made everything much better and I took another drink.

"Tell me when you're tired," I said. Then a little later, "Watch out the oar doesn't pop you in the tummy."

"If it did"—Catherine said between strokes—"life might be much simpler."

I took another drink of the brandy.

"How are you going?"

"All right."

"Tell me when you want to stop."

"All right."

I took another drink of the brandy, then took hold of the two gunwales of the boat and moved forward.

"No. I'm going beautifully."

"Go on back to the stern. I've had a grand rest."

For a while, with the brandy, I rowed easily and steadily. Then I began to catch crabs and soon I was just chopping along again with a thin brown taste of bile from having rowed too hard after the brandy.

"Give me a drink of water, will you?" I said.

"That's easy," Catherine said.

Before daylight it started to drizzle. The wind was down or we were protected by mountains that bounded the curve the lake had made. When I knew daylight was coming I settled down and rowed hard. I did not know where we were and I wanted to get into the Swiss part of the lake. When it was beginning to be daylight we were quite close to the shore. I could see the rocky shore and the trees.

"What's that?" Catherine said. I rested on the oars and listened. It was a motor boat chugging out on the lake. I pulled close up to the shore and lay quiet. The chugging came closer; then we saw the motor boat in the rain a little astern of us. There were four *guardia di finanza* in the stern, their *alpini* hats pulled down, their cape collars turned up and their carbines slung across their backs. They all looked sleepy so early in the morning. I could see the yellow on their hats and the yellow marks on their cape collars. The motor boat chugged on and out of sight in the rain.

I pulled out into the lake. If we were that close to the border I did not want to be hailed by a sentry along the road. I stayed out where I could just see the shore and rowed on for three quarters of an hour in the rain. We heard a motor boat once more but I kept quiet until the noise of the engine went away across the lake.

"I think we're in Switzerland, Cat," I said.

"Really?"

"There's no way to know until we see Swiss troops."

"Or the Swiss navy."

"The Swiss navy's no joke for us. That last motor boat we heard was probably the Swiss navy."

"If we're in Switzerland let's have a big breakfast. They have wonderful rolls and butter and jam in Switzerland."

JOHN HERSEY

(1914–1993)

John Hersey was a correspondent for Time *in the late thirties and covered the Mediterranean and the Pacific theaters for* Time *and* Life *during World War II. Hersey's experience in Italy was the genesis for the novel* A Bell for Adano, *which won the Pulitzer Prize in 1945.* A Bell for Adano, *Hersey's later novel* The Wall, *set in Warsaw's Jewish ghetto, and his nonfiction work* Hiroshima *brought the implications of war home to Americans. In an article in* The Atlantic Monthly *in 1949, Hersey wrote "What should be the aims of a writer who undertakes a novel of contemporary history? . . . Above all, this kind of novel should make anyone who reads it better able to meet life in his generation—whenever that generation may be . . . Journalism allows its readers to witness history; fiction gives its readers an opportunity to live it."*

A Bell for Adano *tells the story of Victor Joppolo, an Italian-American major who heads the occupying American force in the Sicilian village of Adano. Joppolo searches for a replacement for the town's bell, which had been melted down by the Fascists for bullets.*

from A BELL FOR ADANO

Invasion had come to the town of Adano.

An American corporal ran tautly along the dirty Via Favemi and at the corner he threw himself down. He made certain arrangements with his light machine gun and then turned and beckoned to his friends to come forward.

In the Via Calabria, in another part of town, a party of three crept forward like cats. An explosion, possibly of a mortar shell, at some distance to the north but apparently inside the town, caused them to fall flat with a splash of dust. They waited on their bellies to see what would happen.

An entire platoon ducked from grave to grave in the Capucin Cemetery high on the hill overlooking town. The entire platoon was scared. They were out of touch with their unit. They did not know the situation. They were near their objective, which was the rocky crest not far off, but they wanted to find out what was going on in the town before they moved on.

All through the town of Adano, Americans were like this. They were not getting much resistance, but it was their first day of invasion, and they were tight in their muscles.

But at one of the sulphur loading jetties at the port a Major with a brief case under his arm stepped from the sliding gangway of LCI No. 9488, and he seemed to be wholly calm.

"Borth," he said to the sergeant who followed him onto the jetty, "this is like coming home, how often I have dreamed this." And he bent over and touched the palm of his hand to the jetty, then dusted his palm off on his woolen pants.

This man was Major Victor Joppolo, who had been named senior civil affairs officer of the town of Adano, representing Amgot. He was a man of medium height, with the dark skin of his parents, who were Italians from near Florence. He had a mustache. His face was round and his cheeks seemed cheerful but his eyes were intense and serious. He was about thirty-five.

The sergeant with him was Leonard Borth, an M.P., who was to be in charge of matters of security in Adano: he was to help weed out the bad Italians and make use of the good ones. Borth had volunteered to be the first to go into the town with the Major. Borth had no fear; he cared about nothing. He was of Hungarian parentage, and he had lived many places—in Budapest, where he had taken pre-medical studies, in Rome, where he had been a correspondent for *Pester Lloyd*, in Vienna, where he had worked in a travel agency, in Marseille, where he had been

secretary to a rich exporter, in Boston, where he had been a reporter for the *Herald,* and in San Francisco, where he sold radios.
Still he was less than thirty. He was an American citizen and an
enlisted man by choice. To him the whole war was a cynical
joke, and he considered his job in the war to make people take
themselves less seriously.

When the Major touched Italian soil, Borth said: "You are
too sentimental."

The Major said: "Maybe, but you will be the same when you
get to Hungary."

"Never, not me."

The Major looked toward the town and said: "Do you think
it's safe now?"

Borth said: "Why not?"

"Then how do we go?"

Borth unfolded a map case deliberately. He put a freckled finger on the celluloid cover and said: "Here, by the Via Barrino as
far as the Via of October Twenty-eight, and the Piazza is at the
top of the Via of October Twenty-eight."

"October Twenty-eight," the Major said, "what is that, October Twenty-eight?"

"That's the date of Mussolini's march on Rome, in 1922,"
Borth said. "It is the day when Mussolini thinks he began to be
a big shot." Borth was very good at memory.

They started walking. The Major said: "I have lost all count,
so what is today?"

"July tenth."

"We will call it the Via of July Ten."

"So you're renaming the streets already. Next you'll be raising
monuments, Major Joppolo, first to an unknown soldier, then to
yourself. I don't trust you men who are so sentimental and have
too damn much conscience."

"Cut the kidding," the Major said. There was an echo in the
way he said it, as if he were a boy having been called wop by
others in school. In spite of the gold maple leaf of rank on the
collar, there was an echo.

The two men walked up the Via Barrino. There was nobody in the street. All the people had either fled to the hills or were hiding in bomb shelters and cellars. The houses of this street were poor grey affairs, two-storey houses of grey brick, with grey shutters, all dusted over with grey dust which had been thrown up from bomb craters and shell holes. Here and there, where a house had been hit, grey bricks had cascaded into the grey street.

At the corner of the third alley running off the Via of October Twenty-eight, the two men came on a dead Italian woman. She had been dressed in black. Her right leg was blown off and the flies for some reason preferred the dark sticky pool of blood and dust to her stump.

"Awful," the Major said, for although the blood was not yet dry, nevertheless there was already a beginning of a sweet but vomitous odor. "It's a hell of a note," he said, "that we had to do that to our friends."

"Friends," said Borth, "that's a laugh."

"It wasn't them, not the ones like her," the Major said. "They weren't our enemies. My mother's mother must have been like her. It wasn't the poor ones like her, it was the bunch up there where we're going, those crooks in the City Hall."

"Be careful," Borth said, and his face showed that he was teasing the Major again. "You're going to have your office in the City Hall. Be careful you don't get to be a crook too."

"Lay off," the Major said.

Borth said: "I don't trust your conscience, sir, I'm appointing myself assistant conscience."

"Lay off," the Major said, and there was that echo.

They passed a house which had been crushed by a naval shell. The Major said: "Too bad, look at that."

Borth said: "Maybe it was a crook's house, how can you tell? Better forget the house and concern yourself with that." He pointed into an alley at some horse dung and goat dung and straw and melon seeds and old chicken guts and flies. And Borth added: "No question of guilty or not guilty there, Major. Just something to get clean. You've got some business in that alley, not in that house there."

"I know my business, I know what I want to do, I know what it's like to be poor, Borth."

Borth was silent. He found the seriousness of this Major Joppolo something hard to penetrate.

They came in time to the town's main square, which was called Piazza Progresso. And on that square they saw the building they were looking for.

It was a building with a look of authority about it. This was not one of those impermanent-looking, World's-Fair-architecture Fascist headquarters which you see in so many Italian towns, buildings so up to the moment in design that, like airplanes, they were obsolete before they were ever finished. This was an old building, made of stone. At its second floor it had an old balcony, a place of many speeches. This building had served kings before Fascists and now was about to serve democracies after them. In case you couldn't recognize authority in the shape of the building, there stood, in embossed bronze letters across the front, the words *Palazzo di Città*.

There was a clock tower on the left hand front corner. On top of the tower there was a metal frame which must have been designed to hold a bell. It was baroque and looked very old. But there was no bell.

On the side of the clock tower big white letters said: *"Il Popolo Italiano ha creato col suo sangue l'Impero, lo feconderà col sua lavoro e lo difenderà contra chiunque colle sue armi."*

The Major pointed and said: "See, Borth, even after our invasion it says: 'The Italian people built the Empire with their blood, will make it fruitful with their work and will defend it against anyone with their arms.'"

Borth said: "I know you can read Italian. So can I. Don't translate for Borth."

The Major said: "I know, but think of how that sounds today."

Borth said: "It sounds silly, sure."

The Major said: "If they had seen any fruit of their work, they would have fought with their arms. I bet we could teach them to want to defend what they have. I want to do so much here, Borth."

Borth said: "That sounds silly, too. Remember the alley, clean up the alleyway, sir, it is the alley that you ought to concentrate on."

The Major walked across the Piazza up to the big black door of the Palazzo, put his brief case down, took a piece of chalk out of his pocket, and wrote on a panel of the door: "Victor Joppolo, Major, U.S.A., AMGOT, Town of Adano."

Then both men went inside and up some marble stairs, looking all around them as they climbed. They took a turn and went through a door marked *Podestà*. The office on the other side of that door took Victor Joppolo's breath away.

In the first place, it was so very big. It must have been seventy feet long and thirty feet wide. The ceiling was high, and the floor was marble.

After all the poverty which had shouted and begged in the streets, this room was stiflingly rich. The furniture was of a heavy black Italian style which seemed to be bursting with some kind of creatures half man and half fruit. The curtains were of rich brocade, and the walls were lined with a silken stuff.

The door where the men came in was near the southwest corner of the room. To the right of it a huge table stood, with some maps and aerial photos on it which had been left behind by the officers of an American regiment, who had used the room as a command post early in the morning. There was an incongruous bundle of Italian brooms in the corner. The south wall had a double white door in the middle, and on either side a huge sofa bound in black leather. Then on the opposite side, facing the street and giving onto the place of speeches, there were two big French doors.

Scattered along the wall and pressed against it, as if frightened, were a heavy table, several throne-like chairs of various sizes, another couch and, in the far corner, a white stone statue of a saint. She, besides being decently swathed in a marble scarf, had a piece of American signal corps telephone wire wound around her neck on its way from the nearest French door to the desk, where a field phone had evidently been set up. To the left of the door there was a tremendous bookcase with a glass front, beyond it an enamel washstand with a big stone pitcher beside it, and then a weirdly ornate upright piano.

Up to the right, over the two sofas, there were huge pictures of Italy's King Victor Emmanuel and his Queen, facing each other in sympathetic misery. On the outside wall there was a picture of Crown Prince Umberto, smiling at everything that happened in the room. Over the Saint of the Telephone there was a photograph of Princess Marie José of Belgium, Umberto's wife, dressed as a Red Cross nurse. Above the bookcase there was a great dustless square where a picture had been but was not now.

All this, both the heavy furniture and the ironic pictures, seemed placed there merely to press the eye toward the opposite end of the room, toward the biggest picture in the room, a romantic oil of a group of men pointing into the distance, and especially toward the desk.

The scale of everything in that room was so big that hugeness in the desk did not seem unnatural. It was of wood. On either end there were wooden bas-reliefs of fasces and of the phrase Anno XV, for the fifteenth year of Fascism, or 1937, when the desk was presumably made. Under the desk there was a wooden scrollwork footstool.

"Say," said Major Joppolo, "this is okay."

"Looks like that office of Mussolini's," Borth said. "Come to think of it, you look quite a lot like Mussolini, sir, except the mustache. Will it be okay with you to be a Mussolini?"

"Cut the kidding," the Major said. "Let's look around."

They went out through the white door at the end of the room and walked through several offices, all of which were crowded with desks and files and bookcases. The files had not been emptied or even disturbed. "Good, said Borth, "lists of names, every one registered and all their records. It'll be easy for us here."

The Major said: "What a difference between my office and these others. It is shameful."

All Borth said was: "Your office?"

When the two went back into the big office there was an Italian there. He had evidently been hiding in the building. He was a small man, with a shiny linen office coat on, with his collar buttoned but no tie.

The small Italian gave the Fascist salute and with an eager face said in Italian: "Welcome to the Americans! Live Roosevelt! How glad I am that you have arrived. For many years I have hated the Fascists."

The Major said in Italian: "Who are you?"

The little man said: "Zito Giovanni. I have been well known as anti-Fascist."

Major Joppolo said: "What do you do?"

Zito said: "I greet the Americans."

Borth said in an Italian which was heavily accented: "Idiot, what was your job before the disembarkation?"

Zito said: "Zito Giovanni, usher in the *Palazzo di Città*, native of Adano."

Major Joppolo said: "You were the usher here?"

"Every day from eight to eight."

"Why did you work for the Fascists if you hated them?"

"I have hated them many years, I am well known as anti-Fascist, I have lived under a great suspicion."

The Major said: "Usher, I love the truth, you will find that out. If you lie to me, you will be in very serious trouble. Do not lie to me. If you were a Fascist, you were a Fascist. There is no need to lie."

Zito said: "One had to eat, one had to earn a living. I have six children."

Major Joppolo said: "So you were a Fascist. Now you will have to learn to live in a democracy. You will be my usher."

The little Zito was delighted.

The Major said: "Do not salute me that way."

Zito bowed and said: "The fascist salute, no sir."

Major Joppolo said: "Do not bow. There is no need to grovel

here. I am only a Major. Borth here is a Sergeant. Are you a man?"

Little Zito was getting very mixed up. "No sir," he said cautiously. Then he saw by the Major's expression that he should have said yes, and he did.

The Major said: "You may greet me by shaking my hand. You will greet Sergeant Borth in the same way."

Borth said, and his expression showed that he was teasing the Italian: "First I will find out if he's a dangerous Fascist."

Little Zito did not know whether to laugh or cry. He was frightened but he was also flattered by these men. He said: "I will never lie to you, Mister Major. I am anti-Fascist, Mister Sergeant. I will be usher here."

Major Joppolo said: "Be here at seven o'clock each morning."

"Seven o'clock," said Zito.

A brief burst of machine gun and rifle fire echoed from distant streets. Zito cringed.

Borth said: "You are perhaps a man but you are also frightened."

Major Joppolo said: "Has it been bad here?"

Zito started jabbering about the bombardments and the air raids. "We are very hungry," he said when he had cooled down a little. "For three days we have not had bread. All the important ones ran away and left me here to guard the Palazzo. The stink of dead is very bad, especially in the Piazza San Angelo. Some people are sick because the drivers of the water carts have not had the courage to get water for several days, because of the planes along the roads. We do not believe in victory. And our bell is gone."

Major Joppolo said: "Your bell?"

Zito said: "Our bell which was seven hundred years old. Mussolini took it. It rang with a good tone each quarter hour. Mussolini took it to make rifle barrels or something. The town was very angry. Everyone begged the Monsignor, who is the uncle of the Mayor, to offer some church bells instead. But the

Monsignor is uncle of the Mayor, he is not the sort to desecrate churches, he says. It meant we lost our bell. And only two weeks before you came. Why did you not come sooner?"

"Where was this bell?"

"Right here." Zito pointed over his head. "The whole building tingled when it rang."

Major Joppolo said to Borth: "I saw the framework for the bell up on the tower, did you?" Then he added to Zito: "That is your reason for wanting us to have come sooner, is it?"

Zito was careful. "Partly," he said.

Borth said: "Usher, if you were a good Fascist you would be able to tell me why there is a big blank space up there on the wall over which there used to hang a picture. It is easy to see by the square of dust that there was a rather large picture there."

Zito smiled and said: "The picture does not exist. It has been destroyed."

Borth said: "You are not hiding it in the basement? You are not afraid that the Americans will be driven out by your German allies and that your leader will return some day and see the square of dust on the wall and ask questions?"

Zito said: "It is destroyed, I swear it. I cannot lie before the Mister Major."

Major Joppolo said: "Usher, what is that big picture over my desk?"

This was where the little Zito told a beautiful lie. The picture was of a group of men in antique costume. One of them, by expression of face, position in the picture and by the accident of being the only one in the sunlight of all the men, was obviously their leader, and he was pointing out the side of the picture to the left.

Zito thought quickly and said: "That, Mister Major, is Columbus discovering America."

Zito smiled because it was a beautiful lie. Major Joppolo did not discover for three weeks that the picture was really a scene from the Sicilian Vespers, that bloody revolt which the Sicilians mounted against a previous invader.

Now Major Joppolo said in English more or less to himself: "It's a nice picture, I wonder how old it is, maybe it's by somebody famous."

The Major went to the desk, pulled out the high-backed chair and sat in it, carefully putting his feet on the scrollwork footstool.

Borth said: "How does it feel, Duce?"

The Major said: "There is so much to do, I hardly know where to begin."

Borth said: "I know what I must do. I've got to find the offices of the Fascist Party, to see if I can find more records. May I take the Mister Usher and look for the Fascio?"

"Go ahead, Borth," the Major said.

When the two had left, Major Joppolo opened his brief case and took out some papers. He put them in a neat pile on the desk in front of him and began to read:

INSTRUCTIONS TO CIVIL AFFAIRS OFFICERS. *First day:* Enter the city with the first column. Cooperate with C.I.C. in placing guards and seizing records. Place all food warehouses, enemy food dumps, wholesale food concerns, and other major food stocks under guard. Secure an estimate from local food distributors of the number of days of food supplies which are on hand or available. Make a report through channels on food situation in your area. See that the following establishments are placed under guard or protection: foundries, machine shops, electrical works, chemical plants, flour mills, breweries, cement plants, refrigeration plants, ice plants, warehouses, olive oil refineries, sulphur refineries, tunny oil mills, soap manufacturing plants, and any other important establishments. Locate and make available to port authorities all known local pilots. . . ."

And the list went on and on. When he had read three pages, Major Joppolo looked at his wrist watch. It was eleven thirty. Almost half of this first day was gone. He took the sheets of instructions up from the desk and tore them in half, and tore the halves in quarters, and crumbled up the quarters and threw them into a cane wastebasket under the desk.

Then he sat and stared out the nearest French door into the empty street for a long time. He looked tired and defeated.

He stirred and reached into his brief case again and took out a small black loose leaf notebook. The pages were filled with notes on his Amgot school lectures: notes on civilian supply, on public safety, on public health, on finance, on agriculture, industry, utilities, transportation, and all the businesses of an invading authority. But he passed all these pages by, and turned to the page marked: *Notes to Joppolo from Joppolo.*

And he read: "Don't make yourself cheap. Always be accessible to the public. Don't play favorites. Speak Italian whenever possible. Don't lose your temper. When plans fall down, improvise. . . ."

That was the one he wanted. When plans fall down, improvise.

Plans for this first day were in the wastebasket. They were absurd. Enough was set forth in those plans to keep a regiment busy for a week.

Now Victor Joppolo felt on his own, and he no longer looked tired. He got up briskly, went out onto the balcony and saw that there were two flagpoles there. He went back in, reached in his brief case and pulled out two flags, one American, the other British.

He tucked the Union Jack under his arm as he walked out again, felt for the toggles on the American flag, mounted them on the halyard on the left-hand flagpole, and raised the flag.

Before the flag reached the top of the pole there were five Italians in the Piazza. Before he had the British flag attached to the halyard on the right-hand pole, there were twenty. By the time he had both flags up, forty people were shouting: *"Buon giorno, buon giorno, Americano."*

PAUL HOFMANN

(1912–   )

Italy is no longer Percy Bysshe Shelley's "paradise of exiles," notes for-
mer New York Times *Rome bureau chief Paul Hofmann. "Italy is no*
quaint idyll of permanent comedy or aesthete's dream. It must be taken
on the Italians' own terms." Hofmann has been an observer of Italy
since before World War II, when he first traveled there as a hitchhiking
college student.

Born in Vienna in 1912, Hofmann moved to Rome during World
War II. "Self-exiled, I did not think of myself as being uprooted," he
wrote. "I felt at home." After a first job in a Mafia-run hotel near the
train station, Hofmann began work as a newspaperman. When Italy en-
tered World War II, he found himself drafted into Hitler's army as an
interpreter. Hofmann wrote, "I kept in touch with the Italian anti-Nazi
underground and was able to shed the hated Nazi uniform on the heady
day of Rome's liberation by the Allied forces in June 1944. Shortly after-
ward I joined the staff of The New York Times. *"*

A naturalized American citizen, Hofmann reported for the Times
from over forty countries, but always returned to Rome. Besides That
Fine Italian Hand, *from which this excerpt is taken, Hofmann has*
written several books on Italy, including Cento Citta, *a guide to*
smaller towns and cities, and Rome: The Sweet Tempestuous Life.
He lives in Rome.

The Art of Arrangement

from THAT FINE ITALIAN HAND

Toward the end of each month, one out of every ten Italians trudges to the post office and, if there is enough cash on hand and the staff does not happen to be on strike, lines up to collect the pension that the state pays to its army of invalids. The amount is modest—some get as little as the equivalent of $100 a month—but it helps the beneficiaries and their families to have their pasta on the table every day.

With 5.5 million certified *invalidi* (including 700,000 people officially found to have suffered bodily harm in the nation's last war, which ended in 1945), Italy would seem to be one of the world's most hazardous countries, writhing under plagues like biblical Egypt, endangered by accidents lurking in homes, fields, and factories, and racked by crippling diseases. Catastrophe is indeed familiar to Italy. Five deaths out of every 100,000 are caused by one of the frequent floods, earthquakes, or other natural calamities; the statistical average for most other Western countries is about one death in 100,000. Gunfire and bombings by terrorists, mafiosi, and other criminals punctuate life in Italy, and the hectic motor traffic exacts its daily toll of casualties. Yet Italians live on average longer than do Britons, French, or West Germans. Spry and lucid octogenarians abound. In the Alps, great-grandmothers walk for hours to and from church; in Rome, old men hold sway in the national government and in the Vatican; in Sicily, aged godfathers call the tune. The longevity and vitality of the Italians is enviable—convincing proof of their knack for survival.

Few of the 5.5 million supposedly handicapped Italians are permanently disabled, and many are chipper as the birds in the trees. The overwhelming majority of those who receive monthly invalidity pensions are nursing questionable if not imaginary ailments that do not prevent them from tackling life as everybody else does, and from getting old. By far the major part of the spurious infirm live in the sunny Mezzogiorno, where, one would think, the environment is healthier than in the foggy, industrial North. Southerners, to be sure, have a hard time finding jobs; to be pronounced an invalid by an official commission and thus become entitled to a state pension is a substitute for a guaranteed minimum wage or unemployment compensation. "In the North they have the Earnings Integration Fund, and the South has the invalidity pensions," said Ciriaco De Mita, a Christian Democratic leader whose rocklike political base is Avellino near Naples. He was soon to become government chief.

For decades candidates for elective office, mayors, members of Parliament, and cabinet ministers have been busy obtaining pensions for reputedly disabled constituents—a small favor like handing out candy to children or cigars to their fathers. If the officially attested impairment is not—exceptionally—a serious one, the person claiming to be afflicted with it may even get a job, because the law obliges some public employers, like the state railroads, to set aside a quota for *invalidi* when they hire new personnel.

Despite all the interventions by powerful personages, the procedures for getting an invalidity pension are slow and complicated, of course. In 1988 the Court of Accounts in Rome reported about 10,000 pending claims that referred to injuries said to have been suffered or diseases contracted during military service in World War I. Probably few of the original would-be *invalidi* were still alive, but their spouses and children had kept pressing their cases. The backlog from World War II was 180,000 claims.

The monthly payment from the state that helps millions of Italians, especially in the South, in the business of surviving is, unsurprisingly, a handy tool for assembling and operating political machines. It is also a prime example of the Italian art of arrangement—a technique for taking life's hurdles, surviving by one's wits, coasting along, making ends meet, and striking deals that are not exactly illegal, or only slightly so, and may bring advantages to more than one party (even though less clever people, the anonymous ranks of taxpayers, and the even vaguer interests of the national community might be directly or indirectly damaged).

Arrangiarsi, a verb that uncounted Italians conjugate every day, does not mean "to arrange oneself," as newcomers to the country and beginning students of its language may wrongly assume before hearing it said again and again in disparate circumstances—a transport strike, an adulterous affair, money trouble, crowded accommodations, odds and ends from the refrigerator for dinner, and a thousand other challenges large and small. *Arrangiarsi* in its various applications translates accurately as "to make do," or "to find a way out of a predicament," also "to make the best of a lousy situation." The important thing is never to crumple in adversity. The gift for getting out of a tight spot is coupled with uncommon resilience—a national trait that has been cultivated and celebrated since the days of Boccaccio's *Decameron.*

Innumerable are the routine "arrangements" in Italian everyday life. If you want to beat the ubiquitous lines, don't line up at all—pay someone who will do it for you. That is one thing the many messengers, doormen, drivers, and characters with undefined tasks who hang around the lobbies and corridors of most offices can handle. For a pack of cigarettes or the price of a bottle of wine your or somebody else's *usciere* (doorkeeper or office attendant) will pay electricity and phone bills at the post office and cash a check at the bank; he will be glad to run such errands because they give him an excuse for staying away all morning and taking care also of his own affairs. An *usciere* with years of experience and a long-established network of contacts may be able during one of the many bank strikes to make a subarrangement with an employee who will honor a check via the branch office's back door (a favor worth an extra consideration for both).

Instead of lining up with a bunch of others at a municipal office to get one of those birth or residence certificates continually needed in Italy so that one can line up at some other agency, turn to one of the storefront businesses that specialize in dealing with the authorities; they will get that piece of official paper for you. They work like travel agents and are usually combined with driving schools, also selling car insurance and taking care of vehicle registrations.

Every motorist in Italy sooner or later becomes a customer of one or another of the self-appointed car attendants who are "arrangement" personified. They fill a need because parking meters have not been much of a success in the cities that have tried them; the devices were constantly being rifled or vandalized. The Italian Automobile Club runs some parking lots, watched by its uniformed personnel, but these facilities are themselves far from sufficient. However, any few square feet of available space in the streets and piazzas of the crowded inner cities and in the neighborhoods of restaurants, movie houses, theaters, sports stadiums, and beaches will provide a chance for someone to make a living. He will wear an official-looking cap with the word *guardiamacchine* (car watcher) in gold embroidery. He will preside over double and triple parking, will always accommodate a good tipper, and will alone be able to extricate your auto from a jumble of other vehicles. If you don't pay him what he expects for his services or even try to freeload, you may find a scratch on your car's body or a flat tire next time. Of course such a curbside entrepreneur must have made his own arrangements with the traffic police and possibly also with some shadowy power that allots street space in the area.

Speaking of that Italian popular idol, the automobile, watch the mechanic who fixes your car. A spare part is hard to get? He will find it at the flea market, take it from a cannibalized auto, hammer it out himself, or maybe even swipe it from somewhere. If there is no space in his cramped two-man workshop, he will put your car out on the sidewalk and, with his assistant, will be tinkering on it while pedestrians respectfully step into the street, fully aware that important work and an inspiring exercise in "arrangement" are in progress.

Or observe how that famous national institution, Italian opera, works. The great shrines of musical drama elsewhere—the Metropolitan Opera of New York, the San Francisco Opera, Covent Garden in London, the Vienna and Munich state operas—map their programs and sign up casts years ahead (with stars who may have been eclipsed or lost their voices by the time they are to sing the parts assigned to them). Nothing of the kind happens in Italian operatic institutions, from La Scala in Milan to the Teatro Bellini in Catania.

If the performing season is to start in, say, December, it will still be highly uncertain in October whether it can open at all: The promised subsidies from the government in Rome, the regional authorities, and the city have not arrived, the banks are reluctant to grant another loan, the musicians and chorus demand higher pay and threaten to strike, the renowned guest producer insists on expensive new sets and costumes, and the singers miss scheduled rehearsals or show up at the last minute. Managements grope from one "arrangement" to the next. Maybe *Carmen* will have to perform without singing tobacco girls, street urchins, and soldiers, as happened at the Teatro dell'Opera in Rome after the entire chorus walked out; or La Scala will have to postpone a scheduled ballet production until the next season. Once in a while, nevertheless, all the frantic improvisations and make-do end up just right on some magic evening at La Scala or at the San Carlo in Naples or even at the Sferisterio in Macerata (a colonnaded ball-playing court from the early nineteenth century in a remote town near the Adriatic coast, where by dint of "arrangements," occasionally quite brilliant ones, outdoor opera is performed every summer).

The Italian cinema, which has disseminated around the world the imagery of *la dolce vita* and the philosophy of not taking anything too seriously, is all "arrangement." A real-estate tycoon is talked into putting up money for a picture in which his young girlfriend is to get a role; the producer insists that the scriptwriters come up with a scene in a southern village street because a suitable set, a holdover from a Mafia film, still stands in the Cinecittà studios; the director invents an entirely new sequence on the spur of the moment when the *trovarobe* ("things finder," propman) returns from the Porta Portese flea market with what looks like the very first espresso machine ever built, an antique that will yield a couple of gags; and so on, from bright idea to brainstorm to improvisation.

When Ingrid Bergman came to Rome in 1949 to film under the director Roberto Rossellini, then her lover and soon to become her second husband, she was stunned by the absence of any production schedule. In Hollywood the Swedish actress had been used to being told weeks in advance what she was supposed to do on the set almost minute by minute on any given day. On location in Southern Italy, Rossellini seemed to worry much more about the *spaghetti alle vongole* and the right wine for lunch than about the picture he was shooting, and appeared vague as to which scene would come next. A generation later Marcello Mastroianni said he liked working under Federico Fellini: "I show up at the set in the morning, and ask Fellini, 'Hey, Federì, what do you want me to do today?'"

Improvising scenes and dialogues goes back to the comedia dell'arte, in which Harlequin, Columbine, and other stock characters of popular farce quarreled and made up in allusive, topical language to the amusement of sixteenth-century audiences. Today one does not have to be in touch with Italian show business to meet stars of "arrangement." Everyone who has lived in the country for a little while knows a few of them. You haven't seen them for some time, and on meeting them again you ask: "What are you doing these days?" If the answer is, as it often will be, "Oh, *m'arrangio*" (meaning something like "I'm getting along"), don't persist, just change the subject.

Living by arrangements, one may be riding in a chauffeur-driven Mercedes or wearing an expensive designer dress while having only pizza for dinner. The Mercedes may be registered in the name of a company with a mailbox in the Principality of Liechtenstein as its only other tangible asset, and the haute couture number may be a gift from a rich friend. Even the bill for the pizza may be payable in a week under the famed Neapolitan food-on-credit scheme.

Naples especially has long been notorious for cultivating the art of getting along by "arrangement," the way Cremona is celebrated for its Stradivarius violins and Venice for its gondolas. When Goethe visited Naples in 1787 he was told that in the city, then one of Europe's most populous capitals, 30,000 to 40,000 *lazzaroni* (idlers) could always be found in the streets. The clear-eyed German looked hard but couldn't detect a single one. What he did see he described in his *Italian Journey*: porters for hire looking for customers; seamen smoking their pipes while waiting for an unfavorable wind to abate; small boys picking up horse droppings, which they would sell as manure to farmers in the countryside; children carrying fish from the Santa Lucia waterfront to the markets, or gathering wood chips that the carpenters in the Arsenal were scattering, which they put into baskets and would take home for the kitchen stove; street vendors selling lemonade and cakes; Punchinello in a mock quarrel on a stage set up on a noisy street corner, nearby a quack peddling his nostrums and above them, "a balcony on which a quite nice girl was offering her charms." To paint a true portrait of Naples, Goethe remarked, would require lots of talent and years of observation, and one would perhaps come to the conclusion that the so-called *lazzaroni* were not a bit less active than all other classes of people, and were in their own way "working not only to live but also to enjoy."

Two centuries later, thousands of Neapolitans still invent their day and their livelihood every morning, and they seem to enjoy doing so. Maybe the relatives of someone who has just died in a hospital will want to have the body brought home—which is illegal, unless one acquires a fake certificate attesting that the patient is still alive—so that the family and their friends can hold a good, traditional Neapolitan wake. The going tariff for such a macabre service, certificate included, is around $1,200, to be split among four or five people. Another method to get gainfully through the day is to acquire a carton of smuggled American cigarettes on commission and sell packs, or even batches of two or three cigarettes, to smokers in the warren of small streets in the center of the city. Even small boys can do that.

The Neapolitan genius for "arrangement" flowered most memorably in a golden age of finagling that started in the autumn of 1943 and lasted through the late 1940s. It has become an often repeated theme of modern Italian folklore, evoked by Curzio Malaparte in his best-sellers *Kaputt* and *The Skin*. (Malaparte, though no Neapolitan, was a virtuoso in inventing for himself a new persona every time the vicissitudes of his stormy era suggested the need. His real name was Kurt Erich Suckert. He was of German ancestry but, having been born in Prato, considered himself a Tuscan. An earlier follower of Mussolini, he turned anti-Fascist and eventually professed himself an admirer of Mao Zedong. When Malaparte died in 1957, both an Italian Communist party official and a Roman Catholic priest stood at his bedside. He willed his villa on the Isle of Capri to the People's Republic of China, which did not know what to do with it.)

When the Nazis evacuated Naples in 1943 after the Allied landing operations near Salerno, the city's urchins and *lazzaroni* pelted the retreating Wehrmacht troops with stones and bottles, and fired at them with guns long hidden in basements and under floorboards. (The Roman populace did nothing of the kind when the Germans moved out of the capital, undisturbed, in June 1944.)

Under Allied occupation Naples became a major supply base for Southern and Central Europe in an atmosphere anticipating to some extent that of Saigon during the Vietnam War. Italians still tell each other the legendary feats of the Neapolitan shoeshine boys doubling as underage pimps who "sold" blind-drunk American servicemen to prostitutes who would then roll them and strip them to their underpants before dumping them on some street corner where they could sober up. Another classic is the reputed disappearance in the Bay of Naples of an American freighter with many thousands of pairs of footwear for the troops; U.S. quartermaster services thereupon cleverly (they thought) sent to Naples one shipload of all right shoes followed by another of all left shoes, but the thefts continued and a new Neapolitan cottage industry sprang up—workshops specializing in converting stolen left shoes into right ones, and vice versa.

Today the poor neighborhoods of Naples are still honeycombed with poky workshops. Local officials keep repeating that although the city has not one glove factory it produces and exports millions of pairs of gloves ever year: They are being stitched together on a piecework basis by women in stuffy one-room apartments in decrepit buildings that open right into the street known as *bassi*; the cutting and sewing machines, on loan from subcontractors, stand close to the kitchen ranges, where the pasta for the entire large family is being cooked, and are moved aside at night to make room for cots and foldout beds. Other Neapolitan *bassi* turn out plaster statuettes to be sold by souvenir vendors outside the Sanctuary of the Virgin of the Rosary at Pompeii or near the Vatican in Rome, as well as plastic handbags, slippers of imitation leather, and a myriad of other cheap items.

Late in autumn every year some shed or dingy apartment in the Naples area will blow up, all too often with people getting killed or wounded. The police don't have to do much investigating; they know at once what caused the explosion—inexpert handling of pyrotechnic material. Like the Chinese, many Italians and particularly Neapolitans are crazy about fireworks and won't pass up a chance for indulging in the mania. The biggest occasion is New Year's Eve when, at midnight, all of Naples erupts in thunder and flames like Mount Vesuvius during one of its historic outbreaks. For months clandestine workshops in and around the city have manufactured and stored pinwheels, flares, Roman candles, and firecrackers that can be as powerful as small bombs. The authorities have issued their ritual warnings against the dangerous industry, raided a few pyrotechnic factories, and arrested dozens of street peddlers caught selling their products. Motorcycle patrols have checked trucks on the highways from Naples to the North and South and have regularly discovered boxes of firecrackers under layers of tomatoes and artichokes. But only a tiny part of the flammable material is ever seized. When the newspapers reappear on January 2 after the New Year's vacation, they carry long casualty lists, as if a battle had been fought—Neapolitans and people elsewhere killed and maimed while setting off their beloved fireworks or when hit by a fun rocket.

The glove industry in the *bassi* of Naples and the clandestine pyrotechnic shops are among the more picturesque of many hundreds of thousands of small enterprises spread over the length and breadth of Italy like the cells of a vigorous organism. Others include furniture and knitwear factories in various parts of the country, each with a few dozen workers; hole-in-the-wall operations in Apulia specializing in fake Louis Vuitton bags ("genuine" fakes that are sold as such and snapped up by Japanese tourists); small hotels and pensions along the coast and in resorts, run by the owners and their relatives; innumerable dressmakers and leatherware suppliers working for famous-label firms; goldsmiths clustered in Vicenza and Arezzo; some seventy ceramics makers in the majolica town of Faenza alone and many more in other places; manufacturers of fashion accessories and television antennas; and family establishments in the Alpine valleys whose computer-guided machines turn out "hand-carved" wooden sculptures of the Virgin Mary or of Walt Disney characters (unauthorized) that are shipped to distant outlets. Such small industries, immensely varied, account for nearly one-half of all the goods and services produced by Italy.

HENRY JAMES

(1843–1916)

*The clash of American and European cultures fascinated Henry James.
As an American expatriate in Europe for most of his life, he witnessed
the contest first-hand. As a young man, James made several trips to Europe before deciding to make it his home, and in 1876 he settled in London. He became a British subject in 1915, a year before his death. He is
one of the few Americans honored in the Poet's Corner of Westminster
Abbey.*

A trip to Florence in 1880 provided the setting for The Portrait of a
Lady, *first published serially in* The Atlantic. The Portrait of a Lady
*is probably James's finest novel, and is considered one of the best in the
English language. It tells the story of a young American heiress who
marries a middle-aged widower, Gilbert Osmond, only to find that she
was wed for her money and betrayed by Madame Merle, a woman she
took for a friend. The novel revisited James's familiar theme: the straight-
forward, newly rich American meeting the cultured, corrupt European.*

from THE PORTRAIT OF A LADY

It would certainly have been hard to see what injury could arise
to her from the visit she presently paid to Mr. Osmond's hill-top.
Nothing could have been more charming than this occasion—a
soft afternoon in May, in the full maturity of the Italian spring.
The two ladies drove out of the Roman Gate, beneath the enormous blank superstructure which crowns the fine clear arch of

that portal and makes it nakedly impressive, and wound between high-walled lanes, into which the wealth of blossoming or-chards overdrooped and flung a perfume, until they reached the small superurban piazza, of crooked shape, of which the long brown wall of the villa occupied in part by Mr. Osmond, formed the principal, or at least the most imposing, side. Isabel went with her friend through a wide, high court, where a clear shadow rested below, and a pair of light-arched galleries, facing each other above, caught the upper sunshine upon their slim columns and the flowering plants in which they were dressed. There was something rather severe about the place; it looked somehow as if, once you were in, it would not be easy to get out. For Isabel, however, there was of course as yet no thought of getting out, but only of advancing. Mr. Osmond met her in the cold ante-chamber—it was cold even in the month of May—and ushered her, with her companion, into the apart-ment to which we have already been introduced. Madame Merle was in front, and while Isabel lingered a little, talking with Mr. Osmond, she went forward, familiarly, and greeted two per-sons who were seated in the drawing-room. One of these was little Pansy, on whom she bestowed a kiss; the other was a lady whom Mr. Osmond presented to Isabel as his sister, the Count-ess Gemini. "And that is my little girl," he said, "who has just come out of a convent."

Pansy had on a scanty white dress, and her fair hair was neatly arranged in a net; she wore a pair of slippers, tied, sandal-fashion, about her ankles. She made Isabel a little conventual curtsey, and then came to be kissed. The Countess Gemini simply nodded, without getting up; Isabel could see that she was a woman of fashion. She was thin and dark, and not at all pretty, having fea-tures that suggested some tropical bird—a long beak-like nose, a small, quickly-moving eye, and a mouth and chin that receded extremely. Her face, however, thanks to a very human and fem-inine expression, was by no means disagreeable, and, as regards her appearance, it was evident that she understood herself and made the most of her points. The soft brilliancy of her toilet had the look of shimmering plumage, and her attitudes were light and sudden, like those of a creature that perched upon the twigs. She had a great deal of manner; Isabel, who had never known any one with so much manner, immediately classified the Countess Gemini as the most affected of women. She remembered that Ralph had not recommended her as an acquaintance; but she was ready to acknowledge that on a casual view the Countess presented no appearance of wickedness. Nothing could have been kinder or more innocent than her greeting to Isabel.

"You will believe that I am glad to see you when I tell you that it is only because I knew you were to be here that I came myself. I don't come and see my brother—I make him come and see me. This hill of his is impossible—I don't see what possesses him. Really, Osmond, you will be the ruin of my horses some day; and if they receive an injury you will have to give me another pair. I heard them panting to-day; I assure you I did. It is very disagreeable to hear one's horses panting when one is sitting in the carriage; it sounds, too, as if they were not what they should be. But I have always had good horses; whatever else I may have lacked, I have always managed that. My husband doesn't know much, but I think he does know a horse. In general the Italians don't, but my husband goes in, according to his poor light, for everything English. My horses are English—so it is all the greater pity they should be ruined. I must tell you," she went on, directly addressing Isabel, "that Osmond doesn't often invite me; I don't think he likes to have me. It was quite my own idea, coming to-day. I like to see new people, and I am sure you are very new. But don't sit there; that chair is not what it looks. There are some very good seats here, but there are also some horrors."

These remarks were delivered with a variety of little jerks and glances, in a tone which, although it expressed a high degree of good-nature, was rather shrill than sweet.

"I don't like to have you, my dear?" said her brother. "I am sure you are invaluable."

"I don't see any horrors anywhere," Isabel declared, looking about her. "Everything here seems to me very beautiful."

"I have got a few good things," Mr. Osmond murmured; "indeed I have nothing very bad. But I have not what I should have liked."

He stood there a little awkwardly, smiling and glancing about; his manner was an odd mixture of the indifferent and the expressive. He seemed to intimate that nothing was of much consequence. Isabel made a rapid induction: perfect simplicity was not the badge of his family. Even the little girl from the convent, who, in her prim white dress, with her small submissive face and her hands locked before her, stood there as if she were about to partake of her first communion—even Mr. Osmond's diminutive daughter had a kind of finish which was not entirely artless.

"You would have liked a few things from the Uffizi and the Pitti—that's what you would have liked," said Madame Merle.

"Poor Osmond, with his old curtains and crucifixes!" the Countess Gemini exclaimed; she appeared to call her brother only by his family-name. Her ejaculation had no particular object; she smiled at Isabel as she made it, and looked at her from head to foot.

Her brother had not heard her; he seemed to be thinking what he could say to Isabel. "Won't you have some tea?—you must be very tired," he at last bethought himself of remarking.

"No, indeed, I am not tired; what have I done to tire me?" Isabel felt a certain need of being very direct, of pretending to nothing; there was something in the air, in her general impression of things—she could hardly have said what it was—that deprived her of all disposition to put herself forward. The place, the occasion, the combination of people, signified more than lay on the surface; she would try to understand—she would not simply utter graceful platitudes. Poor Isabel was perhaps not aware that many women would have uttered graceful platitudes to cover the working of their observation. It must be confessed that her pride was a trifle alarmed. A man whom she had heard spoken of in terms that excited interest, and who was evidently capable of distinguishing himself, had invited her, a young lady not lavish of her favours, to come to his house. Now that she had done so, the burden of the entertainment rested naturally upon himself. Isabel was not rendered less observant, and for the moment, I am afraid, she was not rendered more indulgent, by perceiving that Mr. Osmond carried his burden less complacently than might have been expected. "What a fool I was to have invited these women here!" she could fancy his exclaiming to himself.

"You will be tired when you go home, if he shows you all his *bibelots* and gives you a lecture on each," said the Countess Gemini.

"I am not afraid of that; but if I am tired, I shall at least have learned something."

"Very little, I suspect. But my sister is dreadfully afraid of learning anything," said Mr. Osmond.

"Oh, I confess to that; I don't want to know anything more—I know too much already. The more you know, the more unhappy you are."

"You should not undervalue knowledge before Pansy, who has not finished her education," Madame Merle interposed, with a smile.

"Pansy will never know any harm," said the child's father. "Pansy is a little convent-flower."

"Oh, the convents, the convents!" cried the Countess, with a sharp laugh. "Speak to me of the convents. You may learn anything there; I am a convent-flower myself. I don't pretend to be good, but the nuns do. Don't you see what I mean?" she went on, appealing to Isabel.

Isabel was not sure that she saw, and she answered that she was very bad at following arguments. The Countess then declared that she herself detested arguments, but that this was her brother's taste—he would always discuss. "For me," she said, "one should like a thing or one shouldn't; one can't like everything, of course. But one shouldn't attempt to reason it out—you never know where it may lead you. There are some very good feelings that may have bad reasons; don't you know? And then there are very bad feelings, sometimes, that have good reasons. Don't you see what I mean? I don't care anything about reasons, but I know what I like."

"Ah, that's the great thing," said Isabel, smiling, but suspecting that her acquaintance with this lightly-flitting personage would not lead to intellectual repose. If the Countess objected to argument, Isabel at this moment had as little taste for it, and she put out her hand to Pansy with a pleasant sense that such a gesture committed her to nothing that would admit of a divergence of views. Gilbert Osmond apparently took a rather hopeless view of his sister's tone, and he turned the conversation to another topic. He presently sat down on the other side of his daughter, who had taken Isabel's hand for a moment; but he ended by drawing her out of her chair, and making her stand between his knees, leaning against him while he passed his arm round her little waist. The child fixed her eyes on Isabel with a still, disinterested gaze, which seemed void of an intention, but conscious of an attraction. Mr. Osmond talked of many things; Madame Merle had said he could be agreeable when he chose, and to-day, after a little, he appeared not only to have chosen, but to have determined. Madame Merle and the Countess Gemini sat a little apart, conversing in the effortless manner of persons who knew each other well enough to take their ease; every now and then Isabel heard the Countess say something extravagant. Mr. Osmond talked of Florence, of Italy, of the pleasure of living in that country, and of the abatements to such pleasure. There were both satisfactions and drawbacks; the drawbacks were pretty numerous; strangers were too apt to see Italy in rose-colour. On the whole it was better than other countries, if one was content to lead a quiet life and take things as they came. It was very dull sometimes, but there were advantages in living in the country which contained the most beauty. There were certain impressions that one could get only in Italy. There were others that one never got there, and one got some that were very bad. But from time to time one got a delightful

one, which made up for everything. He was inclined to think
that Italy had spoiled a great many people; he was even fatuous
enough to believe at times that he himself might have been a
better man if he had spent less of his life there. It made people
idle and dilettantish, and second-rate; there was nothing tonic in
an Italian life. One was out of the current; one was not *dans le
mouvement,* as the French said; one was too far from Paris and
London. "We are gloriously provincial, I assure you," said Mr.
Osmond, "and I am perfectly aware that I myself am as rusty as
a key that has no lock to fit it. It polishes me up a little to talk with
you—not that I venture to pretend I can turn that very complicated lock I suspect your intellect of being! But you will be going away before I have seen you three times, and I shall perhaps
never see you after that. That's what it is to live in a country that
people come to. When they are disagreeable it is bad enough;
when they are agreeable it is still worse. As soon as you find you
like them they are off again! I have been deceived too often; I
have ceased to form attachments; to permit myself to feel at-
tractions. You mean to stay—to settle? That would be really
comfortable. Ah yes, your aunt is a sort of guarantee; I believe
she may be depended upon. Oh, she's an old Florentine; I mean
literally an old one; not a modern outsider. She is a contemporary of the Medici; she must have been present at the burning of
Savonarola, and I am not sure she didn't throw a handful of chips
into the flame. Her face is very much like some faces in the early
pictures; little, dry, definite faces, that must have had a good deal
of expression, but almost always the same one. Indeed, I can
show you her portrait in a fresco of Ghirlandaio's. I hope you
don't object to my speaking that way of your aunt, eh? I have an
idea you don't. Perhaps you think that's even worse. I assure you
there is no want of respect in it, to either of you. You know I'm
a particular admirer of Mrs. Touchett."

While Isabel's host exerted himself to entertain her in this
somewhat confidential fashion, she looked occasionally at
Madame Merle, who met her eyes with an inattentive smile in
which, on this occasion, there was no infelicitous intimation

that our heroine appeared to advantage. Madame Merle eventually proposed to the Countess Gemini that they should go into the garden, and the Countess, rising and shaking out her soft plumage, began to rustle toward the door.

"Poor Miss Archer!" she exclaimed, surveying the other group with expressive compassion. "She has been brought quite into the family."

"Miss Archer can certainly have nothing but sympathy for a family to which you belong," Mr. Osmond answered, with a laugh which, though it had something of a mocking ring, was not ill-natured.

"I don't know what you mean by that! I am sure she will see no harm in me but what you tell her. I am better than he says, Miss Archer," the Countess went on. "I am only rather light. Is that all he has said? Ah then, you keep him in good humour. Has he opened on one of his favourite subjects? I give you notice that there are two or three that he treats *à fond*. In that case you had better take off your bonnet."

"I don't think I know what Mr. Osmond's favourite subjects are," said Isabel, who had risen to her feet.

The Countess assumed, for an instant, an attitude of intense meditation; pressing one of her hands, with the fingertips gathered together, to her forehead.

"I'll tell you in a moment," she answered. "One is Machiavelli, the other is Vittoria Colonna, the next is Metastasio."

"Ah, with me," said Madame Merle, passing her arm into the Countess Gemini's, as if to guide her course to the garden, "Mr. Osmond is never so historical."

"Oh you," the Countess answered as they moved away, "you yourself are Machiavelli—you yourself are Vittoria Colonna!"

"We shall hear next that poor Madame Merle is Metastasio!" Gilbert Osmond murmured, with a little melancholy smile.

Isabel had got up, on the assumption that they too were to go into the garden; but Mr. Osmond stood there, with no apparent inclination to leave the room, with his hands in the pockets of his jacket, and his daughter, who had now locked her arm into one of his own, clinging to him and looking up, while her eyes moved from his own face to Isabel's. Isabel waited, with a certain unuttered contentedness, to have her movements directed; she liked Mr. Osmond's talk, his company; she felt that she was being entertained. Through the open doors of the great room she saw Madame Merle and the Countess stroll across the deep grass of the garden; then she turned, and her eyes wandered over the things that were scattered about her. The understanding had been that her host should show her his treasures; his pictures and cabinets all looked like treasures. Isabel, after a moment, went toward one of the pictures to see it better; but just as she had done so Mr. Osmond said to her abruptly—

"Miss Archer, what do you think of my sister?"

Isabel turned, with a good deal of surprise.

"Ah, don't ask me that—I have seen your sister too little."

"Yes, you have seen her very little; but you must have observed that there is not a great deal of her to see. What do you think of our family tone?" Osmond went on, smiling. "I should like to know how it strikes a fresh, unprejudiced mind. I know what you are going to say—you have had too little observation of it. Of course this is only a glimpse. But just take notice, in future, if you have a chance. I sometimes think we have got into a rather bad way, living off here among things and people not our own, without responsibilities or attachments, with nothing to hold us together or keep us up; marrying foreigners, forming artificial tastes, playing tricks with our natural mission. Let me add, though, that I say that much more for myself than for my sister. She's a very good woman—better than she seems. She is rather unhappy, and as she is not of a very serious disposition, she doesn't tend to show it tragically; she shows it comically instead. She has got a nasty husband, though I am not sure she makes the best of him. Of course, however, a nasty husband is an awkward thing. Madame Merle gives her excellent advice, but it's a good deal like giving a child a dictionary to learn a language with. He can look out the words, but he can't put them together. My sister needs a grammar, but unfortunately she is not grammatical. Excuse my troubling you with these details; my sister was very right in saying that you have been taken into the family. Let me take down that picture; you want more light."

He took down the picture, carried it toward the window, related some curious facts about it. She looked at the other works of art, and he gave her such further information as might appear to be most acceptable to a young lady making a call on a summer afternoon. His pictures, his carvings and tapestries were interesting; but after a while Isabel became conscious that the owner was more interesting still. He resembled no one she had ever seen; most of the people she knew might be divided into groups of half-a-dozen specimens. There were one or two exceptions to this; she could think, for instance, of no group that would contain her Aunt Lydia. There were other people who were, relatively speaking, original—original, as one might say, by courtesy—such as Mr. Goodwood, as her cousin Ralph, as Henrietta Stackpole, as Lord Warburton, as Madame Merle. But in essentials, when one came to look at them, these individuals belonged to types which were already present to her mind. Her mind contained no class which offered a natural place to Mr. Osmond—he was a specimen apart. Isabel did not say all these things to herself at the time; but she felt them, and afterwards they became distinct. For the moment she only said to herself that Mr. Osmond had the interest of rareness. It was not so much what he said and did, but rather what he withheld, that distinguished him; he indulged in no striking deflections from common usage; he was an original without being an eccentric. Isabel had never met a person of so fine a grain. The peculiarity was physical, to begin with, and it extended to his immaterial part. His dense, delicate hair, his overdrawn, retouched features, his clear complexion, ripe without being coarse, the very evenness of the growth of his beard, and that light, smooth, slenderness of structure which made the movement of a single one of his fingers produce the effect of an expressive gesture—these personal points struck our observant young lady as the signs of an unusual sensibility. He was certainly fastidious and critical; he was probably irritable. His sensibility had governed him—possibly governed him too much; it had made him impatient of vulgar troubles and had led him to live by himself, in a serene, impersonal way, thinking about art and beauty and history. He had consulted his taste in everything—his taste alone, perhaps; that was what made him so different from every one else. Ralph had something of this same quality, this appearance of thinking that life was a matter of connoisseurship; but in Ralph it was an anomaly, a kind of humorous excrescence, whereas in Mr. Osmond it was the key-note, and everything was in harmony with it. Isabel was certainly far from understanding him completely; his meaning was not at all times obvious. It was hard to see what he meant, for instance, by saying that he was gloriously provincial—which was so exactly the opposite of what she had supposed. Was it a harmless paradox, intended to puzzle her? or was it the last refinement of high culture? Isabel trusted that she should learn in time; it would be very interesting to learn. If Mr. Osmond were provincial, pray what were the characteristics of the capital? Isabel could ask herself this question, in spite of having perceived that her host was a shy personage; for such shyness as his—the shyness of ticklish nerves and fine perceptions—was perfectly consistent with the best breeding. Indeed, it was almost a proof of superior qualities. Mr. Osmond was not a man of easy assurance, who chatted and gossiped with the fluency of a superficial nature; he was critical of himself as well as of others, and exacting a good deal of others (to think them agreeable), he probably took a rather ironical view of what he himself offered: a proof, into the bargain, that he was not grossly conceited. If he had not been shy, he would not have made that gradual, subtle, successful effort to overcome his shyness, to which Isabel felt that she owed both what pleased and what puzzled her in his conversation to-day. He suddenly asked her what she thought of the Countess Gemini—that was doubtless a proof that he was interested in her feelings; it could scarcely be as a help to knowledge of his own sister. That he should be so interested showed an inquiring mind; but it was a little singular that he should sacrifice his fraternal feeling to his curiosity. This was the most eccentric thing he had done.

There were two other rooms, beyond the one in which she had been received, equally full of picturesque objects, and in these apartments Isabel spent a quarter of an hour. Every thing was very curious and valuable, and Mr. Osmond continued to be the kindest of ciceroni, as he led her from one fine piece to another, still holding his little girl by the hand. His kindness almost surprised our young lady, who wondered why he should take so much trouble for her; and she was oppressed at last with the accumulation of beauty and knowledge to which she found herself introduced. There was enough for the present; she had ceased to attend to what he said; she listened to him with attentive eyes, but she was not thinking of what he told her. He probably thought she was cleverer than she was; Madame Merle would have told him so; which was a pity, because in the end he would be sure to find out, and then perhaps even her real cleverness would not reconcile him to his mistake. A part of Isabel's fatigue came from the effort to appear as intelligent as she believed Madame Merle had described her, and from the fear (very unusual with her) of exposing—not her ignorance; for that she cared comparatively little—but her possible grossness of perception. It would have annoyed her to express a liking for something which her host, in his superior enlightenment, would think she ought not to like; or to pass by something at which the truly initiated mind would arrest itself. She was very careful, therefore, as to what she said, as to what she noticed or failed to notice—more careful than she had ever been before.

They came back into the first of the rooms, where the tea had been served; but as the two other ladies were still on the terrace, and as Isabel had not yet been made acquainted with the view, which constituted the paramount distinction of the place, Mr. Osmond directed her steps into the garden without more delay. Madame Merle and the Countess had had chairs brought out, and as the afternoon was lovely, the Countess proposed they should take their tea in the open air. Pansy, therefore, was sent to bid the servant bring out the tray. The sun had got low, the golden light took a deeper tone, and on the mountains and the plain that stretched beneath them, the masses of purple shadow seemed to glow as richly as the places that were still exposed. The scene had an extraordinary charm. The air was almost solemnly still, and the large expanse of the landscape, with its gardenlike culture and nobleness of outline, its teeming valley and delicately-fretted hills, its peculiarly human-looking touches of habitation, lay there in splendid harmony and classic grace.

"You seem so well pleased that I think you can be trusted to come back," Mr. Osmond said, as he led his companion to one of the angles of the terrace.

"I shall certainly come back," Isabel answered, "in spite of what you say about its being bad to live in Italy. What was that you said about one's natural mission? I wonder if I should forsake my natural mission if I were to settle in Florence."

"A woman's natural mission is to be where she is most appreciated."

"The point is to find out where that is."

"Very true—a woman often wastes a great deal of time in the inquiry. People ought to make it very plain to her."

"Such a matter would have to be made very plain to me," said Isabel, smiling.

"I am glad, at any rate, to hear you talk of settling. Madame Merle had given me an idea that you were of a rather roving disposition. I thought she spoke of your having some plan of going round the world."

"I am rather ashamed of my plans; I make a new one every day."

"I don't see why you should be ashamed; it's the greatest of pleasures."

"It seems frivolous, I think," said Isabel. "One ought to choose something very deliberately, and be faithful to that."

"By that rule, then, I have not been frivolous."

"Have you never made plans?"

"Yes, I made one years ago, and I am acting on it to-day."

"It must have been a very pleasant one," said Isabel.

"It was very simple. It was to be as quiet as possible."

"As quiet?" the girl repeated.

"Not to worry—not to strive nor struggle. To resign myself. To be content with a little." He uttered these sentences slowly, with little pauses between, and his intelligent eyes were fixed upon Isabel's with the conscious look of a man who has brought himself to confess something.

"Do you call that simple?" Isabel asked, with a gentle laugh.

"Yes, because it's negative."

"Has your life been negative?"

"Call it affirmative if you like. Only it has affirmed my indifference. Mind you, not my natural indifference—I had none. But my studied, my wilful renunciation."

Isabel scarcely understood him; it seemed a question whether he were joking or not. Why should a man who struck her as having a great fund of reserve suddenly bring himself to be so confidential? This was his affair, however, and his confidences were interesting. "I don't see why you should have renounced," she said in a moment.

"Because I could do nothing. I had no prospects, I was poor, and I was not a man of genius. I had no talents even; I took my measure early in life. I was simply the most fastidious young gentleman living. There were two or three people in the world I envied—the Emperor of Russia, for instance, and the Sultan of Turkey! There were even moments when I envied the Pope of Rome—for the consideration he enjoys. I should have been delighted to be considered to that extent; but since that couldn't be, I didn't care for anything less, and I made up my mind not to go in for honours. A gentleman can always consider himself, and fortunately, I was a gentleman. I could do nothing in Italy— I couldn't even be an Italian patriot. To do that, I should have had to go out of the country; and I was too fond of it to leave it. So I have passed a great many years here, on that quiet plan I spoke of. I have not been at all unhappy. I don't mean to say I have cared for nothing; but the things I have cared for have been definite—limited. The events of my life have been absolutely unperceived by any one save myself; getting an old silver crucifix at a bargain (I have never bought anything dear, of course), or discovering, as I once did, a sketch by Correggio on a panel daubed over by some inspired idiot!"

This would have been rather a dry account of Mr. Osmond's career if Isabel had fully believed it; but her imagination supplied the human element which she was sure had not been wanting. His life had been mingled with other lives more than he admitted; of course she could not expect him to enter into this. For the present she abstained from provoking further revelations; to intimate that he had not told her everything would be more familiar and less considerate than she now desired to be. He had certainly told her quite enough. It was her present inclination, however, to express considerable sympathy for the success with which he had preserved his independence. "That's a very pleasant life," she said, "to renounce everything but Correggio!"

"Oh, I have been very happy; don't imagine me to suggest for a moment that I have not. It's one's own fault if one is not happy."

"Have you lived here always?"

"No, not always. I lived a long time at Naples, and many years in Rome. But I have been here a good while. Perhaps I shall have to change, however; to do something else. I have no longer myself to think of. My daughter is growing up, and it is very possible she may not care so much for the Correggios and crucifixes as I. I shall have to do what is best for her."

"Yes, do that," said Isabel. "She is such a dear little girl."

"Ah," cried Gilbert Osmond, with feeling, "she is a little saint of heaven! She is my great happiness!"

D. H. LAWRENCE

(1885–1930)

More than sixty years after his death, critics are still divided about the work of D. H. Lawrence. He is regarded by some as one of the greatest modern English writers; others find his work didactic and obscure. But while his fiction and poetry are both revered and excoriated, his travel writing is almost universally admired.

D. H. Lawrence never settled in one place for very long. He lived in England, Germany, Italy, France, Australia, India, Mexico, and New Mexico. Ironically, Lawrence and his wife, Frieda, claimed to be homebodies and could set up housekeeping quickly, marking each residence with their personal belongings and taste. It was perhaps his adaptability that made Lawrence a brilliant observer. His work includes Mornings in Mexico, Twilight in Italy, Etruscan Places, *and* Sea and Sardinia, *which includes the selection "To Sorgono." About his travel writing Diana Trilling wrote, "What most writers fail to suggest at fullest length, Lawrence creates with almost a single stroke of the pen, so that we come away from a few sentences about a momentary meeting on the road, in an inn, on a bus, not with the sense of having made a fleeting acquaintance, but with the conviction of having had a complete social, human experience."*

To Sorgono

from SEA AND SARDINIA

The various trains in the junction squatted side by side and had long, long talks before at last we were off. It was wonderful to be running in the bright morning towards the heart of Sardinia, in the little train that seemed so familiar. We were still going third class, rather to the disgust of the railway officials at Mandas.

At first the country was rather open: always the long spurs of hills, steep-sided, but not high. And from our little train we looked across the country, across hill and dale. In the distance was a little town, on a low slope. But for its compact, fortified look it might have been a town on the English downs. A man in the carriage leaned out of the window holding out a white cloth, as a signal to someone in the far off town that he was coming. The wind blew the white cloth, the town in the distance glimmered small and alone in its hollow. And the little train pelted along.

It was rather comical to see it. We were always climbing. And the line curved in great loops. So that as one looked out of the window, time and again one started, seeing a little train running in front of us, in a diverging direction, making big puffs of steam. But lo, it was our own little engine pelting off around a loop away ahead. We were quite a long train, but all trucks in front, only our two passenger coaches hitched on behind. And for this reason our own engine was always running fussily into sight, like some dog scampering in front and swerving about us, while we followed at the tail end of the thin string of trucks.

I was surprised how well the small engine took the continuous steep slopes, how bravely it emerged on the sky-line. It is a queer railway. I would like to know who made it. It pelts up hill and down dale and round sudden bends in the most unconcerned fashion, not as proper big railways do, grunting inside deep cuttings and stinking their way through tunnels, but running up the hill like a panting, small dog, and having a look round, and starting off in another direction, whisking us behind unconcernedly. This is much more fun than the tunnel-and-cutting system.

They told me that Sardinia mines her own coal: and quite enough for her own needs: but very soft, not fit for steam-purposes. I saw heaps of it: small, dull, dirty-looking stuff. Truck-loads of it too. And truck-loads of grain.

At every station we were left ignominiously planted, while the little engines—they had gay gold names on their black little bodies—strolled about along the sidelines, and snuffed at the various trucks. There we sat, at every station, while some truck was discarded and some other sorted out like a branded sheep, from the sidings and hitched on to us. It took a long time, this did.

ALL THE STATIONS so far had had wire netting over the windows. This means malaria-mosquitoes. The malaria climbs very high in Sardinia. The shallow upland valleys, moorland with their intense summer sun and the riverless, boggy behaviour of the water breed the pest inevitably. But not very terribly, as far as one can make out: August and September being the danger months. The natives don't like to admit there is any malaria: a tiny bit, they say, a tiny bit. As soon as you come to the *trees* there is no more. So they say. For many miles the landscape is moorland and downlike, with no trees. But wait for the trees. Ah, the woods and forests of Gennargentu: the woods and forests higher up: no malaria there!

The little engine whisks up and up, around its loopy curves as

if it were going to bite its own tail: we being the tail: then suddenly dives over the sky-line out of sight. And the landscape
changes. The famous woods begin to appear. At first it is only
hazel-thickets, miles of hazel-thickets, all wild, with a few black
cattle trying to peep at us out of the green myrtle and arbutus
scrub which forms the undergrowth; and a couple of rare, wild
peasants peering at the train. They wear the black sheepskin tunic, with the wool outside, and the long stocking-caps. Like cattle they too peer out from between deep bushes. The myrtle
scrub here rises man-high, and cattle and men are smothered in
it. The big hazels rise bare above. It must be difficult getting
about in these parts.

Sometimes in the distance one sees a black-and-white peasant riding lonely across a more open place, a tiny vivid figure. I
like so much the proud instinct which makes a living creature
distinguish itself from its background. I hate the rabbity khaki
protection-colouration. A black-and-white peasant on his pony,
only a dot in the distance beyond the foliage, still flashes and
dominates the landscape. Ha-ha! proud mankind! There you
ride! But alas, most of the men are still khaki-muffled, rabbit-
indistinguishable, ignominious. The Italians look curiously rabbity in the grey-green uniform: just as our sand-coloured khaki
men look doggy. They seem to scuffle rather abased, ignominious on the earth. Give us back the scarlet and gold, and devil
take the hindmost.

THE LANDSCAPE REALLY begins to change. The hillsides
tilt sharper and sharper. A man is ploughing with two small red
cattle on a craggy, tree-hanging slope as sharp as a roof-side. He
stoops at the small wooden plough, and jerks the ploughlines.
The oxen lift their noses to heaven, with a strange and beseech-
ing snake-like movement, and taking tiny little steps with their
frail feet, move slantingly across the slope-face, between rocks
and tree-roots. Little, frail, jerky steps the bullocks take, and
again they put their horns back and lift their muzzles snakily to

heaven, as the man pulls the line. And he skids his wooden plough round another scoop of earth. It is marvellous how they hang upon that steep, craggy slope. An English labourer's eyes would bolt out of his head at the sight.

There is a stream: actually a long tress of a waterfall pouring into a little gorge, and a stream-bed that opens a little, and shows a marvellous cluster of naked poplars away below. They are like ghosts. They have a ghostly, almost phosphorescent luminousness in the shadow of the valley, by the stream of water. If not phosphorescent, then incandescent: a grey, goldish-pale incandescence of naked limbs and myriad cold-glowing twigs, gleaming strangely. If I were a painter I would paint them: for they seem to have living, sentient flesh. And the shadow envelops them.

Another naked tree I would paint is the gleaming mauve-silver fig, which burns its cold incandescence, tangled, like some sensitive creature emerged from the rock. A fig tree come forth in its nudity gleaming over the dark winter-earth is a sight to behold. Like some white, tangled sea anemone. Ah, if it could but answer! or if we had tree-speech!

Y E S, the steep valley sides become almost gorges, and there are trees. Not forests such as I had imagined, but scattered, grey, smallish oaks, and some lithe chestnuts. Chestnuts with their long whips, and oaks with their stubby boughs, scattered on steep hillsides where rocks crop out. The train perilously winding round, half way up. Then suddenly bolting over a bridge and into a completely unexpected station. What is more, men crowd in—the station is connected with the main railway by a post motor-omnibus.

An unexpected irruption of men—they may be miners or navvies or land-workers. They all have huge sacks: some lovely saddle-bags with rose-coloured flowers across the darkness. One old man is in full black-and-white costume, but very dirty and coming to pieces. The others wear the tight madder-brown breeches and sleeved waistcoats. Some have the sheepskin tunic, and all wear the long stocking-cap. And how they smell! of sheep-wool and of men and goat. A rank scent fills the carriage.

They talk and are very lively. And they have mediæval faces, *rusé,* never really abandoning their defences for a moment, as a badger or a pole-cat never abandons its defences. There is none of the brotherliness and civilized simplicity. Each man knows he must guard himself and his own: each man knows the devil is behind the next bush. They have never known the post-Renaissance Jesus. Which is rather an eye-opener.

Not that they are suspicious or uneasy. On the contrary, noisy, assertive, vigorous presences. But with none of that implicit belief that everybody will be and ought to be good to them which is the mark of our era. They don't expect people to be good to them: they don't want it. They remind me of half-wild dogs that will love and obey, but which won't be handled. They won't have their heads touched. And they won't be fondled. One can almost hear the half-savage growl.

The long stocking caps they wear as a sort of crest, as a lizard wears his crest at mating time. They are always moving them, settling them on their heads. One fat fellow, young, with sly brown eyes and a young beard round his face, folds his stocking-foot in three, so that it rises over his brow martial and handsome. The old boy brings his stocking-foot over the left ear. A handsome fellow with a jaw of massive teeth pushes his cap back and lets it hang a long way down his back. Then he shifts it forward over his nose, and makes it have two sticking-out points, like fox-ears, above his temples. It is marvellous how much expression these caps can take on. They say that only those born to them can wear them. They seem to be just long bags, nearly a yard long, of black stockinette stuff.

The conductor comes to issue them their tickets. And they all take out rolls of paper money. Even a little mothy rat of a man who sits opposite me has quite a pad of ten-franc notes. Nobody seems short of a hundred francs nowadays: nobody.

They shout and expostulate with the conductor. Full of coarse life they are: but so coarse! The handsome fellow has his sleeved waistcoat open, and his shirt-breast has come unbuttoned. Not looking, it seems as if he wears a black undervest. Then suddenly, one sees it is his own hair. He is quite black inside his shirt, like a black goat.

But there is a gulf between oneself and them. They have no inkling of our crucifixion, our universal consciousness. Each of them is pivoted and limited to himself, as the wild animals are. They look out, and they see other objects, objects to ridicule or mistrust or to sniff curiously at. But "thou shalt love thy neighbour as thyself" has never entered their souls at all, not even the thin end of it. They might love their neighbour, with a hot, dark, unquestioning love. But the love would probably leave off abruptly. The fascination of what is beyond them has not seized on them. Their neighbour is a mere external. Their life is centripetal, pivoted inside itself, and does not run out towards others and mankind. One feels for the first time the real old mediæval life, which is enclosed in itself and has no interest in the world outside.

And so they lie about on the seats, play a game, shout, and sleep, and settle their long stocking-caps: and spit. It is wonderful in them that at this time of day they still wear the long stocking-caps as part of their inevitable selves. It is a sign of obstinate and powerful tenacity. They are not going to be broken in upon by world-consciousness. They are not going into the world's common clothes. Coarse, vigorous, determined, they will stick to their own coarse dark stupidity and let the big world find its own way to its own enlightened hell. Their hell is their own hell, they prefer it unenlightened.

And one cannot help wondering whether Sardinia will resist right through. Will the last waves of enlightenment and world-unity break over them and wash away the stocking-caps? Or is the tide of enlightenment and world-unity already receding fast enough?

Certainly a reaction is setting in, away from the old universality, back, away from cosmopolitanism and internationalism. Russia, with her Third International, is at the same time reacting most violently away from all other contact, back, recoiling on herself, into a fierce, unapproachable Russianism. Which motion will conquer? The workman's International, or the centripetal movement into national isolation? Are we going to merge into one grey proletarian homogeneity?—or are we going to swing back into more-or-less isolated, separate, defiant communities?

Probably both. The workman's International movement will finally break the flow towards cosmopolitanism and world-assimilation, and suddenly in a crash the world will fly back into intense separations. The moment has come when America, that extremist in world-assimilation and world-oneness, is reacting into violent egocentricity, a truly Amerindian egocentricity. As sure as fate we are on the brink of American empire.

For myself, I am glad. I am glad that the era of love and oneness is over: hateful homogeneous world-oneness. I am glad that Russia flies back into savage Russianism, Scythism, savagely self-pivoting. I am glad that America is doing the same. I shall be glad when men hate their common, world-alike clothes, when they tear them up and clothe themselves fiercely for distinction, savage distinction, savage distinction against the rest of the creeping world: when America kicks the billy-cock and the collar-and-tie into limbo, and takes to her own national costume: when men fiercely react against looking all alike and being all alike, and betake themselves into vivid clan or nation-distinctions.

The era of love and oneness is over. The era of world-alike should be at an end. The other tide has set in. Men will set their bonnets at one another now, and fight themselves into separation and sharp distinction. The day of peace and oneness is over, the day of the great fight into multifariousness is at hand. Hasten the day, and save us from proletarian homogeneity and khaki all-alikeness.

I love my indomitable coarse men from mountain Sardinia, for their stocking-caps and their splendid, animal-bright stupidity. If only the last wave of all-alikeness won't wash those superb crests, those caps, away.

R. W. B. LEWIS

(1917–   )

In 1920 Anglican clergyman Leicester Lewis came to Italy with his family to study church history. His son, three-year-old Richard Warrington Baldwin Lewis, was carried up Mt. Vesuvius on the back of a guide. It is the literary scholar's first memory of Italy. R. W. B. Lewis returned to Italy many times, as a soldier with the American army during World War II and again for more than a dozen extended visits to Florence since 1950. Lewis explains, "These were not 'visits' properly speaking, for on every one we were living in the city; we were (increasingly) at home in it."

Lewis is fiercely devoted to Florence. Once asked by the Italian novelist Ignazio Silone, "Why do you live in that dusty backwater?" he was at a loss for a reply. Lewis recalls fumbling for a satisfactory answer and finally, decades later, concluding, it is not "any particular building or painting or statue or piazza or bridge, not even the whole unrivaled array of works of art. It is the city itself—the city understood as a self; as a whole, a miraculously developed design."

For many years Lewis was a professor at Yale University, and he now divides his time between Florence and Connecticut. His personal chronicle The City of Florence: Historical Vistas and Personal Sightings, from which this excerpt is taken, was published in 1995.

Vespucci Territory: 1987

from THE CITY OF FLORENCE

SUMMERTIME

Summer in Florence has a bad reputation. Florence-wise friends, when told we planned to spend the months of July and August in the city, expressed alarm for our well-being and praise for our courage. The *heat,* they kept exclaiming. Sheila Hale, the author of the often knowing and witty *American Express Guide to Florence and Tuscany,* takes note of a beautiful old pharmacy on Via Cavour that was founded in the fifteenth century by the monks from nearby San Marco: "Their specifics," she writes, "include an anti-hysteric, which might come in handy if you are visiting Florence in August." We had lunch in the third week of July at the Orologio, a particularly nice trattoria on the south side of the river, and asked Franco, the gentlest and kindest of waiters (we had come to know him the year before), if the place would be closing soon. Yes, said Franco with a kind of violence. He pressed his hands together, then yanked them apart in a savage ripping motion, to indicate desperation and imminent collapse. Without an immediate period of *riposo,* he said, he would not survive.

The heat can be oppressive at times. It seems to get caught in Florence's topographical curvature; one walks perspiring and mostly in the morning; local nerves do get frazzled after a while. But except for a mean little spell toward the end of our stay (a spell washed away by a tumultuous *temporale*), the temperature

rarely rose above 90 degrees Fahrenheit during our 1987 summer. It was hotter in Rome and Naples, according to the daily
reports, and murderously hot in Calabria. New Yorkers were
much worse off than we were, so we read. And anyhow we are
among those who feel about Florence as Cole Porter did about
Paris, and love it when it sizzles.

In fact, no few of our Florentine acquaintances speak fondly
of the summer here, and of August as their favorite month. The
city empties out delightfully, and, as it does, things close down
all over town. The majority of the restaurants, like the Orologio,
close for up to a month, as they do in other Italian cities and
with an annual clang in Paris. Many food stores are shut, as are a
number of luxury shops. The streets become invitingly vacant.
Nor are the tourists any sort of menace. We counted twenty-
one tour buses one morning, lined up on the Lungarno stretching eastward away from Ponte alle Grazie, and the newspaper
informed us that the number of tourists had increased a good
deal since the previous summer, when varieties of fear and fool-
ishness had kept Americans out of Europe. But tourists were
hardly visible in most parts of the city.

As in some surrealist movie, they tended to tramp about on
the Ponte Vecchio and the street running north from it; to cluster at the entrance to San Lorenzo's New Sacristy and the
Medici tombs; and to push together in thickets around the
Duomo. The line of people waiting to get into the Uffizi
stretched most mornings in snakelike fashion halfway across the
Piazza Signoria; but the depressing spectacle was caused in part
by the Uffizi authorities, who instructed the ticket takers—as a
symbolic protest against some ministerial action—to delay matters by scrutinizing each ticket with care, turning it over and
back and peering at the stamp. Elsewhere, the casual visitor was
rarely in evidence; and elsewhere was where we lived.

WE LIVED in a quite remarkably spacious and high-ceilinged
apartment on Borgo Ognissanti, a street at the edge of the "his-

toric center" of the city that departs from Piazza Goldoni and
Ponte alla Carraia and runs parallel to Lungarno Vespucci and
the river. An official of the American consulate generously put
it at our disposal when he took his family back to Texas for
home leave. This was our tenth stay of any duration in Florence,
and never have we inhabited rooms of such airy vastness. Henry
James, after inspecting similar large chambers in several old Florentine palazzi in 1873, commented with almost unmixed approval on "the echoing excess of space" he observed in them;
and thought that "the spaciousness of some of these ancient
drawing-rooms is that of the Russian steppes . . . Such quarters," he ventured, "seem a translation into space of the old-
fashioned idea of leisure." Leisure was certainly a requisite just to
get around in the place. It took a measurable amount of time for
one of us to walk across the apartment—shouting would have
been useless—to summon the other to the telephone.

The apartment occupied much of the second floor (European
style: fifty-nine steps up, or ascend by the hard-breathing little
elevator) in a building known as the Palazzo della Marescialla.
The name goes back to the early-seventeenth century and one
Eleanora Dori, who married the lowborn Florentine Concino
Concini, and who in time became the confidante of Maria de'
Medici, the Queen of France. The latter, the daughter of
Francesco I, the second Medici Grand Duke of Tuscany, had
married Henri IV, and had helped bring things Florentine to
Paris and the French court. After the king's death, Concino
Concini became a special favorite of the widowed queen, who
made him governor of Picardy and Normandy and gave him the
title of Marshall (*Maresciallo*). Concini and Eleanora were profit-
ing happily from their situation until the new king, the adolescent Louis XIII, vexed by their influence with his mother,
decided to get rid of them. The *Maresciallo* was assassinated in
front of the Louvre in 1617, and a few weeks later the *Marescialla*
was beheaded and then burned as a witch.

Long before this, Eleanora Dori, in status-seeking moves in
Florence, had renamed herself Poponelli and then Galigai. The

palazzo bears the coat-of-arms of the illustrious Galigai family—crossed chains—to which the *Marescialla* had no claim
whatever. A satirical verse about her circulated in Florence. In
rough translation:

> Now Dori, now Poponelli, and now Galigai,
> What in hell will you ever be satisfied by?

It is a beguiling neighborhood, both in its ongoing life and its
history. Fashionable shops along Via de' Fossi down the way, offering *antichità,* neoclassic statuary, ceramics, and exquisite silk,
give way, upward on Ognissanti, to the food stores: the *ortolano*
(for fruit and vegetables), the *macellaio* (for beautiful cuts of veal
and beef), the *panificio* (for bread), the *alimentari* (cheese, *pro-
sciutto crudo,* staples), the *latteria* (for milk). Shopping, as all foreign residents in Florence come to discover, is a daily exercise in
neighborliness, a round of visits and talk. Our excellent wine
merchant delivered on call from the other side of Ponte Carraia,
bringing up heavy cartons of mineral water, that indispensable
summer item, and such assorted wines as the occasion called
for—especially, that year, a marvelous 1985 Cacchiano red.

On our way to the *panificio* and the *ortolano,* we walked through
Florentine history, as represented in this quarter-mile by the
church of Ognissanti, built in 1256 by the Umiliati, a colony of
Lombard monks who founded the wool industry, which was the
basis of the city's wealth, and of all the wealth it gave rise to, for
two centuries. The Umiliati had charge of Ponte alla Carraia,
near at hand, the oldest of the great medieval Florentine bridges.
They rebuilt it in 1269, and, as we said in an earlier chapter, it
took its name— "cart road"—from the *carri* which hauled wool
across it to the section of San Frediano, where most of the wool
workers lived. The church itself has an early-seventeenth century
baroque facade and a modest square-topped bell tower from the
thirteenth century.

Inside, at one of the altars to the right, is a Madonna of
Mercy, an early painting by Domenico Ghirlandaio which dis-

plays members of the Vespucci family (donors of the chapel and Ghirlandaio's "guardians") and, among them, the youthful Amerigo, looking alert and watchful. Next door to the church, and with its own entrance, is the former refectory, which contains a Last Supper of Ghirlandaio, at once serene and dramatic, with glimpses in the background of a gracious garden with abundant foliage and skylarks in flight. It is a variant of Ghirlandaio's *Last Supper* in the Convent of San Marco, and students of the artist may be reminded that this is the one without the cat.

Ognissanti is Vespucci territory. The family, from Peretola, a few kilometers west of Florence (the name seems derived from *vespa,* the word for "wasp," and in our day for a motor scooter of arguable charm), made their original fortune in silk, though they also went in for wool and banking. They had their houses on Borgo Ognissanti, directly across from our palazzo; Amerigo was born in one of them in 1454. Another of them was made into a hospital in 1388 by the prosperous silk merchant Simone Vespucci, and when the hospital was enlarged in the later sixteenth century by Grand Duke Ferdinand I and given its present name of San Giovanni di Dio, it absorbed all the Vespucci holdings. San Giovanni di Dio is now a day clinic offering varieties of services.

The *quartiere* of which Ognissanti is a part is called Santa Maria Novella, for the church of the same name. Via de' Fossi at its far end opens into the piazza over which the church presides. William Dean Howells, in *Tuscan Cities,* tells of coming to Florence for the winter of 1882–83 with the notion of writing about it. He took lodgings for the family in Piazza Santa Maria Novella, and soon was wondering "why I should have thought of writing of the whole city, when one piazza in it was interesting enough to make a book about."

Howells was aware that the twenty-one-year-old Longfellow had lodged in Piazza Santa Maria Novella in 1828, in virtually the same building as the Howells family, on the west side of the square; and that Boccaccio (to whom Longfellow later paid tribute as a master teller of tales) had set the opening of the *De-*

cameron in the church. He was even more conscious that Henry James had spent a productive period, completing *Roderick Hudson,* in rooms overlooking the piazza from the south end, on Via della Scala. It was from this address that James had written Howells in the spring of 1874 to say that Florence now seemed to him an old literary masterpiece of which one turned the pages with constantly renewed pleasure.

James, after another stay in Florence, in 1877, recorded visiting the church of Santa Maria Novella—always, for James, the best of the Florentine churches—bearing in hand a copy, just acquired, of Ruskin's *Mornings in Florence.* He "looked about for a while at the beautiful church"—lingering under the multi-tiered frescoes of Ghirlandaio in the choir, and no doubt pausing before the Trinity of Masaccio and, in the Strozzi chapel, the frescoes of Filippino Lippi—and then sat down to peruse the Ruskin essays. There he learned that he had been all wrong in his enjoyment of "the good old city of Florence" and most of its art works. "I had taken great pleasure in certain frescos by Ghirlandaio in the choir of that very church; but it appeared from one of the little books that the frescos were as naught." (Ruskin had said that the paintings were "simply—good for nothing.") "I had much admired Santa Croce and had thought the Duomo a very noble affair; but I had now the most positive assurance that I knew nothing about them." Finally, wrote James, it was with Ruskin himself that he "lost patience . . . not the stupid Brunelleschi, not the vulgar Ghirlandaio." He lost patience with the view that there is rigid truth and unforgivable error in the human response to works of art; with the "apocalyptic terminology" that suggests a kind of damnation in not seeing things correctly; with the total absence of any portion of *joy* in the aesthetic experience.

The piazza's irregular shape is punctuated by two imposing stone obelisks, by Giambologna (1608), set on the backs of two bronze turtles. The obelisks served as goal posts for an annual chariot race that was one of the chief public spectacles introduced by the Medici dukes. One of the spectators seated in the grandstands in June 1581 was Michel de Montaigne, who found the event extremely stimulating. The chariots made three turns around the square, and the Strozzi charioteer, to the cautious enthusiasm of the crowd, was declared to have arrived at the post an instant ahead of the Grand Duke's man. Montaigne thought the verdict plainly wrong, but wrote that he "liked this spectacle more than any other I saw in Italy." Some two hundred and fifty years later, James Fenimore Cooper, who had been in Florence for the winter and spring of 1829, gave his own account of the *corso dei còcchi* (carriages). He felt that the effect of the whole scene was impressive: the parade of guards on horse and foot, the well-dressed populace, the balconies "garnished by tapestry and fine women." But the race itself seemed to him a bumpy and unskilled performance. "One may witness the same any fine evening in New York," he said, "between two drunken Irish cartmen who are on their way home."

The great railway station behind the church—it too is called Santa Maria Novella ("FIRENZE S.M.N." is the sign that greets you as your train is pulling in)—was the scene of chaos and distress on the last weekend of July. A new and independent union known as Cobas—the word comes from *comitato della base,* and means essentially a union directly representative of the workers—brought about a nationwide strike of railway employees. Almost 80 percent of all local trains across the country stopped running for twenty-four hours, more than 60 percent of all long-distance trains came to a halt, and there was no movement of freight at all. The entire system was paralyzed. It was, of course, one of the most heavily scheduled weekends of the summer for Italian and foreign travelers, and among the untold scores of thousands left stranded were those many seeking to escape the literally killing temperatures of Calabria. The Florence station, when we looked in on it, was a sea of despondently milling stranded passengers.

The strike was in protest against a contract recently proposed for the railroad workers by the ministry of transport in Rome, which offered a modest pay increase to take leisurely effect over

a three-year period, and some slight reduction in the number of
hours per week. The terms were rejected by the Cobas, who ral-
lied a quite unexpected majority of workers to the cause. In the
wake of the strike, charges and countercharges filled the air, ac-
cusations of lying, wild exaggerations. But what impressed the
American onlooker was the almost total absence of concern for
the public welfare, for the interests of the average citizen. This
was true of the Cobas as it was of the ministerial spokesman;
and not less so of the large established unions (CGIL to the left,
CISI to the right, UIL somewhere in the middle), as they regarded the affair with skeptical eye. There were vague references
to the need for union self-discipline; but these seemed to be old
refrains, an accepted part of the *spettacolo,* the histrionics, of the
process.

I felt the same lack of concern, the same fundamental indifference (*menefregismo*—fuckyouism, in American—is the earthy
Italian word for it), to the well-being of the citizenry during a
series of strikes by the Florentine bus services earlier in the summer. Buses stopped running for an entire morning, or for two
hours at several different periods during the day. The strike times
were announced in advance by the Florence newspapers, but the
resulting inconvenience was enormous; on five separate days
over a two-week stretch, the life of the city was thrown into
calamitous disarray. And during all the heated public discussion
of the strikes and the issues that lay behind them, I failed to hear
a single note of genuine anxiety about their effect upon the
city's people.

This indifference causes one a peculiar pang in Florence, for
it was here that the very notion of the public welfare first came
into being, at least on the European continent: *la cosa pubblica,*
the public thing, as understood by the *Primo Popolo* and the *Sec-
ondo Popolo* in the thirteenth century. The edict ordering
Arnolfo di Cambio to prepare models for the cathedral enjoined
him that, like all other works commissioned by the Commune,
his should "correspond to the noble soul which is composed of
the souls of all [the Commune's] citizens united in one will."

The force, one might say the allure, of that principle persisted into the sixteenth century, when it gradually lost all vitality and died under Medici rule. If there are faint signs of a revival today, as some would like to claim, they are not to be found in the sphere of the public services. It does not altogether become an American in the 1990s to complain about the decline of the public sentiment in other countries; but even the most chastened American can feel a spurt of good national feeling when he is made to undergo the miseries of the Italian postal system.

Matters were not so bad during the summer of 1987 as they were during a long stay a good many years ago when, in the course of a months-long postal strike, tons of mail (so we heard) were routinely destroyed, dumped into the sea, thrown into the furnaces. But it is, without competition, the worst delivery service in the Western world; even an Italian government report not long back described the "disservice" as intolerable (Edith Wharton arrived at the same finding before the First World War.) Anything larger than an airmail letter can be held up indefinitely. A visit to the storeroom in the station where packages accumulate from incoming freight trains is enough to make your hair stand on end. There is obviously no plan on the part of the attendants—as they sit about and smoke and laugh—for sorting and distributing the items in the foreseeable future.

A small clasp-envelope packet of letters and bills, all of some urgency, was sent to us from America at the end of June. It reached Florence in a fortnight, but no action was taken about it for another two weeks. We were then informed by a notice that we could pick the thing up at the office on Via G. B. Foggini. No one we consulted locally had heard of the street; in our *quartiere* post office, the clerks fell to arguing good-naturedly over its whereabouts. We finally located it on a large-scale map: several miles away on the southwest outskirts of town. We proceeded to the general area but failed to hit upon Via Foggini after several tries. Finally we approached an aged woman who was buying vegetables. She had lived in the neighborhood for years, she said, but still wasn't sure which street was Foggini. She thought it was the one veering off to the left. We peered through binoculars: she was right. "*Mille grazie!*" we said fervently. "*A voi!*" ("Thanks to *you!*"), she replied with quavering, ancient courtesy. We went on, paid 250 lire for some inexplicable charge, and collected our packet.

BERNARD MALAMUD

(1914–1986)

"My work, all of it, is an idea of dedication to the human," said Bernard Malamud in an interview. "If you don't respect man, you cannot respect my work." Although Malamud was best known for fiction that reflected Jewish themes, his first novel, The Natural, *was a mythic fantasy about baseball. His subsequent books, including* The Assistant, The Fixer, *and* The Tenants *explored the nature of the Jewish experience. Malamud once wrote, "The Jews are absolutely the very stuff of dreams."*

In the mid-1950s Malamud received a grant and took a sabbatical in Rome. His experience in Italy was the basis for many of the short stories in his collections The Magic Barrel *and* Pictures of Fidelman. *Although Malamud deserted the familiar Brooklyn setting of most of his fiction, his characters and themes remain unchanged. In "The Maid's Shoes," Orlando Krantz, a Jewish American professor on sabbatical in Rome, is foiled by his Italian maid, Rosa. Like most Malamud heroes, Krantz becomes unwillingly engaged in life and is ultimately disillusioned, but not crushed.*

The Maid's Shoes

from THE STORIES OF
BERNARD MALAMUD

The maid had left her name with the porter's wife. She said she was looking for steady work and would take anything but pre–

ferred not to work for an old woman. Still, if she had to she would. She was forty-five and looked older. Her face was worn but her hair was black, and her eyes and lips were pretty. She had few good teeth. When she laughed she was embarrassed around the mouth. Although it was cold in early October, that year in Rome, and the chestnut vendors were already bent over their pans of glowing charcoals, the maid wore only a threadbare black cotton dress which had a split down the left side, where about two inches of seam had opened on the hip, exposing her underwear. She had sewn the seam several times but this was one of the times it was open again. Her heavy but well-formed legs were bare and she wore house slippers as she talked to the portinaia; she had done a single day's washing for a signora down the street and carried her shoes in a paper bag. There were three comparatively new apartment houses on the hilly street and she left her name in each.

The portinaia, a dumpy woman wearing a brown tweed skirt she had got from an English family that had once lived in the building, said she would remember the maid but then she forgot; she forgot until an American professor moved into a furnished apartment on the fifth floor and asked her to help him find a maid. The portinaia brought him a girl from the neighborhood, a girl of sixteen, recently from Umbria, who came with her aunt. But the professor, Orlando Krantz, did not like the way the aunt played up certain qualities of the girl, so he sent her away. He told the portinaia he was looking for an older woman, someone he wouldn't have to worry about. Then the portinaia thought of the maid who had left her name and address, and she went to her house on the Via Appia Antica near the catacombs and told her an American was looking for a maid, mezzo servizio; she would give him her name if the maid agreed to make it worth her while. The maid, whose name was Rosa, shrugged her shoulders and looked stiffly down the street. She said she had nothing to offer the portinaia.

"Look at what I'm wearing," she said. "Look at this junk pile, can you call it a house? I live here with my son and his bitch of a wife who counts every spoonful of soup in my mouth. They treat me like dirt and dirt is all I have to my name."

"In that case I can do nothing for you," the portinaia said. "I have myself and my husband to think of." But she returned from the bus stop and said she would recommend the maid to the American professor if she gave her five thousand lire the first time she was paid.

"How much will he pay?" the maid asked the portinaia.

"I would ask for eighteen thousand a month. Tell him you have to spend two hundred lire a day for carfare."

"That's almost right," Rosa said. "It will cost me forty one way and forty back. But if he pays me eighteen thousand I'll give you five if you sign that's all I owe you."

"I will sign," said the portinaia, and she recommended the maid to the American professor.

Orlando Krantz was a nervous man of sixty. He had mild gray eyes, a broad mouth, and a pointed clefted chin. His round head was bald and he had a bit of a belly, although the rest of him was quite thin. He was a somewhat odd-looking man but an authority in law, the portinaia told Rosa. The professor sat at a table in his study, writing all day, yet was up every half hour on some pretext or other to look nervously around. He worried how things were going and often came out of his study to see. He would watch Rosa working, then went in and wrote. In a half hour he would come out, ostensibly to wash his hands in the bathroom or drink a glass of cold water, but he was really passing by to see what she was doing. She was doing what she had to. Rosa worked quickly, especially when he was watching. She seemed, he thought, to be unhappy, but that was none of his business. Their lives, he knew, were full of troubles, often sordid; it was best to be detached.

This was the professor's second year in Italy; he had spent the first in Milan, and the second was in Rome. He had rented a large three-bedroom apartment, one of which he used as a study. His wife and daughter, who had returned for a visit to the States in August, would have the other bedrooms; they were due

back before not too long. When the ladies returned, he had told
Rosa, he would put her on full time. There was a maid's room
where she could sleep; indeed, which she already used as her
own though she was in the apartment only from nine till four.
Rosa agreed to a full-time arrangement because it would mean
all her meals in and no rent to pay her son and his dog-faced wife.

While they were waiting for Mrs. Krantz and the daughter to
arrive, Rosa did the marketing and cooking. She made the professor's breakfast when she came in, and his lunch at one. She offered to stay later than four, to prepare his supper, which he ate
at six, but he preferred to take that meal out. After shopping she
cleaned the house, thoroughly mopping the marble floors with
a wet rag she pushed around with a stick, though the floors did
not look particularly dusty to him. She also washed and ironed
his laundry. She was a good worker, her slippers clip-clopping as
she hurried from one room to the next, and she frequently finished up about an hour or so before she was due to go home; so
she retired to the maid's room and there read *Tempo* or *Epoca,* or
sometimes a love story in photographs, with the words printed
in italics under each picture. Often she pulled her bed down and
lay in it under blankets, to keep warm. The weather had turned
rainy, and now the apartment was uncomfortably cold. The custom of the condominium in this apartment house was not to
heat until the fifteenth of November, and if it was cold before
then, as it was now, the people of the house had to do the best
they could. The cold disturbed the professor, who wrote with
his gloves and hat on, and increased his nervousness so that he
was out to look at her more often. He wore a heavy blue
bathrobe over his clothes; sometimes the bathrobe belt was
wrapped around a hot-water bottle he had placed against the
lower part of his back, under the suit coat. Sometimes he sat on
the hot-water bag as he wrote, a sight that caused Rosa, when
she once saw this, to smile behind her hand. If he left the hot-
water bag in the dining room after lunch, Rosa asked if she
might use it. As a rule he allowed her to, and then she did her
work with the rubber bag pressed against her stomach with her
elbow. She said she had trouble with her liver. That was why the

professor did not mind her going to the maid's room to lie down before leaving, after she had finished her work.

Once after Rosa had gone home, smelling tobacco smoke in the corridor near her room, the professor entered it to investigate. The room was not more than an elongated cubicle with a narrow bed that lifted sideways against the wall; there was also a small green cabinet, and an adjoining tiny bathroom containing a toilet and a sitz bath fed by a cold-water tap. She often did the laundry on a washboard in the sitz bath, but never, so far as he knew, had bathed in it. The day before her daughter-in-law's name day she had asked permission to take a hot bath in his tub in the big bathroom, and though he had hesitated a moment, the professor finally said yes. In her room, he opened a drawer at the bottom of the cabinet and found a hoard of cigarette butts in it, the butts he had left in ashtrays. He noticed, too, that she had collected his old newspapers and magazines from the wastebaskets. She also saved cord, paper bags, and rubber bands; also pencil stubs he had thrown away. After he found that out, he occasionally gave her some meat left over from lunch, and cheese that had gone dry, to take with her. For this she brought him flowers. She also brought a dirty egg or two her daughter-in-law's hen had laid, but he thanked her and said the yolks were too strong for his taste. He noticed that she needed a pair of shoes, for those she put on to go home in were split in two places, and she wore the same black dress with the tear in it every day, which embarrassed him when he had to speak to her; however, he thought he would refer these matters to his wife when she arrived.

As jobs went, Rosa knew she had a good one. The professor paid well and promptly, and he never ordered her around in the haughty manner of some of her Italian employers. This one was nervous and fussy but not a bad sort. His main fault was his silence. Though he could speak a better than passable Italian, he preferred, when not at work, to sit in an armchair in the living room, reading. Only two souls in the whole apartment, you would think they would want to say something to each other once in a while. Sometimes when she served him a cup of coffee as he read, she tried to get in a word about her troubles. She wanted to tell him about her long, impoverished widowhood, how badly her son had turned out, and what her miserable daughter-in-law was like to live with. But though he listened courteously; although they shared the same roof, and even the same hot-water bottle and bathtub, they almost never shared speech. He said no more to her than a crow would, and clearly showed he preferred to be left alone. So she left him alone and was lonely in the apartment. Working for foreigners had its advantages, she thought, but it also had disadvantages.

After a while the professor noticed that the telephone was ringing regularly for Rosa each afternoon during the time she usually was resting in her room. In the following week, instead of staying in the house until four, after her telephone call she asked permission to leave. At first she said her liver was bothering her, but later she stopped giving excuses. Although he did not much approve of this sort of thing, suspecting she would take advantage of him if he was too liberal in granting favors, he informed her that, until his wife arrived, she might leave at three on two afternoons of the week, provided that all her duties were fully discharged. He knew that everything was done before she left but thought he ought to say it. She listened meekly—her eyes aglow, lips twitching—and meekly agreed. He presumed, when he happened to think about it afterwards, that Rosa had a good spot here, by any standard, and she ought soon to show it in her face, change her unhappy expression for one less so. However, this did not happen, for when he chanced to observe her, even on days when she was leaving early, she seemed sadly preoccupied, sighed much, as if something on her heart was weighing her down.

He never asked what, preferring not to become involved in whatever it was. These people had endless troubles, and if you let yourself get involved in them you got endlessly involved. He knew of one woman, the wife of a colleague, who had said to her maid: "Lucrezia, I am sympathetic to your condition but I don't want to hear about it." This, the professor reflected, was basically good policy. It kept employer-employee relationships where they belonged—on an objective level. He was, after all, leaving Italy in April and would never in his life see Rosa again. It would do her a lot more good if, say, he sent her a small check at Christmas, than if he needlessly immersed himself in her miseries now. The professor knew he was nervous and often impatient, and he was sometimes sorry for his nature; but he was what he was and preferred to stay aloof from what did not closely and personally concern him.

But Rosa would not have it so. One morning she knocked on his study door, and when he said avanti, she went in embarrassedly, so that even before she began to speak he was himself embarrassed.

"Professore," Rosa said, unhappily, "please excuse me for bothering your work, but I have to talk to somebody."

"I happen to be very busy," he said, growing a little angry. "Can it wait a while?"

"It'll take only a minute. Your troubles hang on all your life but it doesn't take long to tell them."

"Is it your liver complaint?" he asked.

"No. I need your advice. You're an educated man and I'm no more than an ignorant peasant."

"What kind of advice?" he asked impatiently.

"Call it anything you like. The fact is I have to speak to somebody. I can't talk to my son, even if it were possible in this case. When I open my mouth he roars like a bull. And my daughter-in-law isn't worth wasting my breath on. Sometimes, on the roof, when we're hanging the wash, I say a few words to the portinaia, but she isn't a sympathetic person so I have to come to you, I'll tell you why."

Before he could say how he felt about hearing her confidences, Rosa had launched into a story about this middle-aged government worker in the tax bureau, whom she had happened to meet in the neighborhood. He was married, had four children, and sometimes worked as a carpenter after leaving his office at two o'clock each day. His name was Armando; it was he who telephoned her every afternoon. They had met recently on a bus, and he had, after two or three meetings, seeing that her shoes weren't fit to wear, urged her to let him buy her a new pair. She had told him not to be foolish. One could see he had very little, and it was enough that he took her to the movies twice a week. She had said that, yet every time they met he talked about the shoes he wanted to buy her.

"I'm only human," Rosa frankly told the professor, "and I need the shoes badly, but you know how these things go. If I put on his shoes they may carry me to his bed. That's why I thought I would ask you if I ought to take them."

The professor's face and bald head were flushed. "I don't see how I can possibly advise you—"

"You're the educated one," she said.

"However," he went on, "since the situation is still essentially hypothetical, I will go so far as to say you ought to tell this generous gentleman that his responsibilities should be to his family. He would do well not to offer you gifts, as you will do, not to accept them. If you don't, he can't possibly make any claims upon you or your person. This is all I care to say. Since you have requested advice, I've given it, but I won't say any more."

Rosa sighed. "The truth of it is I could use a pair of shoes. Mine look as though they've been chewed by goats. I haven't had a new pair in six years."

But the professor had nothing more to add.

After Rosa had gone for the day, in thinking about her problem, he decided to buy her a pair of shoes. He was concerned that she might be expecting something of the sort, had planned, so to speak, to have it work out this way. But since this was conjecture only, evidence entirely lacking, he would assume, until proof to the contrary became available, that she had no ulterior motive in asking his advice. He considered giving her five thousand lire to make the purchase of the shoes herself and relieve him of the trouble, but he was doubtful, for there was no guarantee she would use the money for the agreed purpose. Suppose she came in the next day, saying she had had a liver attack that had necessitated calling the doctor, who had charged three thousand lire for his visit; therefore would the professor, in view of these unhappy circumstances, supply an additional three thousand for the shoes? That would never do, so the next morning, when the maid was at the grocer's, the professor slipped into her room and quickly traced on paper the outline of her miserable shoe—a task but he accomplished it quickly. That evening, in a store on the same piazza as the restaurant where he liked to eat, he bought Rosa a pair of brown shoes for fifty-five hundred lire, slightly more than he had planned to spend; but they were a solid pair of ties, walking shoes with a medium heel, a practical gift.

He gave them to Rosa the next day, a Wednesday. He felt embarrassed to be doing that, because he realized that despite his warnings to her, he had permitted himself to meddle in her affairs; but he considered giving her the shoes a psychologically proper move in more ways than one. In presenting her with them he said, "Rosa, I have perhaps a solution to suggest in the matter you discussed with me. Here are a pair of new shoes for you. Tell your friend you must refuse his. And when you do, perhaps it would be advisable also to inform him that you intend to see him a little less frequently from now on."

Rosa was overjoyed at the professor's kindness. She attempted to kiss his hand but he thrust it behind him and retired to his study. On Thursday, when he opened the apartment door to her ring, she was wearing his shoes. She carried a large paper bag from which she offered the professor three small oranges still on a branch with green leaves. He said she needn't have brought them, but Rosa, smiling half hiddenly in order not to show her teeth, said that she wanted him to see how grateful she was. Later she requested permission to leave at three so she could show Armando her new shoes.

He said dryly, "You may go at that hour if your work is done."

She thanked him profusely. Hastening through her tasks, she left shortly after three, but not before the professor, in his hat, gloves, and bathrobe, standing at his open study door as he was inspecting the corridor floor she had just mopped, saw her hurrying out of the apartment, wearing a pair of dressy black needle-point pumps. This angered him; and when Rosa appeared the next morning, though she begged him not to when he said she had made a fool of him and he was firing her to teach her a lesson, the professor did. She wept, pleading for another chance, but he would not change his mind. So she desolately wrapped up the odds and ends in her room in a newspaper and left, still crying. Afterwards he was upset and very nervous. He could not stand the cold that day and he could not work.

A week later, the morning the heat was turned on, Rosa appeared at the apartment door, and begged to have her job back. She was distraught, said her son had hit her, and gently touched her puffed black-and-blue lip. With tears in her eyes, although she didn't cry, Rosa explained it was no fault of hers that she had accepted both pairs of shoes. Armando had given her his pair first; had, out of jealousy of a possible rival, forced her to take them. Then when the professor had kindly offered his pair of shoes, she had wanted to refuse them but was afraid of angering him and losing her job. This was God's truth, so help her St. Peter. She would, she promised, find Armando, whom she had not seen in a week, and return his shoes if the professor would take her back. If he didn't, she would throw herself into the Tiber. He, though he didn't care for talk of this kind, felt a certain sympathy for her. He was disappointed in himself at the way he had handled her. It would have been better to have said a few appropriate words on the subject of honesty and then philosophically dropped the matter. In firing her he had only made things difficult for them both, because, in the meantime, he had tried two other maids and found them unsuitable. One stole, the other was lazy. As a result the house was a mess, impossible for him to work in, although the portinaia came up for an hour each morning to clean. It was his good fortune that Rosa had appeared at the door just then. When she removed her coat, he noticed with satisfaction that the tear in her dress had finally been mended.

She went grimly to work, dusting, polishing, cleaning everything in sight. She unmade beds, then made them, swept under them, mopped, polished head- and footboards, adorned the beds with newly pressed spreads. Though she had just got her job back and worked with her usual efficiency, she worked, he observed, in sadness, frequently sighing, attempting a smile only when his eye was on her. This is their nature, he thought; they have hard lives. To spare her further blows by her son he gave her permission to live in. He offered extra money to buy meat for her supper but she refused it, saying pasta would do. Pasta and green salad was all she ate at night. Occasionally she boiled an artichoke left over from lunch and ate it with oil and vinegar. He invited her to drink the white wine in the cupboard and take fruit. Once in a while she did, always telling what and how much, though he repeatedly asked her not to. The apartment was nicely in order. Though the phone rang, as usual, daily at three, only seldom did she leave the house after she had talked to Armando.

Then one dismal morning Rosa came to the professor and in her distraught way confessed she was pregnant. Her face was lit in despair; her white underwear shone through her black dress.

He felt annoyance, disgust, blaming himself for having re-employed her.

"You must leave at once," he said, trying to keep his voice from trembling.

"I can't," she said. "My son will kill me. In God's name, help me, professore."

He was infuriated by her stupidity. "Your sexual adventures are none of my responsibility."

"Was it that Armando?" he asked almost savagely.

She nodded.

"Have you informed him?"

"He says he can't believe it." She tried to smile but couldn't.

"I'll convince him," he said. "Do you have his telephone number?"

She told it to him. He called Armando at his office, identified himself, and asked the government clerk to come at once to the apartment. "You have a grave responsibility to Rosa."

"I have a grave responsibility to my family." Armando answered.

"You might have considered them before this."

"All right, I'll come over tomorrow after work. It's impossible today. I have a carpentering contract to finish up."

"She'll expect you," the professor said.

When he hung up he felt less angry, although still more emotional than he cared to feel. "Are you quite sure of your condition?" he asked her, "that you are pregnant?"

"Yes." She was crying now. "Tomorrow is my son's birthday. What a beautiful present it will be for him to find out his mother's a whore. He'll break my bones, if not with his hands, then with his teeth."

"It hardly seems likely you can conceive, considering your age."

"My mother gave birth at fifty."

"Isn't there a possibility you are mistaken?"

"I don't know. It's never been this way before. After all, I've been a widow—"

"Well, you'd better find out."

"Yes, I want to," Rosa said. "I want to see the midwife in my neighborhood but I haven't got a single lira. I spent all I had left when I was working, and I had to borrow carfare to get here. Armando can't help me just now. He has to pay for his wife's teeth this week. She has very bad teeth, poor thing. That's why I came to you. Could you advance me two thousand of my pay so I can be examined by the midwife?"

After a minute he counted two one-thousand-lire notes out of his wallet. "Go to her now," he said. He was about to add that if she was pregnant, not to come back, but he was afraid she might do something desperate, or lie to him so she could go on working. He didn't want her around any more. When he thought of his wife and daughter arriving amid this mess, he felt sick with nervousness. He wanted to get rid of the maid as soon as possible.

The next day Rosa came in at twelve instead of nine. Her

dark face was pale. "Excuse me for being late," she murmured. "I was praying at my husband's grave."

"That's all right," the professor said. "But did you go to the midwife?"

"Not yet."

"Why not?" Though angry he spoke calmly.

She stared at the floor.

"Please answer my question."

"I was going to say I lost the two thousand lire on the bus, but after being at my husband's grave I'll tell you the truth. After all, it's bound to come out."

This is terrible, he thought, it's unending. "What did you do with the money?"

"That's what I mean," Rosa sighed. "I bought my son a present. Not that he deserves it, but it was his birthday." She burst into tears.

He stared at her a minute, then said, "Please come with me."

The professor left the apartment in his bathrobe, and Rosa followed. Opening the elevator door he stepped inside, holding the door for her. She entered the elevator.

They stopped two floors below. He got out and nearsightedly scanned the names on the brass plates above the bells. Finding the one he wanted, he pressed the button. A maid opened the door and let them in. She seemed frightened by Rosa's expression.

"Is the doctor in?" the professor asked the doctor's maid.

"I will see."

"Please ask him if he'll see me for a minute. I live in the building, two flights up."

"Sì, signore." She glanced again at Rosa, then went inside.

The Italian doctor came out, a short middle-aged man with a beard. The professor had once or twice passed him in the cortile of the apartment house. The doctor was buttoning his shirt cuff.

"I am sorry to trouble you, sir," said the professor. "This is my maid, who has been having some difficulty. She would like to determine whether she is pregnant. Can you assist her?"

The doctor looked at him, then at the maid, who had a hand-kerchief to her eyes.

"Let her come into my office."

"Thank you," said the professor. The doctor nodded.

The professor went up to his apartment. In a half hour the phone rang.

"Pronto."

It was the doctor. "She is not pregnant," he said. "She is frightened. She also has trouble with her liver."

"Can you be certain, doctor?"

"Yes."

"Thank you," said the professor. "If you write her a prescription, please have it charged to me, and also send me your bill."

"I will," said the doctor and hung up.

Rosa came into the apartment. "The doctor told you?" the professor said. "You aren't pregnant."

"It's the Virgin's blessing," said Rosa.

Speaking quietly, he then told her she would have to go. "I'm sorry, Rosa, but I simply cannot be constantly caught up in this sort of thing. It upsets me and I can't work."

She turned her head away.

The doorbell rang. It was Armando, a small thin man in a long gray overcoat. He was wearing a rakish black Borsalino and a slight mustache. He had dark, worried eyes. He tipped his hat to them.

Rosa told him she was leaving the apartment.

"Then let me help you get your things," Armando said. He followed her to the maid's room and they wrapped Rosa's things in newspaper.

When they came out of the room, Armando carrying a shopping bag, Rosa holding a shoe box wrapped in a newspaper, the professor handed Rosa the remainder of her month's wages.

"I'm sorry," he said, "but I have my wife and daughter to think of. They'll be here in a few days."

She answered nothing. Armando, smoking a cigarette butt, gently opened the door for her and they left together.

Later the professor inspected the maid's room and saw that Rosa had taken all her belongings but the shoes he had given her. When his wife arrived in the apartment, shortly before Thanksgiving, she gave the shoes to the portinaia, who wore them a week, then gave them to her daughter-in-law.

MARY McCARTHY

(1912–1989)

Mary McCarthy's literary range was impressive—short stories, essays, criticism, novels, and books on Italian society and art. Although best known for her novel The Group, *she also wrote about her Catholic childhood, Vietnam, Watergate, and, scathingly, about American intellectuals and academia. Her diverse work is unified by a "diamond-edged" satire and an autobiographical core. McCarthy once said, "What I really do is take real plums and put them in an imaginary cake."*

Italy appealed to McCarthy's wit, her sense of the ludicrous. McCarthy produced two volumes of non-fiction about Italy, The Stones of Florence *and* Venice Observed. *She combined first-hand observation of the cities with art criticism and social and political history. In* Venice Observed, *from which this selection is taken, she wrote, "Everything that happens in Venice has this inherent improbability, of which the gondola, floating, insubstantial, at once romantic and haunting, charming and absurd, is the symbol. 'Why don't they put outboard motors on them?' an American wondered."*

The Loot

from VENICE OBSERVED

The signore and the signora were separated for tax purposes, explained the real-estate agent. *"J'ai une bonne place pour vous,"* he had told me, a few days before, as he led me along a fondamenta, jingling a set of house keys. The apartment was very pretty: four large rooms overlooking the garden of a palazzo and furnished, for the most part, in a gay Venetian rococo, blue-and-white stripes, pink rosebuds, cabinets painted in the manner of Tiepolo, chairs with scallop-shell backs. But now I wanted to know precisely how many persons were going to occupy the apartment above, sharing a common entrance-hall and a bathtub with me—"only when you are out," the agent had hastily stipulated. "You do not have to worry; they do not take many baths." I had accepted this reassurance, joining rather thinly in his crackling laugh. The signora, he went on, would have her own washbowl and toilet and kitchenette in the quarters she was fixing for herself upstairs. She and her teen-age daughter and son would take most of their meals at the grandmother's. This son had not been specified in the original invoice; he had transpired as the deal progressed. And only the night before, I had been told by a Venetian acquaintance that there was a signore too and had him pointed out to me as he was leaving a restaurant—a dark, red-fleshed man with an oiled moustache. "You did not *say* there was a husband!" I now reproached the real-estate agent in his office, pushing the lease aside. "He will not be at home; you will not see him," the agent promised. For tax reasons, the signore had a separate domicile, over the Taverna La Fenice. "*Madame et vous,*" the agent applied his pet formula, like a soothing lotion, "*serez des bonnes amies.*" "I hope so," I retorted darkly. The speciality of this little man, I had discovered, seemed to be renting apartments that were already occupied. He had begun by trying to rent me his own apartment, with himself in it. "*Des bonnes amies,*" he now repeated, and I took out my fountain pen and signed.

Contrary to everyone's predictions, it has not worked out badly. The agent was right when he reiterated. "*C'est une bonne place pour vous, Madame.*" The signora is a tall ash-blonde stringbean of a woman, with a long droll, Modigliani face—a good-natured, feckless comedian, the "second" female part in a Goldoni play, who scolds and winks as she slaps about with her dustcloth, a cigarette hanging from one corner of her mouth. And it is true; I do not see the signore, though he sleeps here, I find, after all. Lying in their matrimonial bed—a vast Florentine gilt affair of the cinquecento with life-size Cupids, more like a barge than a bed—I hear his step on the stair, late at night, as he ascends with the signora after a supper at the Mamma's or at the Colomba restaurant. In the mornings, I sometimes hear his voice raised in anger, in a matrimonial dispute, or I catch a glimpse of a pair of pomaded moustaches disappearing out the door, followed by a flash of svelte polo-coat. But that is all he is to me: a stormy, uxorious voice, a whisk of moustache and coat-tails, a surreptitious step on the stair. Like Jove, he visits his premises by stealth, and I come to think of him as simply a male totem, a bull or a shower of coins. He is gone by eight in the morning. The signora says he is in the construction business and is putting up some houses near San Giobbe. They have come down in the world—like nearly everyone in Venice. I can see this from their wedding photograph, which hangs beside my bed. They are standing by the Grand Canal, with the Dogana and the Salute in the background; the signore, thinner and paler, with a mere sketch of his present moustache, wears a morning coat and striped trousers; the signora is in white satin, with veil and pearls and orange blossoms. The picture is over-exposed, which gives it a filmy sadness, fully justified by subsequent events. He was a *dottore delle Belle Arti,* the signora tells me, and he lists himself in the telephone book as "Professor Giuliano." For ten years, says the signora, they have not got along together. "*Ah, Elva, Elva!*" she commiserates with herself, yawning. "*Poverina.*"

The signora is a matter-of-fact person, shrewd, candid, and naive. With her long face, fair hair, and wide-set, almost Mongoloid, rolling blue-green eyes, she seems to me a true daughter of Venice, which in fact she is. The signore, whom I do not care for, I decide to classify as southern. Dottore delle Belle Arti or not, he is too coarse-grained and swart to be a real Venetian. It is only his marital situation ("separated for tax purposes") that seems to have been inspired by the playful genius loci. There is much wry humour in Venice and very little pretence. There is no syrup either, nothing cloying or gluey; the gondolier's taut, erect pose sets the pattern. Where Naples is operatic, Venice is chamber music or, if you wish, Mozartian opera—Leporello, Cherubino, Figaro, whose arias, indeed, were composed on the text of the Venetian librettist, Lorenzo da Ponte.

Like sailors and ship's captains, the Venetians are fond of pets. They prefer cats to dogs, which are impractical in a city which has so little open space; most of the dogs one sees being led about on leashes have a touristic air and in fact they usually belong to foreigners, English or American. The signora has a cat, I discover, from hearing it claw at my windows, trying to get in. Its persistence tells me that it must live here, though the signora does not at first confess this. It is another displaced person, like the signore, and has been put out to live on the roof-tiles during the period when the apartment is rented. *"Permesso,"* says the signora, bursting into my sitting-room one morning with a paper full of garbage. She opens the window and thrusts the paper out. The cat eats, ravenously. *"Poverino,"* she cries, making a sad noise, while she glances apologetically in my direction. I do not understand why, if she pities the cat, she does not take it upstairs to live in her quarters; she has a terrace there. Perhaps the signore has objected. But I am determined not to take it as *my* lodger. The apartment is crowded with fragile china objects, which the signore values extortionately, as I have already learned on offering to pay for one that my coatsleeve had brushed off the table. Moreover, I am afraid of the cat, which pounds on the windows in a clawed frenzy, knowing that it belongs here and that I do not. It has become a perfect tiger, thanks to its life on the tiles.

In the kitchen reside two other candidates for the SPCA, if there only were one in Venice: a pair of pet goldfish in a blue-and-white-china bowl. In the bottom of the bowl is a pile of five- and ten-lire pieces. That is all—no greenery, no algae, no scum. The water is clear and still. The fish are extremely pale, almost white, as though their colour had been bled from them, and very lethargic in their movements, not to say torpid. When I first looked at the apartment, I noted the fish and supposed they would go upstairs with the family. But when I moved in, they were still there in the kitchen, and the signora, drawing one of her most apologetic faces, as though she were about to ask me for a loan of one million lire, inquired whether they were in my way, whether I should mind if they stayed there. I did not mind, I said, but she must tell me what to feed them. Nothing, declared the signora, with a droll, sidelong look; she delights in mystifications. "*Non capisco,*" I had to admit. "*Niente, niente!*" airily repeated the signora. They did not have to be fed; that was the principle of this aquarium. The coins generated some sort of chemical in the water, and the fish lived on that; she had copied the idea from a fountain in Milan. I expressed doubt. Those poor blanched creatures were dying. Certainly not, scoffed the signora; she had had them nearly two years and they were in excellent health. As a proof of this, she plunged her long forefinger with its red-painted nail into the water and tickled one fish's tail; he feebly crept away from her touch. "*Ecco!*" she said, opening her pocketbook and tossing a fresh coin into the bowl. It was a bank too, she pointed out: if I needed change for my breakfast rolls, I had only to borrow from the fish. And there was nothing to clean; between the fish and the lire, the water stayed fresh. I nodded mutely, not being fluent enough in Italian to argue further.

Left to myself in the kitchen, I have tried feeding them bread crumbs. But they refuse this nourishment, rising languidly to inspect it and then turning their heads aside like peckish invalids; if they ingest a morsel, their flaccid jaws wanly seeking a purchase on it, they at once sink, inert, to the bottom, where they lie, spent, on their silvery bed of coins. Doubtless, they are accustomed to their diet, which keeps them in a state of bare animation, between life and death. The signora does not like it if she comes down and finds the water floury from the dissolving crumbs. I watch meekly while she dumps it out and pours in fresh water; the only excuse I can give for putting her to this trouble is that the fish look so very pale. "'*Pallidi*,' '*pallidi*,'" she scolds, between indignation and amusement. "*Non sono pallidi.*"

She laughs at the idea, which she finds typical of a foreigner, that a fish can turn white from hunger. And though she does not understand English or French, she knows very well that the fish are being criticized when she hears exclamations proceeding from the kitchen if I am entertaining friends. "'*Pallidi*,' '*smorti*'"—we are all the same, she jests. What can I do? I am too cowardly to put the poor creatures out of their misery, which a square meal of fish food would almost certainly bring about. I do not wish to incur the signora's wrath; in her brusque way, she has an affection for these fish that is based on their prodigious powers of survival. So I conclude that I had best leave them as they are and take them as an allegory on Venice, a society which lived in a bowl and drew its sustenance from the filth of lucre. Once flame-coloured, today it is a little pale and moribund, like the fish after two years of the signora's regimen.

Venice Preserved

from VENICE OBSERVED

No stones are so trite as those of Venice, that is, precisely, so well worn. It has been part museum, part amusement park, living off the entrance fees of tourists, ever since the early eighteenth century, when its former sources of revenue ran dry. The carnival that lasted half a year was not just a spontaneous expression of Venetian license; it was a calculated tourist attraction. Francesco Guardi's early "views" were the postcards of that period. In the Venetian preserve, a thick bitter-sweet marmalade, tourism itself became a spicy ingredient, suited to the foreign taste; legends of dead tourists now are boiled up daily by gondoliers and guides. Byron's desk, Gautier's palace, Ruskin's boarding house, the room where Browning died, Barbara Hutton's plate-glass window—these memorabilia replace the Bucintoro or Paolo Sarpi's statue as objects of interest. The Venetian crafts have become sideshows—glass-blowing, bead-stringing, lace-making; you watch the product made, like pink spun sugar at a circus, and bring a sample home, as a souvenir. Venetian manufactures today lay no claim to beauty or elegance, only to being "Venetian."

And there is no use pretending that the tourist Venice is not the real Venice, which is possible with other cities—Rome or Florence or Naples. The tourist Venice *is* Venice: the gondolas, the sunsets, the changing light, Florian's, Quadri's, Torcello, Harry's Bar, Murano, Burano, the pigeons, the glass beads, the vaporetto. Venice is a folding picture postcard of itself. And though it is true (as is sometimes said, sententiously) that nearly two hundred thousand people live their ordinary working lives in Venice, they too exist in it as tourists or guides. Nearly every Venetian is an art appreciator, a connoisseur of Venice, ready to talk of Tintoretto or to show you, at his own suggestion, the spiral staircase (said to challenge the void), to demonstrate the Venetian dialect or identify the sound of the Marangona, the bell of the Campanile, when it rings out at midnight.

A count shows the Tiepolo on the ceiling of his wife's bedroom; a dentist shows his sitting room, which was formerly a ridotto. Everything has been catalogued, with a pride that is more in the knowledge than in the thing itself. "A fake," genially says a gentleman, pointing to his Tintoretto. "Réjane's," says a house owner, pointing to the broken-down bed in the apartment she wants to let. The vanity of displaying knowledge can outweigh commercial motives or the vanity of ownership. "Eighteenth century?" you say hopefully to an antique dealer, as you look at a set of china. "No, nineteenth," he answers with firmness, losing the sale. In my apartment, I wish everything to be Venetian, but "No," says the landlady, as I ask about a cabinet: "Florentine." We stare at a big enthroned Madonna in the bedroom— very bad. She would like me to think it a Bellini and she measures the possibility against the art knowledge she estimates me to possess. "*School* of Giovanni Bellini," she announces, nonchalantly, extricating herself from the dilemma.

A Venetian nobleman has made a study of plants peculiar to Venice and shows slides on a projector. He has a library of thirty thousand volumes, mainly devoted to Venetian history. In the public libraries, in the wintertime the same set of loungers pores over Venetian archives or illustrated books on Venetian art; they move from the Correr library, when it closes, to the heatless Marciana, where they sit huddled in their overcoats, and finally to the Querini-Stampaglia, which stays open until late at night.

The Venetians catalogue everything, including themselves. "These grapes are brown," I complain to the young vegetable dealer in Santa Maria Formosa. "What is wrong with that? *I* am brown," he replies. "I am the housemaid of the painter Vedova," says a maid, answering the telephone. "I am a Jew," begins a cross-eyed stranger who is next in line in a bakeshop. "Would you care to see the synagogue?"

Almost any Venetian, even a child, will abandon whatever he is doing in order to show you something. They do not merely give directions; they lead, or in some cases follow, to make sure you are still on the right way. Their great fear is that you will miss an artistic or "typical" sight. A sacristan, who has already been tipped, will not let you leave until you have seen the last Palma Giovane. The "pope" of the Chiesa dei Greci calls up to his housekeeper to throw his black hat out the window and settles it firmly on his broad brow so that he can lead us personally to the Archaeological Museum in the Piazza San Marco; he is afraid that, if he does not see to it, we shall miss the Greek statuary there.

This is Venetian courtesy. Foreigners who have lived here a long time dismiss it with the observation: "They have nothing else to do." But idleness here is alert, on the *qui vive* for the opportunity of sightseeing; nothing delights a born Venetian so much as a free gondola ride. When the funeral gondola, a great black-and-gold ornate hearse, draws up beside a fondamenta, it is an occasion for esthetic pleasure. My neighborhood was especially favored in this way, because across the campo was the Old Men's Home. Everyone has noticed the Venetian taste in shop displays, which extends down to the poorest bargeman, who cuts his watermelons in half and shows them, pale pink, with green rims against the green side-canal, in which a pink palace with oleanders is reflected. *Che bello, che magnifico, che luce, che colore!*—they are all *professori delle Belle Arti*. And throughout the Veneto, in the old Venetian possessions, this internal tourism, this expertise, is rife. In Bassano, at the Civic Museum, I took the Mayor for the local art critic until he interrupted his discourse on the jewel tones ("like Murano glass") in the Bassani pastorals to look at his watch and cry out: "My citizens are calling me." Nearby, in a Palladian villa, a Venetian lady suspired, *"Ah, bellissima,"* on being shown a hearthstool in the shape of a life-size stuffed leather pig. Harry's Bar has a drink called a Tiziano, made of grapefruit juice and champagne and colored pink with grenadine or bitters. "You ought to have a Tintoretto," someone remonstrated, and the proprietor regretted that he had not yet invented that drink, but he had a Bellini and a Giorgione.

When the Venetians stroll out in the evening, they do not avoid the piazza San Marco, where the tourists are, as the Romans do with Doney's on the Via Veneto. The Venetians go to look at the tourists, and the tourists look back at them. It is all for the ear and eye, this city, but primarily for the eye. Built on water, it is an endless succession of reflections and echoes, a mirroring. Contrary to popular belief, there are no back canals where a tourist will not meet himself, with a camera, in the person of the other tourist crossing the little bridge. And no word can be spoken in this city that is not an echo of something said before. *"Mais c'est aussi cher que Paris!"* exclaims a Frenchman in a restaurant, unaware that he repeats Montaigne. The complaint against foreigners, voiced by a foreigner, chimes querulously through the ages, in unison with the medieval monk who found St. Mark's Square filled with "Turks, Libyans, Parthians, and other monsters of the sea." Today it is the Germans we complain of, and no doubt they complain of the Americans, in the same words.

Nothing can be said here (including this statement) *that has not been said before.* One often hears the Piazza described as an open-air drawing room; the observation goes back to Napoleon, who called it "the best drawing room in Europe." A friend likens the ornamental coping of St. Mark's to sea foam, but Ruskin thought of this first: ". . . at last, as if in ecstasy, the crests of the arches break into a marbly foam, and toss themselves far into the blue sky in flashes and wreaths of sculptured spray . . ." Another friend observes that the gondolas are like hearses; I was struck by the novelty of the fancy until I found it, two days later, in Shelley: "that funereal bark." Now I find it everywhere. A young man, boarding the vaporetto, sighs that "Venice is so urban," a remark which at least *sounds* original and doubtless did when Proust spoke of the "always urban impression" made by Venice in the midst of the sea. And the worst of it is that nearly all these clichés are true. It is true, for example, that St. Mark's at night looks like a painted stage flat; this is a fact which everybody notices and which everybody thinks he has discovered for himself. I blush to remember the sound of my own voice, clear in its own conceit, enunciating this proposition in the Piazza, nine years ago.

"I envy you, writing about Venice," says the newcomer. "I pity you," says the old hand. One thing is certain. Sophistication, that modern kind of sophistication that begs to differ, to be paradoxical, to invert, is not a possible attitude in Venice. In time, this becomes the beauty of the place. One gives up the struggle and submits to a classic experience. One accepts the fact that what one is about to feel or say has not only been said before by Goethe or Musset but is on the tip of the tongue of the tourist from Iowa who is alighting in the Piazzetta with his wife in her furpiece and jewelled pin.

HERMAN MELVILLE

(1819–1891)

In 1856, Herman Melville, plagued by depression, visited Italy to restore his health. His eighteen-month tour of Europe, including Italy and the Holy Land, was financed by his father-in-law—one of many attempts to shore up his son-in-law's precarious finances. Melville stopped in Naples, Rome, Venice, and Florence. Like many writers at the time, he hoped to spin his journey into a series of profitable magazine articles and lectures. He gathered material for a lecture series on "Statues in Rome" and wrote the poems "Venice," "In a Bye–Canal," called by R. W. B. Lewis a "powerful and twisting lyric," and "In a Church of Padua." Ultimately, Melville's trip did not alleviate his long-term mental and financial problems. For the last fifteen years of his life there were no printings of his books and he died without knowing that in the twentieth century he would be recognized as one of America's great authors.

Venice

With Pantheist energy of will
The little craftsman of the Coral Sea
Strenuous in the blue abyss,
Up-builds his marvellous gallery
    And long arcade,
Erections freaked with many a fringe
    Of marble garlandry,
Evincing what a worm can do.

Laborious in a shallower wave,
Advanced in kindred art,
A prouder agent proved Pan's might
When Venice rose in reefs of palaces.

In a Bye-Canal

A swoon of noon, a trance of tide,
The hushed siesta brooding wide
    Like calms far off Peru;
No floating wayfarer in sight,
Dumb noon, and haunted like the night
    When Jael the wiled one slew.

A languid impulse from the oar
Plied by my indolent gondolier
Tinkles against a palace hoar,
    And, hark, response I hear!
A lattice clicks; and, lo, I see,
Between the slats, mute summoning me,
What loveliest eyes of scintillation,
What basilisk glance of conjuration!

    Fronted I have, part taken the span
Of portents in nature and peril in man.
I have swum—I have been
'Twixt the whale's black flukes and the white shark's fin;
The enemy's desert have wandered in,
And there have turned, have turned and scanned,
Following me how noiselessly,
Envy and Slander, lepers hand in hand.
All this. But at the latticed eye—

"Hey! Gondolier, you sleep, my man;
Wake up!" And, shooting by, we ran;
The while I mused, This, surely, now,
Confutes the Naturalists, allow!
Sirens, true sirens verily be,
Sirens, waylayers in the sea.

Well, wooed by these same deadly misses,
    Is it shame to run?
No! flee them did divine Ulysses,
    Brave, wise, and Venus' son.

In a Church of Padua

In vaulted place where shadows flit,
An upright sombre box you see:
A door, but fast, and lattice none.
But punctured holes minutely small
In lateral silver panel square
Above a kneeling-board without,
Suggest an aim if not declare.

Who bendeth here the tremulous knee
No glimpse may get of him within,
And he immured may hardly see
The soul confessing there the sin;
Nor yields the low-sieved voice a tone
Whereby the murmurer may be known.

Dread diving-bell! In thee inurned
What hollows the priest must sound,
Descending into consciences
    Where more is hid than found.

MARY MORRIS

(1947–   )

Mary Morris is a self-described "wanderer of the planet." Most of the characters in her fiction are defined by a journey, although the trip may be emotional rather than actual. "As a writer my life has always been connected with journeys, I have been a kind of compulsive traveler since I can remember. My stories evolve out of those experiences," she said. Morris's first book, Vanishing Animals and Other Stories, *was published in 1979. Critics took note and labeled her a writer to watch. Four years later she published a novel,* Crossroads. *Morris returned to short fiction in her next book,* The Bus of Dreams and Other Stories— *tales pervaded by transience. Her next novel,* The Waiting Room, *a story of three generations of women, was published in 1989, and in 1993 she edited an anthology of writing by women travelers,* Maiden Voyages. *In fiction or non-fiction, Morris is never far from the central metaphor of travel. "For me writing is a kind of journey," she said, "whether it evolves from the world outside or the world within."*

Morris's essay "On Italian Time" first appeared in Travel and Leisure. *In it, her initial frustration with the Italian inattention to timetables, schedules, and regimen gives way to understanding.*

On Italian Time

Recently my family and I traveled by train from Zurich to Milan. Having just spent the night on a plane, we collapsed into the train compartment intending to sleep during the six-hour ride.

Shortly after we left Zurich a Swiss conductor told us the train separated at the border. We would have to move into one of the front cars, but the half-hour stop in Chiesa would give us ample time to make the shift.

Somewhere, as we dozed through Switzerland, our conductor left the train. Another one who was younger, Italian, and seemingly wiser, woke us, shouting that we'd be in Lugano in ten minutes. The train would separate there, but it was a short stop. "You'd better hurry."

At Lugano my husband and I dragged our luggage, sleeping daughter, and assorted paraphernalia onto the platform and dashed toward the front. As we approached another trainman I said to him in Italian, "Excuse us, sir, but which cars go to Italy?" He looked at me with slight disdain as he uttered in a resonant baritone, "Signora, tutto il treno va in Italia." He said it three times to make sure I understood. The whole train goes to Italy.

It was a difficult moment. We had given up our secluded little compartment for what looked like a long section of second-class smoking cars. Too tired to return, we climbed on. A high school soccer team was celebrating, but our daughter had fallen back asleep, and we didn't have the heart to move her again. In Chiesa, when I got off to change money, I watched the part of the train we had originally been sitting in divide off and head for Austria.

I am not a cynic and I love Italy. But I have discovered that time and space are relative notions there. I have followed signs to the Palazzo Grassi that led directly into a wall, and floated the wrong way down a one-way canal, the gondolier shouting all the way. I've read timetables that had no relation to actual departure times, and followed a sign to Verona that in fifteen minutes brought me back full circle to the place on Lake Garda where I had begun.

No one maliciously puts you on the wrong part of the train or sends you in the wrong direction. It's just that arrivals and departures matter much less than wines and sauces, the state of your frescoes, and lovemaking. Italy, like Mexico, is fundamentally a pagan land that has embraced Christianity out of necessity, guilt, and belief. Scratch the surface and you'll find heathens, and heathens don't really care what day it is, let alone what time. What matters is seeing, smelling, tasting. Who cares if you turn left, when right is just as beautiful and the wine is just as good.

In Verona we rented a small green Fiat from a disgruntled Eurocar representative named Gemania who had dyed red hair. When I stopped by to extend our rental, she asked for the contract. "I'm sorry," I said, "I can't seem to locate it."

"But you must find it," she insisted. "If you do not have the contract, we cannot give you the weekly rate." The message was clear: without the rental agreement we were essentially buying the car. That night my husband and I went through every bag and every shred of paper, but we found no contract. I decided to call Gemania. I would plead, bribe, do anything. But when I explained the situation she said, "Oh, don't worry. No problem. It's fine."

What had happened to Gemania since the previous day? Had she eaten a wonderful meal, had a troublesome tooth pulled, received a letter from a long-lost love? Sheer whimsy seems to be a national trait. Terra firma becomes quicksand. For some reason I find this charming.

Later, on the train to Venice, the conductor kindly suggested we would save time if we got off in Vicenza and waited for the direct train to Venice on Binario 3 (Track 3). He held up three fingers. "Numero tre," he said emphatically. We sat contentedly with our luggage at Binario 3, thinking how lucky we were to be the only people going to Venice that day. Look at the poor people stuffing themselves into that overcrowded train on Binario 2.

As we watched the train for Venice depart from Binario 2, I was left once again to ponder the Italian character. Our conductor could not have been more self-assured. After all, we are helpless tourists and he has this one job: to collect our money and tell us where to go. Perhaps we tourists are victims of intentional misinformation—a plot whose purpose is to drive us away.

However, the natives suffer similar fates. When we visited

Manuela, a friend who lives in Vicenza, she served us lunch on her patio. Afterward she came with us to spend an afternoon touring Vicenza. We returned to her house to find her sons and husband missing and messages on her answering machine from people concerned about her well-being.

It turned out that a local doctor, a family friend, had noticed that a woman with a name similar to Manuela's had been admitted to the hospital. She had been bitten by a tiger mosquito, an aggressive insect, and had swollen up like a balloon. Coincidentally, she resembled Manuela, if Manuela were blown up like a balloon.

The doctor phoned his wife who phoned her sister who phoned Manuela's sister who phoned the sons and so on. Several families rushed to the hospital to stand at the swollen woman's bedside, debating whether or not this was Manuela (who, at the time, was having gelato with us in the piazza).

Manuela insisted we drive with her to her friend Marina's house. That was where everyone had assembled to await word on whether the woman in the hospital was Manuela. The sun was setting as we arrived at a beautiful villa in the countryside surrounded by cypresses and Roman pines. There under the trees sat all the friends and family. "Manuela vive!" they cheered as Manuela got out of the car. Champagne corks popped and a celebration began.

I was thinking we should get going, but my husband was drinking wine from unmarked bottles that had been brought out of the cellar. I decided to stroll through the vineyards. When I returned, Marina had set a long table outside with a red-checked cloth. She had a salami; someone else had olives. Pepino, Marina's husband, went to pick tomatoes. One of Manuela's sons fetched some mozzarella from my car. Marina asked me to light the candles and I replied, in my best Italian, "Dov'è il semaforo?" Everyone laughed because I'd asked for the traffic lights.

The table was spread with cheese and tomatoes and Tuscan bread and salami. Though we had reservations elsewhere and other places to be, we all sat and drank wine under the stars until it was time for bed.

JOHN MORTIMER

(1923–   )

*British barrister, playwright, and novelist John Mortimer is best known
for his television series "Rumpole of the Bailey." His two professions,
writing and the law, are entwined in his fiction. Early in his career critics allied him with Britain's "Angry Young Men" of the 1950s. Mortimer said, "I was quite different from them because I wasn't a North
Country working class boy. . . . But I've become more of an 'Angry
Young Man' as I've grown older." Mortimer's greatest success came in the
late 1970s and 1980s with "Rumpole of the Bailey." He also adapted
Evelyn Waugh's "Brideshead Revisited" for television and published
his autobiography,* Clinging to the Wreckage: A Part of Life.

*Summer's Lease, from which this excerpt was taken, was published
in 1988 and also became a BBC television series. The novel's heroine,
Molly Pargeter, has leased a house, La Felicità, in Tuscany for her family. During their vacation the Pargeters become enmeshed in the bizarre
life of La Felicità's owner, S. Kettering.* Summer's Lease *combines mystery, comedy, and social commentary. Its title is from Shakespeare's Sonnet XVIII, "And summer's lease hath too short a date."*

from SUMMER'S LEASE

The woman walked round the corner of the house and saw a
snake consuming a large Tuscan toad.

The victim was motionless, looking about it only slightly
puzzled, blinking, whilst the snake attacked its leg. The toad had

the appearance of a fat businessman being done some sexual service by a hard-faced girl on the make and doing his best not to
notice. The snake, with its sleek, shiny head and curled body,
was long and smartly patterned in grey and black.

The woman, wishing to put an end to this outrage and feeling involved on the side of the toad, picked up a stick. But as she
straightened, armed, the nervous snake abandoned its prey and
slithered away into the shadows under a fig tree. There it was lost
among the wild flowers and in the spring grass. The toad sat on,
unafraid, bleeding slightly and blinking into the sun. The woman
dropped her stick and stood looking at it, bewildered.

"Mrs. Pargeter." A man came up behind her and she turned
towards him. He was dressed in a blue blazer and white trousers
as though for some pre-war cruise. The sunlight behind him
penetrated the thinness of his ginger hair and polished his scalp.
"Is there anything more I can show you?"

"No, thanks. Nothing more."

She looked back towards the fig tree and saw that the toad
had lumbered off into the tangled garden, perhaps to rejoin its
tormentor. "Do you honestly think," she asked, standing in front
of the stone walls and cool archways of the villa, "that it'll be
suitable?"

"Suitable for what?"

"For children, of course."

"My dear Mrs. Pargeter. You've read the advertisement?"

Read it? She had learnt it by heart. *Villa to let near small Tuscan town. Suit couple, early forties, with three children (females preferred). Recently installed swimming-pool may compensate for sometimes
impassable road. Owner suggests preliminary viewing to prevent disappointment or future misunderstandings.*

"Doesn't it say, *Suit couple . . . with three children?*"

"It says that." She had noticed it particularly.

"I should've thought that was pretty plain." The man smiled
as though that were quite enough on the subject of children.
"I'll be around in the summer to show you the ropes, depend
upon it. You'll want to know a source of Gordon's gin, angos-

tura bitters, streaky bacon. All life's little essentials. I can even find potted shrimps when the wind's in the right direction. The *Financial Times* may be a bit of a problem. Hard to come by in Mondano-in-Chianti. I happen to know of a supply in Siena but I'd rather you kept it dark. It's not the sort of knowledge one likes to have spread around."

"Don't bother." There was sunshine on her face, an unusual sensation in March, and she felt light-hearted now that the snake and its co-operative victim had withdrawn. "The *Financial Times* is probably the least of our worries." And then she added, as casually as possible, "Grey with sort of black markings. Would that be a grass snake?"

"I don't know. I've never seen one."

"No grass snakes around here at all?"

"No snakes of any kind," he said firmly. "Not as far as I'm concerned. And don't worry, Mrs. Pargeter. No scorpions getting into your slippers at night either. Seen all you want to see, have you?"

She looked for the last time. The doves gave up strutting and whitening the old Ping-Pong table and set off, flapping busily towards the purple hillside. However, their flight was soon aborted and they settled back on the table.

"Yes." She had seen all she wanted to see.

"Then perhaps you'll run me into Mondano?"

The seat in the rented Fiat was warm under her skirt. The man sat beside her and, after asking her permission, lit one of the thin Havana cigars he happened to know where to come by. His features were regular but he had a distinct cast in one eye, so that he couldn't stare straight at her without looking somewhere else. Apart from that he was rather a handsome man, she thought, if you happened to like that type of thing.

MOLLY PARGETER'S DRIVE down the long, rutted track across the hills to Mondano was part of a journey that had started in her childhood and only reached its present stage when, in the middle of a freezing London January, she read the advertisement in the *Daily Telegraph: Villa to let near small Tuscan town.* She had always had, as she would say with that breathless half of a nervous laugh with which she met anyone's emotions including her own, this sort of a "thing" about Italy. Her father had wanted her to turn out to be something exotic, an actress perhaps, or even, in the camera-obsessed sixties, a model, and he couldn't conceal his disappointment at the growth of a big-boned daughter who seemed without ambition. Her mother spent most of her afternoons resting and Molly's was a lonely childhood. She would kneel on the floor behind the sofa and pull out the tall books of art reproductions. Avoiding those which formed part of her father's collection of naked Indian or Japanese bodies locked together in unusually gymnastic postures, she had, throughout her childhood, stuck to the Italian schools of painting. So she gazed and her finger traced the outlines of nymphs—thinner, higher cheek-boned than she could ever hope to be, garlanded with flowers, stepping barefoot through the forest; and sometimes she saw an exhausted Venus, a hand below her belly, lying in a countryside where oxen were driven and ships set sail on uncharted seas. She had looked seriously at soft-eyed young men, pierced, as often as not, by arrows. At the chilly boarding-school to which her parents sent her in the mistaken belief that she would be less lonely among girls of her own age, the prizes for mathematics—a subject which she didn't particularly care for but which came easily to her—were framed reproductions of the works of Italian painters. Duccios and Signorellis and Martinis hung by her bedside at a time when other girls pinned up Elvis and Cliff or even Paul Anka. Such pictures she always found calming to her nerves and she had no need of the large net which was hung at the top of the staircase, to catch those distracted adolescents who attempted suicide in the converted country house where she received her education.

Villa to let near small Tuscan town Suit couple,
early forties with three children (females preferred).

WHEN she was sixteen, in the age of Gucci shoes and Lambrettas, and being taken by her father on birthday treats to his favourite trattoria in the King's Road (white lavatory tiles and low-slung lights, waiters singing "O Sole Mio" and her father embarrassingly ordering *"due cannelloni, per favore,* and *molto formaggio* for my daughter"), Molly was conscious of becoming attracted to men with a lot of black hair round the bracelets of their wrist-watches.

She went on a school trip to Tuscany and saw many of the pictures she had known for so long. At first they seemed brighter, smaller and cruder than she had been led to expect by the polite reproductions. Her friend, Rosie Fortinbras, always getting lost between the Pinacoteca and the Duomo in Siena, boasted of having kissed her way round all the waiters in the restaurant in the Piazza del Campo, saving for the last, like a favourite soft creamy centre, little Vittorio with the face of a page-boy in the corner of an Adoration of the Magi. "Kiss? You can call it kiss if you like. It's a quite different word in Italian." Rosie whispered *"scopare"* to her as they sat beside each other at a concert in a dark and chilly palace behind the square. "What's that mean?" "It means 'he ground himself into me,' as it says in the book I bought at the airport." Rosie's further explanation was lost in a burst of Vivaldi and Molly didn't believe her. All the same, the holiday had excited and disturbed her. She never forgot the sound of Italy, brutal as the sunshine on the hard pavements, and the nightly passage of crowds in the Piazza. Sharing a single ice-cream, she and Rosie watched an ever-circulating stage army of lovers arm in arm, young and old, walking very fast as though to give the illusion of purpose. Among them, young men with shining, pointed shoes astride snarling Vespas shouted, *"Ciao, bellissima,"* but usually to someone else. As the years passed, the sights and sounds became less alarming in her memory and she came to think of Italy as the place where she had been happy.

"Three children. Why *females preferred?* It sounds a bit fishy."
    "Perhaps they think girls do less damage."

"Damage?"

"To the furniture."

"I'm not sure I like the sound of it." Molly's husband frowned. He looked, as always at the prospect of a new departure, an undertaking likely to cost money, desperate for ways of escape. Although he had no dark hairs growing round his wristwatch, Hugh Pargeter had, in his youth, the regular features and slightly curled hair of young men who model knitting patterns. He had gone into his father's firm of solicitors where his looks endeared him to wives in divorce cases, although his extreme reluctance to take decisions prevented them obtaining the best results. As a rule he would wait for others—judges, opponents, even his wife—to decide matters of importance. If things turned out well he would quietly take the credit. If not, his brown eyes wore an expression as helpless and martyred as those of Saint Sebastian in the paintings Molly had always admired.

"What do we know of these people? We know nothing of them." As a lawyer, he had learnt that the safest course was inactivity; if you don't do things, you can't usually be blamed for them. Now he hoped he had found a fatal flaw in his wife's plans and they could, as usual, spend the summer holiday with his mother in Dorset.

"Nothing, until I write to the box number. Of course, I shall get full details."

Hugh sighed. Once she had written, another decision would have been taken, and he would tell them in the office that they were having a stab at Italy this year, he'd managed to track down a villa in Tuscany. So much of their lives, each of the three children, the house in Kensington Park Road and now, it seemed, their summer holiday, followed inexorably after Molly had made a decision.

It was not only the prospect of Tuscany that had captivated Molly, it was the strange provision about three children, females preferred. Her husband had found this fishy, and perhaps for that reason it filled her with intense curiosity. Her life had not been particularly adventurous and at school, where her friend Rosie

Fortinbras courted adventure, she had been regarded as a dull girl and a plodding worker. At night, however, or during the long school holidays, she read detective stories, earning the contempt of her father who told her that his answer to the question "Who dunnit?" was invariably "Who cares?" But, indulging a passion more secret than her love for Italian painting, Molly had early gone off with Holmes and Watson in a cab through the peasouper, or sat on the edge of her chair while Poirot summoned the guests to assemble in the library after tea. She read with great attention, few clues escaped her, and it was with a suppressed little scream of excitement and fear that this large, lonely girl would guess the murderer three or four chapters before the end. She disposed quickly of red herrings, usually sought out the least probable suspect and rarely failed.

So why should anyone advertise their house as being specially suitable for a couple in their *early forties, with three children (females preferred)*? The fact that she and Hugh happened to fit the bill seemed to give her every opportunity for finding out. Accumulating the evidence would be an occupation to keep her going whilst she organized her children's lives with Mrs. O'Keefe, who came in each day to look after them. Some of it arrived about two weeks after she had written to the box number, in the shape of three typewritten pages. There were also several coloured photographs of the villa "La Felicità"; all taken from a low angle, so that it seemed to tower against the sky; a place where the owners might appear on the battlements to a flourish of trumpets and a cry of heralds. The swimming-pool, also shot from ground-level, might have been a sizeable lake, only the distant, slightly blurred figure of a man betrayed the scale. There was a photograph of the bedroom in which the bed appeared gargantuan, with a great carved wooden headboard and foot, neatly made, although somebody's sunglasses had been left on the patchwork quilt. There was a picture of the terrace on which meals were taken "except during thunderstorms" and several of the garden, but none of the kitchen or of the children's accommodation. Each photograph had stamped upon the back the words PRIVATE PROPERTY.

She turned next to the typewritten pages. The work was divided into various sections, the first being headed *General remarks: The villa "La Felicità" can only be enjoyed by the observance of strict rules and a certain discipline. Most of these rules will be obvious. The wasteful use of the bathrooms, for instance, can turn a summer holiday into a time of intense anxiety and the purchase of water by the lorry load may strain the budget of even the best-heeled family. None of the following devices should, on any account, be switched on at the same time: the immersion heater in the master bathroom, the swimming-pool filter or the dishwashing machine. If a hair-drier is in use, it's generally wise to temporarily disconnect the refrigerator. More detailed instructions will be found taped on the walls over the appliances concerned. Above all, avoid flushing the lavatory next to the small sitting-room more than once in any given half hour or serious results may follow.*

Whose was this voice which Molly found to be both bossy and patronizing? She turned to the end of the document and saw a signature S. KETTERING over the address of the villa, LA FE-LICITÀ, MONDANO–IN–CHIANTI, SIENA, ITALY. Probably a Sam and not a Selina Kettering, she thought, and the signs of an absentee male landlord's domination became more pronounced in the final paragraph.

In conclusion, "La Felicità" has a certain atmosphere and is used to special treatment which we ask you to respect. The house is unaccustomed to the sound of transistor radios or record-players by the pool. There is adequate equipment to play music on the lowest shelf of the bookcase in the small sitting-room. We would also ask you to observe the tradition of dinner on the terrace taking place by candlelight. Those alarmed by insect life should consider holidaying in Skegness.

S. Kettering had gone too far. Why should the children be consumed by mosquitoes and confined to three or four scratched LPs? "Frank Sinatra Goes down Memory Lane" she imagined or "The Magic Flute of James Galway," tucked into their disintegrating sleeves on the bottom shelf. And then she read *The villa will appeal in particular to devotees of Italian painting. It makes a perfect centre for the study of the Sienese school. More importantly, perhaps, the work of Piero della Francesca can be followed from the frescos in Arezzo to the pregnant Madonna in the small chapel at*

Monterchi. Enthusiasts can take the trail to Sansepolcro and on, across the Mountains of the Moon, to see the sublime "Flagellation" in the Ducal Palace at Urbino, undoubtedly the greatest small picture in the world. Those making this journey should ensure that the stopcock is closed and all electrical appliances switched off before departure. The pleasures of art tend to be diminished by returning to a complete absence of hot bath water.

Now, in spite of the unsympathetic tone of his letter, S. Kettering had won her. Molly could put up with the mysterious fallibility of the electric devices; she would overcome her husband's reluctance at the prospect of any sort of adventure. She was going, at some time that summer, to follow the Piero della Francesca trail across the Mountains of the Moon to undoubtedly the world's greatest small picture. And if the shadowy Mr. Kettering's requirements had some secret explanation, as she suspected, she was going to find it out.

So she wrote to the box number and suggested a date for a preliminary viewing to avoid disappointment or misunderstandings. Everything was working out more easily than she could have hoped.

Leave the Florence–Siena raccordo and follow signs to Conterchi. In Conterchi take the concealed right-turning between the church and the supermercato, then left under the bridge, following signs to S. Pietro in Crespi. In S. Pietro, turn right by the fountain and immediately left, just past the posto di polizia. After two kilometres you will cross a bridge and see a large ilex tree on your right. You are best advised to turn left down the dirt road which provides a short cut (known only to the Kettering family) to Mondano-in-Chianti. In Mondano, turn left again by Signora Fantoni's alimentari (best mozzarella cheese in the district) and immediately double back to the right down a single-track road which will bring you out behind the Castello Crocetto (most reliable source of Chianti). From then on the unmade road (beware of pot-holes) will take you straight to "La Felicità."

Further orders, typed and duplicated, lay beside Molly on the empty passenger-seat. In front of her the motorway shimmered in the sun like the sands of a desert. She was in a mood of high

excitement, flicking on her indicator light and passing thundering lorries and bucketing Fiats, overloaded with Italian families,
with unexpected expertise. She was elated by a further message,
not typed this time, but written, apparently in haste, on paper
printed with the villa's address. *Will be at the house between two and
three on the afternoon of the 12th, getting things ready for the children's
holidays. Look forward to meeting you then.* The last document was
signed, as always S. KETTERING.

This almost welcoming message kept her going down the *raccordo* to Siena. After she'd turned off, she became tired and nervous. She drove slowly in Conterchi so as not to miss the turning
and Italians hooted at her or raised their fingers in gestures she
knew to be obscene. Once, knowing she couldn't be heard, she
shouted back and was conscious of looking like a pinkish, fair-
haired and flustered fish with its mouth moving silently behind
glass. Her hands sweated and soaked the steering-wheel. In San
Pietro she drove fast to avoid abuse, missed the road by the police station and had to do a U-turn to obey her directions. As
her anxiety grew the small towns and villages looked grey and
inhospitable. Steel shutters barricaded most of the shops and
those that were open displayed only a few boxes of tired vegetables and strings of plastic toys. In Mondano-in-Chianti three old
men, busily engaged in sitting on a wall beside the petrol pumps,
seemed to jeer at her and a child threw a small stone which rattled against her car bonnet.

She had doubts about the road but then found herself driving
along the grey fortress walls of what she hoped might be the
Castello Crocetto. At its gates a tall woman leading a Borzoi dog
viewed her passing with disdain. And then she dived and rattled
down the dirt-track which seemed to go on for ever across an
empty hillside. As the insects met a sticky death on her wind-
screen and brambles and gorse bushes clawed at the bright sides
of her hired Fiat, she wondered if she should have stayed at
home and if she would ever, in fact, see "La Felicità."

Suddenly she did. The track had climbed, twisted, rocked her
in its pot-holes and then swept down in a flurry of loose stones

and flying dust, to a house gradually lit, theatrically, as the sun returned from behind a stray afternoon cloud. Her first thought was that the photographs hadn't lied. The place looked fortified, not as a grim walled castle but impregnable all the same, with thick walls and, in the centre of the square, unornamented two-storey building, a stocky tower from which arrows or muskets might have been shot or red-hot ploughshares hurled down on invaders. The iron-studded door in the central archway looked impervious to battering-rams, but above it, behind a line of sim-ilar arches, was the big open terrace on which S. Kettering ex-pected the family to dine—an instruction, Molly thought, which it would be no particular hardship to follow. Three great stone pots contained geraniums which trailed down to the walls be-neath them, softening the stern appearance of the house.

In the centre of a pavement leading to the front door was a well head with an ornate ironwork structure over it. She had no idea of the age of "La Felicità" but such houses had stood on the white furrowed hillsides in the pictures she knew by heart. She felt then that S. Kettering's almost military orders were appro-priate and added to the feeling of security about the place.

She parked under a straw-covered shelter and got out slowly, still vibrating. The silence was underlined by the drumming of grasshoppers and she noticed that there was no other car which might have brought S. Kettering. The door she tried was un-yielding; the bell she pulled echoed inside some shuttered hall-way but nobody answered. Her confidence, which had returned on her first view of the house, once more ebbed. She wanted to pee and she walked round the house in search of a bush.

It was there that she saw the man lying on the plastic strips of an off-white metal reclining chair beside the pool, which was undoubtedly smaller than it had looked in the photograph. His straw hat was balanced on his forehead, his jacket lay folded on the concrete beside him, and she noticed that he wore balding suede shoes and some form of club or regimental tie.

"You've arrived." He opened one eye and said, "You must be a practical sort of person."

"The directions were brilliant, actually." She knew she

sounded effusive but she remembered the lordliness of S. Kettering's style and wished to propitiate him.

"Some people," he told her, "get horribly lost in Conterchi."

"Poor them!" She wanted to assure him that she wasn't that kind of idiot.

"So you drove here straight from Pisa?"

"Yes." All the bushes she could see were small and scrubby and she couldn't find an excuse to leave S. Kettering and double back to the front of the house.

"Then you'll want to use the facilities." He stood up smartly and she followed him with gratitude as he took from his pocket a large bunch of keys, from each of which dangled a carefully written label.

The chain requires one sharp downward pull. Don't be tentative or give repeated tugs which achieve nothing. So read the notice in the particular facility to which he led her. She pulled sharply and was rewarded. She rejoined the man, embarrassed by the sound of the cascade behind her.

"Managed it first go." He smiled at her. "Unusually masterful."

"This"—she held the fluttering pages of description in her hand—"must be the small sitting-room." The room was lit by a shaft of sunlight from the single open shutter. The furniture seemed large and dark, pieces designed for a grander room. "What's this used for?"

"For anything, I imagine, that you have a mind to. The big sitting-room's downstairs. Converted from the cowsheds. You could do anything in there. Get up a musical comedy."

"Is that what you do?"

"Good heavens, no." He looked at her as though it was she who had made the unusual suggestion. "That's not my style of thing at all."

"And the children's bedrooms?"

"Top floor, I should think. I haven't much personal experience. Not of where children sleep."

"I should like to see them, please."

"I suppose, if you're really keen on it."

"I've come all this way . . ." she smiled.

"And so you have. I'm here to help you. Absolutely all I can." He led her quickly up a staircase which began by being broad and stone and went on up to twist woodenly to the top of the tower. She followed the short-back-and-sides hair-cut of this curious S. Kettering, who, apparently, never said good-night to his children.

"How many have you got?" The rooms he opened for her had few signs of childish occupation. There were some rows of books, bright bed-covers and cushions, some reproductions such as she had once had of Italian paintings. There were no photographs, posters, record-players, piles of clothing from Ox-fam shops, drawings pinned to the wall—nothing much to indi-cate children at all.

"Myself, absolutely none," the man told her. "It's been the experience of my chums that offspring break up marriages. Mother gets wrapped up in the kids and the poor old husband gets left on his ownio."

"But you said you'd be here getting things ready for the chil-dren's holidays . . ."

"Checking up, yes. Seeing that nothing's drowned in the pool recently." The man looked at her with sudden amusement as a penny dropped. "You hadn't taken me for Kettering?" He laughed at her confusion. "I'm not Kettering, or anywhere near it. The name's Fosdyke. William Fosdyke. I'm cursed with living in Mondano all the year round, all through the rains of January and Feb. So I do things for chaps from the U.K. Keep an eye on their properties. And the like."

Of course, she told herself, she should have known at once that he wasn't Kettering. Kettering would have been a less ac-cessible and more commanding presence.

"No, I'm certainly not him," Fosdyke went on, garrulous af-ter her mistake had been discovered. "Wish I were sometimes. Lucky fellow, Kettering. He's got 'La Felicità,' of course. And his marriage; that's something I miss. Mrs. K. thinks the world of Kettering. One hundred per cent devotion. Kettering, not to put too fine a point on it, is the apple of her eye." They stood in the single child's bedroom and Molly joined in a short, silent tribute to the Kettering's marriage, whilst some large, blundering insect bumped against a window that had been long closed.

"I lost my wife," Fosdyke told her. "Many years ago."

"I'm sorry."

"Oh, that's all right. I mean literally lost her. We went shopping in Brighton. We arranged to meet at twelve-thirty under the clock. She never showed up. Missing, believed to have scarpered with the manager of Boots. Women are curious creatures. Nothing personal, Mrs. Pargeter."

She did her best to become businesslike. "I think this will do splendidly for our three." She crossed to the window and looked down to where the pool sparkled in the early sunshine.

"Got snaps of them, have you?" Mr. Fosdyke asked her.

"What?"

"I'll bet you carry snaps of your young. I know Mrs. Kettering does. I'd feel very privileged if you'd let me see them."

So she opened her handbag and produced for the man with the scarpered wife a selection, some faded a little and creased with age. Although mistrusting children, he showed an absorbed interest as he took the photographs and gazed at Henrietta (fourteen), Samantha (just ten) and the baby Jacqueline (now three and born after a long period during which Hugh had displayed a lack of interest in physical contact). As soon as Fosdyke had taken the pictures, she felt that she had shown him too much of her private life and put out her hand to receive them back.

"Fine little family," he said, releasing them. "They look as though they'd fit in jolly well at 'La Felicità.' "

"I think," Molly said firmly, "I'd like to have one more look round. By myself this time."

"Of course. Be my guest. Or rather"—he stood with one hand in his blazer pocket, squinting only a little—"the guest of Mr. Kettering."

When she looked round the house on her own, it seemed more impressive. The big downstairs room might have been a converted cowshed, but when she opened the tall shutters and the sunlight poured in, it looked more like a state apartment. At one end there was a platform with a piano on it, so Fosdyke might, for all she knew, have been right about the musical comedies. The kitchen was a huge stone cavern with an open fireplace, the size of a small room, beside which logs were piled so that she could see herself (but certainly not Hugh) barbecue-ing thick steaks on an iron grill, turning them over with tongs the size of a medieval weapon. In the bedroom cupboard, scented with lavender, a man's shirt and a woman's white skirt swung among the empty coathangers. None of the drawers was locked; all of them were empty. Looking around the bedroom, she saw that it was almost exactly as it had been in the photo-graph, although now there was a book open and face down-wards on the patchwork quilt. She wondered who had been reading so recently on the carefully made bed, or if this fat book, which she now saw to be a collection of Sherlock Holmes stories, were a relic of the past summer, and the maid, or whoever cleared the house, was devotedly keeping her em-ployer's place. She also left the book undisturbed but felt, as soon as she saw the title, a further fellow feeling with S. Kettering.

Her inspection of the bedroom finished, she walked down the staircase into the coolness of the stone-flagged hallway. A large collection of sun-hats hung on pegs in the entrance hall, bowls were filled with dried lavender and a huge pottery jar was crammed with walking-sticks, some of which had ornate silver handles. By the time she reached the front door the house, she knew, had to be hers for the summer. If it had a secret she would do her best to discover it and she was not going to miss the trail across the Mountains of the Moon to what was undoubtedly the greatest small picture in the world.

Molly Pargeter, a woman of forty, whose hair was kept in place with difficulty, might have looked like one of the larger Graces in the paintings she admired had not her size caused her such embarrassment that she lowered her head and stooped a lit-tle as she walked. She was a woman of mixed awkwardness and determination. Now dressed in striped cotton with sensible shoes and a cardigan, she stepped into the sunshine and walked round the corner of the house. And there she caught a snake consuming a large Tuscan toad.

As she drove William Fosdyke back to Mondano he assured her that he would be always at her disposal and could guarantee to make her family holiday a success. "You know what the Brits in this part of Tuscany call me?" he asked her. "Signor Fixit. They know they can rely on me, you see. And I must say that gives me a great pleasure."

She left him in front of a café and as she drove away to follow the complex instructions back to the *raccordo* she saw him in her mirror, standing with his hand still raised in the sort of military salute with which he'd taken his leave of her.

WILLIAM MURRAY

(1926–   )

Born in New York City, William Murray spent his early years in Europe with his Roman mother and did not return to the United States until the mid-1930s. At that time he was eight years old and spoke only Italian and French: "I was a little European boy who just happened to have an American father. And although I quickly became, like many immigrant children, more American than my schoolmates who had grown up here, I never entirely lost touch with my earliest background." After World War II Murray returned to Italy as a music student and felt as if he were "coming home." He has shuttled between countries ever since.

Murray joined The New Yorker *as a fiction editor in 1956 and wrote his first "Letter from Rome" in 1962. For more than thirty years he has been writing about Italy in books and magazines, including a book of observations,* Italy: The Fatal Gift. The Last Italian *is a compilation of Murray's writing from* The New Yorker, The Traveler, *and other magazines. Murray acknowledges that his "beat" is a writer's fantasy. "I can't imagine a more satisfying way for a writer to live, especially because Italy has proven to be a cornucopia providing endless nourishment for the soul and mind."*

The Queen of the Bogs

from THE LAST ITALIAN

"Welcome to the Great Gray Queen of the Bogs!" began the note I found in my message box from a friend of mine, when I checked into my hotel in Milan during a recent visit. It seemed an appropriate greeting, as I had arrived in the city late at night by train to find it, as is often the case, shrouded in fog and bone-chillingly damp. Early the next morning I woke up to rain beating against my window shutters, while outside the narrow streets in the older part of town where I was staying were crowded with figures hunched under umbrellas, threading their way through parked cars on their way to work.

This sight, as well as my friend's salutation, cheered me up. I had not spent much time in Milan since the early 1970s and my first impression was that nothing had changed. I once lived here off and on for over a year and I can't remember ever having seen the sun from November to April, while the strongest memory I've retained from that period is of a constant, hurried coming and going by people impervious to climate and fiercely intent on the day's affairs. Milan is the industrial and commercial capital of the nation, "the most citylike city in Italy," according to the noted Sicilian author Giovanni Verga, who made that observation nearly a century ago. Its inhabitants pride themselves on their energy and business acumen, on their ability to "get things done" while making money, and most of the country's great industrial empires were created here. A typical Milanese tale is always one in which the protagonist rises to the top through imagination, determination, and sheer hard work. "The average Milanese businessman performs labors that would have daunted Sisyphus," Indro Montanelli, the editor of *Il Giornale,* once said. "And because he is a prodigious toiler, he always achieves the summit of whatever he sets out to do. Elsewhere in Italy this is considered luck." Lee Iacocca's autobiography was a clamorous bestseller here, just the kind of self-congratulatory managerial success story the Milanese can identify with.

During most of the seventies, while the country suffered through a prolonged recession, with high inflation, unemployment, and frequent strikes, as well as the terrorist "years of lead," Milan survived better than most other Italian cities. It remained, in Montanelli's words, "a happy island" in a sea of corruption, violence, and misery, where people continued despite everything to work hard and the city government, headed by its popular Socialist mayor, Carlo Tognoli, provided, beginning in 1975, a decade of stability and incorruptible efficiency. "There was once a Milan," a recent story in the weekly *Panorama* observed, with a beloved mayor, efficient public services, and "an enviable autonomy" from the political intrigues being played out in the corridors of Rome's ministerial palazzi. In Milan, Rome, the nation's capital, with its Byzantine bureaucracy and squabbling political factions, has always been considered the quintessential example of everything wrong with the society. The feeling here has always been that only Milan, with its energy and entrepreneurial spirit, could triumph over the inertia to the south and continue to keep Italy, at least the northern half of the peninsula, in the vanguard of the world's industrialized economies. "South of Rome is Africa," is the way I once heard it put, a definition most of my Milanese acquaintances would heartily endorse.

The spirit still dominates Milan and, after only a few hours spent here, it can become contagious; visitors quickly adopt a brisk Milanese pace. One soon discovers, too, that the Milanese are even prouder of their more recent achievements than their earlier ones. The central city bristles with modern skyscrapers, some of them stunningly beautiful. The Milanese design the best modern furniture, and the local fashion industry ranks with Paris as a trendsetter. Ask any Milanese what he likes best about his hometown and he is likely to mention one or all of the above, as well as point out other contemporary features—the many thousands of businesses, large and small; the hundreds of banks and hotels; the best public transportation system in Italy.

No dynamic American executive could fail to appreciate this place. Milan's stock exchange, which now handles about 90 percent of the nation's securities transactions, has recently been modernized. (While the work was under way, a temporary annex was built next door, swallowing up the entire piazza facing the exchange, thus depriving the citizens of badly needed open space. It is typical of Milan that almost no one protested—something that could not happen in Rome or Florence.) The shops seem to be always crowded, the hotels and restaurants full, the economic and scientific sections of the newspapers teeming with news of conventions, trade fairs, technological breakthroughs, international business developments, and announcements of endless opportunities for investment in all sorts of enterprises. Most significant, the want ads indicate a voracious demand for skilled personnel at every level, and there is far less visible misery in Milan than in most American cities. "We have our poor, of course," a friend of mine admitted at lunch one day. "But we take care of them. This is not Naples or New York."

Milan is not merely a commercial center, but, like every other Italian city, has its share of great sights. The Milanese spend a lot of time in and around them. They have a rooted idea that somehow the day has been mismanaged that hasn't put them within walking distance of the historic center, with its great Gothic cathedral, the Galleria and its sidewalk cafés, La Scala, the opera capital of the world, and the majestic Castello Sforzesco, the seat of ducal power in the late Middle Ages. Milan is built like a giant spiderweb with this heart at its center and the Milanese feel irresistibly drawn to it.

The Duomo itself is a fantastic sight. It looks like an enormous white wedding cake, all spires, curlicues, leering gargoyles, and saintly figures. Citizens used to picnic on its rooftop and they still take shelter inside, sitting and gossiping in the pews during the hot, humid summer months. They flock to La Scala during the opera season and are the toughest, most demanding audience in the world. At the cafés under the soaring glass arches of the nearby Galleria, the local buffs will spend hours debating the merits of various singers.

Traditionally, this city has always been receptive to art and kind to artists. In addition to such great public museums as the Brera and the Poldi-Pezzoli, with their dozens of Mantegnas and Bellinis and Tiepolos, Milan has the finest private galleries in Italy, where most of the country's modern art is sold. The town is full of painters and sculptors who feel supported and comfortable here. The tradition is an old one. Henri Beyle, the Frenchman who wrote under the name of Stendhal and haunted La Scala, wanted to be buried here, his tomb to bear the simple epitaph, *"Henri Beyle, Milanese."* And when Giuseppe Verdi lay dying in his hotel room on the Via Manzoni, the citizens laid straw over the cobblestones outside his windows so the maestro would not be disturbed by the rumble of carriage wheels.

And the Milanese also like to celebrate. Milan has by far the most active nightlife in Italy, with elegant late-night spots full of pretty people having a good time. Periodically, this nightlife has come under fire, with revelations that the Mafia owns some of the clubs and that drugs are readily available. "When will Milan decide to open its eyes?" the columnist Giorgio Bocca recently asked in the weekly *L'Espresso*. "When it's like Chicago in the thirties?"

Like every other industrial metropolis, Milan has always had a high crime rate, but in recent years there have been some huge scandals, mostly involving real-estate speculation and drugs. "A distracted, understanding city, Milan," Bocca observed. "Here there are people who buy everything at above-market prices, who keep huge fortunes immobilized in houses, lands, warehouses, but never anyone who asks where this sea of money comes from." He suggested that Milan's coat of arms ought to be redesigned to portray two hands separated by a check, with the left hand obviously ignorant of what the right hand was do-ing. As for what another commentator has called the "river of heroin" flowing undisturbed past the seemingly indifferent gaze of the police, the traffic has served to shed a disquieting light on an underground society of drug dealers, playboys, girls on the loose, and con men. "Milan is the capital of the fast-buck artist," an American businessman told me, "Everything is for sale here."

IN ITS headlong rush to prosperity, Milan has paid little atten-tion to ecological or environmental considerations. The city's traditional colors are various shades of brown, gray, and burnt orange, but some buildings, including many of the elegant eigh-teenth- and nineteenth-century palazzi that line the avenues in the heart of the historic center, are beginning to turn black in the polluted air and some seem to be visibly crumbling before one's eyes. Only recently have the citizens begun to organize in defense of their patrimony. One of the oddest sights I came across was the Columns of San Lorenzo, a grouping of sixteen ancient Roman pillars originally brought here to form a majes-tic portico for the adjacent Church of San Lorenzo, which can trace its own origins back to 350 A.D. The marble shafts had been tightly wrapped in canvas and plastic to protect them from further erosion until they could be restored and the whole mon-ument, one of Milan's most famous sights, resembled a huge package abandoned in the middle of the Corso di Porta Tici-nese, one of the main avenues leading south, as if dropped there by a careless shopper. "We're going to ship them to you in America," I was told facetiously by a young Milanese ecologist, when I inquired about the monument's future. "You can set them up in Arizona, next to the London Bridge."

Sarcasm, irony, and a sort of doomsday wit are the shields be-hind which the people who care most about this city operate. "We are few but nice," I was informed by Luisa Toeschi, a journalist who devotes much of her spare time to working for the local chapter of Italia Nostra, the country's leading ecological organization. She and a colleague named Alberto Ferruzzi, an architect, told me that they keep running into the same people over and over at every meeting and conference having to do with cultural matters or the environment. Italia Nostra was founded in 1958 "to preserve and conserve the historical, artistic and natural patrimony of the nation without hope of gain," as one of the organization's recent bulletins put it. It has sixteen thousand members nationwide, two thousand of them in Milan. "Always the same faces, the same speeches," Signor Ferruzzi said. "It is like talking to oneself."

Nevertheless, over the years, Italia Nostra, aided by a handful of smaller but equally vocal environmental groups that have sprung up during the past decade, has managed to achieve some local victories, mainly by helping to create pedestrian islands inside the *centro storico* and over seventy small parks and gardens within the metropolitan area. WHY DOES MILAN HAVE TO BE UGLY? was the headline over an article published in a newsletter. The piece pointed out that people returning from summer vacations were invariably struck by their hometown's squalor and that there was no reason for such pervasive ugliness.

The traditional answer here to such arguments is that Milan has never been considered a beautiful city, even during its heyday, when it was traversed by its famous *navigli,* or canals, and it can't really compete as a tourist attraction with the rest of Italy, despite its famous sights, elegant palazzi, and splendid private gardens. "You don't go to Milan for beauty," a Roman relative of mine once observed. "You go there to work and that's all."

As the people at Italia Nostra never tire of explaining, however, the quality of life in Milan is no longer merely an aesthetic question but one of survival. There are few controls over the industrial emissions spewing daily from the city's thousands of factories and nearly a million automobiles, nor is there any emergency system in place to warn people of dangerously high pollution levels in the air or to compel factories to shut down and drivers to park their cars. Milan sits in the heart of the Po Valley, Italy's breadbasket, tucked up under the protective rim of the Swiss Alps. It does not benefit from the onshore breezes that protect Naples and Rome or the winds that periodically blow off the peninsula's central mountain ranges. The atmospheric inversion layers that cause the most rapid build-ups of pollutants often last ten days or more here and the area is also subject to thick ground fogs that trap harmful chemicals and prevent them from being dispersed. Almost every day the local newspapers report on the poor quality of the air and often issue warnings of potential disaster, but the authorities seem not to be listening. "It will take a major calamity, with people dropping in the streets, to get our politicians to do anything," a reporter on the daily *Il Giorno* said to me "And it will happen." . . .

Despite its ecological problems, most of which are common to every large industrialized city, Milan seems likely to remain what some local wag once called it, "an international capital in search of a country." It is less than two hours from Paris and London by air, three hours by train from Venice, and less than half an hour by car from the romantic lake country Italy shares with Switzerland. And the city's ferocious concentration on materialism also has its compensations. The Milanese, only about 1.5 million strong, account for less than 7 percent of Italy's population, but 28 percent of the country's national income. With one of the highest per capita earnings in Italy, they own more telephones, computers, household appliances, video games, and cars than other Italians. They drink in the country's best bars and eat in its finest restaurants. They publish most of Italy's books and magazines, put on the biggest trade fairs, sell the most art, and set the fashions for the rest of the nation. If that means the quality of life must suffer a little, many Milanese seem quite ready to pay the price. "In Milan these days everyone's interested only in success and material well-being," the manager of my hotel informed me over a glass of wine one afternoon. "Who cares how you got it or what you did before? The important thing is to have it."

That point of view is also reflected in the activities of the young, few of whom belong to social or political movements and take no interest in politics in general. They are much more likely to join gangs, and all over town there are sizeable contingents of skinheads, punks, "rockabillies," and other groups identifying themselves mainly with pop-music trends. By far the largest and hottest new wave, however, consists of the *paninari,* a term that can only be roughly translated as "sandwichers." They are mainly teenagers, but the fad has now begun to include children of elementary school age and has become an authentic rage.

The movement, if it can be called one, was born sometime in the early eighties at the Panino, a sandwich bar in Piazza Liberty, a small square just off the Corso Vittorio Emanuele, in the heart of the *centro.* Milan, in addition to having some of the best restaurants in the world, has also become the fast-food capital of Italy, with many more Wendys, Burghys, and other junk-food emporiums than any other city. These places are heavily patronized by teenagers, and during the past few years have quite naturally become meeting places and unofficial private hangouts for gangs of kids following a trend or bound together by their own way of looking at the world.

Unlike any other teenage group, the *paninari* are united exclusively by the clothes they wear. Their wardrobes must consist entirely of jackets, shirts, pants, socks, and shoes that not only look American but have been made by one of perhaps a dozen approved designers and companies. They are expensive, with shirts and sweaters priced from a hundred dollars up and shoes as high as two hundred dollars. Each complete outfit costs a minimum of about eight hundred dollars and money-saving imitations of the genuine article will not pass; immediate ostracism is the fate of any would-be *paninaro* who tries to sneak a counterfeit article past the watchful eyes of his contemporaries. "To dress well means to dress with things that cost," a sixteen-year-old named Maurizio Gelati recently told a reporter. When asked if wealth was so important to him, the boy answered, "It's almost everything."

Appearance, however, is more important than reality. The offspring of an unemployed laborer will be accepted into any contingent of *paninari,* provided that he has been able somehow to put together an authentic ensemble that will enable him to blend indistinguishably into the group. Stories in the media of escapades and excesses committed by and for the *paninari* frequently feature episodes in which families of modest means practically bankrupt themselves to keep their children attired in the latest "in" fashion. Few Milanese parents see anything amiss in this attitude. "Let's tell the truth, we adults buy ourselves a Rolex, sports cars, designer clothes," one of them told an interviewer. "Why shouldn't they also have the desire to own the best?"

From Milan the *paninaro* craze has spread to most other major Italian cities, and there are now several magazines and comic books catering to them in which the characters express themselves in a jargon as distinctive, mysterious, and almost untranslatable as the "Valley talk" of Southern California. The phenomenon has alarmed a number of social commentators, who have accused the movement of being right-wing, if not Fascistic. They have pointed out that the *paninari* often greet each other with the Roman salute and that Benito Mussolini is a romantic figure to some of them. The kids themselves deny the political implications. "I have no political ideas," young Gelati declared. "And even my friends who say they are right-wing understand nothing of politics." Another *paninaro* explained that having a photograph of Mussolini in one's room probably meant only that the owner had failed to find a poster of Rambo.

Nevertheless, there is a growing dismay, especially among the young adults who lived through the difficult years between 1968 and 1980, concerning the *paninaro* phenomenon and what they perceive to be the attitude of the young in general. "To think that we educated our children to refute consumerism," one of them observed not long ago. "What surprises us most of all about their gangs, their groups, is the absolute absence of any kind of subversive, contesting messages. All that counts for them is riches, success, power." When I quoted this observation to a Milanese friend of mine, he said, "These kids are not setting any standards; they are merely reflecting the society they live in."

MICHAEL ONDAATJE

(1943–   )

Novelist, film director, and poet, Michael Ondaatje blurs the line between poetry and prose. Born in Colombo, Sri Lanka, and now a resident of Canada, his poetry often has a strong narrative line while his fiction and nonfiction have poetic elements. His best-known book of poetry, The Collected Works of Billy the Kid, *comes close to prose in retelling the American myth. Ondaatje's memoir,* Running in the Family, *poetically recalls his childhood in old Ceylon. One critic wrote, "Moving in and out of imagined landscape, portrait and documentary, anecdote or legend, Ondaatje writes for the eye and the ear simultaneously."*

The author of many books of poetry, literary criticism, and five novels, Ondaatje reached his widest audience with The English Patient, *winner of England's Booker Prize in 1992. Set in the last days of World War II in a bombed villa in northern Italy, the novel is the story of four casualties of the fighting—an emotionally damaged Canadian nurse; her patient, a mysterious victim of severe burns; a thief who is one of the war's heroes and victims; and an Indian "sapper," an expert in bomb disposal. In* The Spectator, *critic Cressida Connolly wrote of* The English Patient, *"The writing is so heady that you have to keep putting the book down between passages so as not to reel from the sheer force and beauty of it. . . . When I finished the book I felt as dazed as if I'd just awoken from a powerful dream."*

from THE ENGLISH PATIENT

Between the kitchen and the destroyed chapel a door led into an oval-shaped library. The space inside seemed safe except for a large hole at portrait level in the far wall, caused by mortar-shell attack on the villa two months earlier. The rest of the room had adapted itself to this wound, accepting the habits of weather, evening stars, the sound of birds. There was a sofa, a piano covered in a grey sheet, the head of a stuffed bear and high walls of books. The shelves nearest the torn wall bowed with the rain, which had doubled the weight of the books. Lightning came into the room too, again and again, falling across the covered piano and carpet.

At the far end were French doors that were boarded up. If they had been open she could have walked from the library to the loggia, then down thirty-six penitent steps past the chapel towards what had been an ancient meadow, scarred now by phosphorus bombs and explosions. The German army had mined many of the houses they retreated from, so most rooms not needed, like this one, had been sealed for safety, the doors hammered into their frames.

She knew these dangers when she slid into the room, walking into its afternoon darkness. She stood conscious suddenly of her weight on the wooden floor, thinking it was probably enough to trigger whatever mechanism was there. Her feet in dust. The only light poured through the jagged mortar circle that looked onto the sky.

With a crack of separation, as if it were being dismantled

from one single unit, she pulled out *The Last of the Mohicans* and even in this half-light was cheered by the aquamarine sky and lake on the cover illustration, the Indian in the foreground. And then, as if there were someone in the room who was not to be disturbed, she walked backwards, stepping on her own footprints, for safety, but also as part of a private game, so it would seem from the steps that she had entered the room and then the corporeal body had disappeared. She closed the door and replaced the seal of warning.

She sat in the window alcove in the English patient's room, the painted walls on one side of her, the valley on the other. She opened the book. The pages were joined together in a stiff wave. She felt like Crusoe finding a drowned book that had washed up and dried itself on the shore. *A Narrative of 1757.* Illustrated by N. C. Wyeth. As in all of the best books, there was the important page with the list of illustrations, a line of text for each of them.

She entered the story knowing she would emerge from it feeling she had been immersed in the lives of others, in plots that stretched back twenty years, her body full of sentences and moments, as if awaking from sleep with a heaviness caused by unremembered dreams.

THEIR ITALIAN hill town, sentinel to the northwest route, had been besieged for more than a month, the barrage focusing upon the two villas and the monastery surrounded by apple and plum orchards. There was the Villa Medici, where the generals lived. Just above it the Villa San Girolamo, previously a nunnery, whose castlelike battlements had made it the last stronghold of the German army. It had housed a hundred troops. As the hill town began to be torn apart like a battleship at sea, by fire shells, the troops moved from the barrack tents in the orchard into the now crowded bedrooms of the old nunnery. Sections of the chapel were blown up. Parts of the top storey of the villa crumbled under explosions. When the Allies finally took over the building and made it a hospital, the steps leading to the third level were sealed off, though a section of chimney and roof survived.

She and the Englishman had insisted on remaining behind when the other nurses and patients moved to a safer location in the south. During this time they were very cold, without electricity. Some rooms faced onto the valley with no walls at all. She would open a door and see just a sodden bed huddled against a corner, covered with leaves. Doors opened into landscape. Some rooms had become an open aviary.

The staircase had lost its lower steps during the fire that was set before the soldiers left. She had gone into the library, removed twenty books and nailed them to the floor and then onto each other, in this way rebuilding the two lowest steps. Most of the chairs had been used for fires. The armchair in the library was left there because it was always wet, drenched by evening storms that came in through the mortar hole. Whatever was wet escaped burning during that April of 1945.

There were few beds left. She herself preferred to be nomadic in the house with her pallet or hammock, sleeping sometimes in the English patient's room, sometimes in the hall, depending on temperature or wind or light. In the morning she rolled up her mattress and tied it into a wheel with string. Now it was warmer and she was opening more rooms, airing the dark reaches, letting sunlight dry all the dampness. Some nights she opened doors and slept in rooms that had walls missing. She lay on the pallet on the very edge of the room, facing the drifting landscape of stars, moving clouds, wakened by the growl of thunder and lightning. She was twenty years old and mad and unconcerned with safety during this time, having no qualms about the dangers of the possibly mined library or the thunder that startled her in the night. She was restless after the cold months, when she had been limited to dark, protected spaces. She entered rooms that had been soiled by soldiers, rooms whose furniture had been burned within them. She cleared out leaves and shit and urine and charred tables. She was living like a vagrant, while elsewhere the English patient reposed in his bed like a king.

From outside, the place seemed devastated. An outdoor staircase disappeared in midair, its railing hanging off. Their life was foraging and tentative safety. They used only essential candle-light at night because of the brigands who annihilated every-thing they came across. They were protected by the simple fact that the villa seemed a ruin. But she felt safe here, half adult and half child. Coming out of what had happened to her during the war, she drew her own few rules to herself. She would not be ordered again or carry out duties for the greater good. She would care only for the burned patient. She would read to him and bathe him and give him his doses of morphine—her only communication was with him.

She worked in the garden and orchard. She carried the six-foot crucifix from the bombed chapel and used it to build a scarecrow above her seedbed, hanging empty sardine cans from it which clattered and clanked whenever the wind lifted. Within the villa she would step from rubble to a candlelit alcove where there was her neatly packed suitcase, which held little besides some letters, a few rolled-up clothes, a metal box of medical supplies. She had cleared just small sections of the villa, and all this she could burn down if she wished.

SHE LIGHTS a match in the dark hall and moves it onto the wick of the candle. Light lifts itself onto her shoulders. She is on her knees. She puts her hands on her thighs and breathes in the smell of the sulphur. She imagines she also breathes in light.

She moves backwards a few feet and with a piece of white chalk draws a rectangle onto the wood floor. Then continues backwards, drawing more rectangles, so there is a pyramid of them, single then double then single, her left hand braced flat on the floor, her head down, serious. She moves farther and farther away from the light. Till she leans back onto her heels and sits crouching.

She drops the chalk into the pocket of her dress. She stands and pulls up the looseness of her skirt and ties it around her waist. She pulls from another pocket a piece of metal and flings it out in front of her so it falls just beyond the farthest square.

She leaps forward, her legs smashing down, her shadow behind her curling into the depth of the hall. She is very quick, her tennis shoes skidding on the numbers she has drawn into each rectangle, one foot landing, then two feet, then one again, until she reaches the last square.

She bends down and picks up the piece of metal, pauses in that position, motionless, her skirt still tucked up above her thighs, hands hanging down loose, breathing hard. She takes a gulp of air and blows out the candle.

Now she is in darkness. Just a smell of smoke.

She leaps up and in midair turns so she lands facing the other way, then skips forward even wilder now down the black hall, still landing on squares she knows are there, her tennis shoes banging and slamming onto the dark floor—so the sound echoes out into the far reaches of the deserted Italian villa, out towards the moon and the scar of a ravine that half circles the building.

TIM PARKS

(1954–   )

British author Tim Parks calls his book Italian Neighbors *an "arrival diary" rather than a travel book, as it chronicles his first year in Italy. Of his adopted home he writes, "I love it . . . but like anyplace that's become home, I hate it too. And, of course, you can't separate the things you love and hate." His transplantation in Italian soil has been fertile for Parks. He is the author of six novels, including the recent thriller* Juggling the Stars, *set in northern Italy.*

In the early 1980s Parks moved to the village of Montecchio outside of Verona with his Italian-born wife, Rita. They rented a condominium on Montecchio's main (and only) street, Via Colombare. The apartment had been owned by the late Umberto Patuzzi and his senile wife, Maria Rosa, and was administered by Patuzzi's niece, Signora Marta, a woman dedicated to circumventing Italy's complicated residency laws. Working against Signora Marta was the local "vigile," who was determined to document Parks's existence. One of Parks's first encounters with Italian bureaucracy was his attempt to change the apartment's phone number from that of the deceased Umberto Patuzzi. His efforts were thwarted by both his landlady and SIP, the Italian telephone company.

Residenza

It would have been some weeks later we tried to change that entry in the phone book. We phoned SIP, the telephone company, and were told that in order to have our names in the phone book with that number we would need a recent certificate of *residenza in bollo* (that is, with a few thousand lire worth of special stamps on it) and signed renunciation of the number by Patuzzi, or his heir. The *contratto* for the phone would then be shifted, for a small charge, into our name and the bills would be addressed to us.

By the standards one has grown used to, this seemed something of a breeze. A check at our local *comune,* a pleasant enough little office with the inevitable crucifix, an impressive collection of rubber stamps, and a large computer on line to the city registry, provided the information that for certificates of residency we would need either proof of ownership of the said flat as first home or a written statement from the owner that we were tenants there. This should be on *carta bollata*—legal paper with, again, a few thousand lire worth of stamps on it.

So we rang Signora Marta. She was very polite but unable to understand why we wanted to change the name, "referring to the number in the phone book." Couldn't we simply tell everybody who wanted to phone us what our number was? We explained that there might be people who wanted to track us down for work. We were *liberi professionisti.* But if, she objected, they knew of our names, then they could ask the people they'd heard of us from, *non è vero?*—people who would surely have our telephone number or know someone who had it. Telephone directories were thus demonstrated to be entirely useless.

No, she added, the point was, it would be extravagant if we were only staying for a year. Because when we were gone we would of course renounce the number, so as not to be listed under it anymore and have bills for it in our names, at which point she could if she chose have the line disconnected, but then God knew how long it might take to get it reconnected and how much that would cost. The result being that she would most probably have to take the number on in her own name (rather than Patuzzi's). And since she already had a phone number, this number (Via Colombare's) would be registered as a second home phone, meaning much higher basic bills even if she made no calls.

So many conversations in Italy follow these serpentine paths, with new laws and regulations constantly raising their ugly heads to turn the most obvious ways forward into dead ends. With the creeping sense of paranoia that results, you occasionally find that people have been imagining rules that don't actually exist, simply because they seem to be the kind of thing the government would invent to make life more difficult and hence probably has. Was it really true, for example, that Marta would be obliged to register the number in her name? Couldn't she register it in a child's or grandmother's? Or was it that if she did that they would then have to switch their *residenza* to Via Colombare with all the problems that entailed?

I proceeded cautiously: when we left the flat, I said, if she asked us to leave it, that is, and we rather hoped she wouldn't because we liked it here, then this would presumably be because she had decided to sell it, or had found someone else to live in it, and in either case the new occupants would want to take over the phone, wouldn't they?

"Not if they already have one in their own name elsewhere," she came back. "Or if they want to retain residency in another province."

Who could have thought of this before starting the phone call? Then when I had already given up and offered a cool *arrivederci,* she suggested by way of an olive branch: "I don't mind writing to say that you live there, though, if you need to have *residenza* for other purposes."

How to explain the elusive yet all important significance of "residency" to a Brit who merely lives where he lives and acts accordingly? Can we hazard a definition? Residency means that the state now recognizes that you live where you live, or say you live (e.g., in the province of X at such and such an address), and henceforth will distinguish you from all the people who live in another province, or country, or who do, yes, live in X but whom the state does not recognize as living where they live (in X), either because those people want to be recognized as living elsewhere (where they don't live) and have managed by some scheme to achieve this, or because they can't get hold of some precious *documento* that would allow them to demonstrate that they do in fact live where they live (in X), and must thus continue to be recognized as living where they no longer live (in Y or Z, for example).

But does it actually matter? Well, yes. Once the state recognizes that one lives where one lives, there are all kinds of benefits: the right to register your car in the area (otherwise you will have to travel to Y or Z to register it), the right to register with a local doctor, the right to apply for local state jobs, the right to have access to certain services and benefits, the right to pay lower phone and utility bills, the right to vote, and most important for us, a 2-percent reduction on the amount of income tax withheld at source on freelance services.

"*Va bene,*" I told Signora Marta; if she could write such a letter we would be very happy. "*La ringrazio.*"

But I was puzzled. She hadn't wanted a formal rent contract. I had half suspected that this was why she hadn't wanted the phone number in our name: she didn't want it to be in any way official that we lived here. And now on the contrary here she was offering to help us get residence. A calculated risk? Generosity?

"The flat," Rita suggested, "is officially owned by Maria Rosa, who is gaga in a nursing home. How is anybody to know that we are paying into Marta's account?"

Still . . . life is complicated. In any event, the drift seems to be that the government makes well-meaning but complicated laws and people very sensibly get smart and get around them. For example, there was this business Marta had mentioned that second homes carry much higher utility bills—a popular tax-the-rich measure. However, it is quite common in Italy for the middle and even lower-middle classes to rent their real home in the city where they work and possess a small holiday flat (second home) by the sea, by one of the lakes, or in the mountains. Result: many people register themselves or their wives or children as residents in the holiday home, so as to avoid higher bills. This in turn will create all kinds of other problems. On election day, the registered residents will have to travel a couple of hundred miles to vote in some place whose local politics they know nothing about. So they don't vote, you object. But in Italy if one doesn't vote three times in succession, one loses certain rights . . . etc., etc. Bureaucracy is a huge tangle of sticky string in which every attempt to loosen one knot tightens another.

And checks, or *accertamenti,* to make sure that each citizen is contributing his length of string to this tangle, are quite common. A few weeks after moving into Via Colombare, I went out on the balcony to see who had buzzed our bell and found a seriously fat man in uniform sitting on a moped with big dispatch boxes. Montecchio's local *vigile.* Taking some papers out of one of these boxes, he asked me something. I asked him if he could please speak Italian. He politely switched from dialect to something more comprehensible, upon which it emerged that he had been asking me whether I lived where quite obviously I was living (wearing pajamas, a piece of toast in my hand). I said I did. He then asked if he could come and see. And in my kitchen he explained at length about the *tassa sui rifiuti,* the garbage-collection tax. This apparently was paid not by the owner or even the renter of a property but by the head of the household actually living there *whether or not resident*—that is, they wanted the money, and red tape was not a problem (similarly, it is perfectly normal for a foreigner to file an income tax return without having a work permit). The person in question was me, I said. I would pay. He scratched his head, cocked it to one side, eyed me carefully from his tubby face. *"Bon,"* he said.

The *vigile* then wrote something amazingly painstakingly on his sheet of paper. While he worked, I noticed how clean his uniform was, how well ironed his shirt, how white the little pouch on his belt. It was another day of sultry heat. Despite the weight of flesh beneath all these clothes and accessories, he was not sweating.

He asked me my name. Then asked me to spell it. Fair enough. We got through Parks quite rapidly, and were speeding through Timothy (Torino Imola Monza Otranto—I say it in my sleep sometimes) when we ran up against the age-old problem of Y. "Hotel, Epsilon," I finished. He hesitated, raised his head, blew out his cheeks, narrowed his eyes. What was epsilon? "Epsilon," I said, "is a letter." *"A sì?"* he said. It was clear that he was used to being *preso in giro*, made a fool of, and so had developed these mannerisms—the suspicion, the slow questioning, the stare—to make himself seem less gullible.

Having studied me for a sufficient length of time, he decided I was not the type, said: *"Sì, sì, sì, d'accordo,"* and scribbled something down, I didn't dare ask him what. But then I had the idea of pulling out my English driving license and offering it, *per una verificazione*. Offended, he waved it away.

"Residenza?" he now inquired, for even if it had no bearing on my paying this tax or not, it was important to write it down. Three or four times.

I was applying for it, I said.

"Stato di famiglia?" (A document describing relationships within the family—who is the mother, the father, the head of the household, who the breadwinner, who dependent.)

I was waiting for my marriage certificate to arrive from England.

"*Professione?*" For everybody must be classified according to his profession.

I told him teacher. Rather flatteringly he wrote down *Professore*.

Then just as he was leaving I made the foolish mistake of remarking that we didn't have this residency business in England.

Again he was clearly concerned that he was being made fun of. There was the same cocking of the head, the puzzlement. He was one of those fat people who are terribly graceful, nimble almost, very aware of their bulk. He turned on his heel away from the door in almost a dance step, pushed back his cap, and lowered himself onto a seat at my kitchen table. This was a serious matter.

How was it possible, he asked, for us not to have residency?

We didn't.

So what do you do? When you move.

You move, I said.

And the registration plates on the car?

You leave them as they are.

And your identity card?

There are no identity cards.

And the doctor?

You go and register at the nearest doctor's office.

He clearly didn't believe me. It couldn't be that easy. Not that I was lying. But I must be ingenuous. There was so much I hadn't understood. He was wondering how he could prove this to me. He had prickly Latin black hair cut short under his cap, and he scratched at it slowly, tugged at the tubby lobe of an ear. Then he had me.

How, he asked, would the postal system work?

In what sense?

How would they know where to bring the mail to, when you moved?

I tried to be equable, offhand. Somebody wrote your address on an envelope, affixed a stamp of the appropriate denomination, and the postal service would take it to that address and ask no questions.

The man got up and left in polite disgust. Obviously it was not a country for *vigili*.

I was not surprised a few weeks later when the first garbage bill arrived addressed to Parks Thimothj. As for the phone, if you open Verona's very handsome telephone directory, you will still to this day find the name of Umberto Patuzzi covering up for whoever is enjoying the pleasure of SIP's services at Via Colombare 10, flat three. Doubtless the gas bills are still in his name too. And the electricity bills, despite the curious fact that these actually include the modest charge of seven thousand lire a year for the votive light over his grave . . . a second home?

JOHN RUSKIN

(1819–1900)

Writer and reformer John Ruskin was twenty-six, a veteran traveler, an Oxford graduate, and the author of the first volume of his work of criti-cism, Modern Painters, *when he went to Italy in 1844. He put aside writing the second volume to study Italian art. His first stop, Genoa, was a disappointment, and he found "half the pictures copies—others bad—others injured or destroyed—others shut up." It was Lucca that moved him, surprisingly more by its architecture than its art. He continued to Pisa, Florence, and finally Venice. He was both affected and distressed by Venice. He feared that botched attempts at modernization—gaslights, iron bridges, railway lines—were being made at the expense of the preservation of the palaces and churches.*

The result was Ruskin's classic architectural series, The Seven Lamps of Architecture *and three volumes of* The Stones of Venice, *a study of the Byzantine and Gothic architecture of that city. Ruskin's knowledge was wide-ranging, and he wove religion, morality, economics, and politics into his analysis of domestic architecture. Brilliant, but also quite mad, Ruskin was plagued with bouts of insanity, especially in the last thirty years of his life.*

This abridged excerpt is a description of St. Mark's Cathedral from The Stones of Venice.

from THE STONES OF VENICE

We find ourselves in a paved alley, some seven feet wide where it is widest, full of people, and resonant with cries of itinerant salesmen,—a shriek in their beginning, and dying away into a kind of brazen ringing, all the worse for its confinement between the high houses of the passage along which we have to make our way. Overhead an inextricable confusion of rugged shutters, and iron balconies and chimney flues pushed out on brackets to save room, and arched windows with projecting sills of Istrian stone, and gleams of green leaves here and there where a fig-tree branch escapes over a lower wall from some inner cortile, leading the eye up to the narrow stream of blue sky high over all. On each side, a row of shops, as densely set as may be, occupying, in fact, intervals between the square stone shafts, about eight feet high, which carry the first floors: intervals of which one is narrow and serves as a door; the other is, in the more respectable shops, wainscotted to the height of the counter and glazed above, but in those of the poorer tradesmen left open to the ground, and the wares laid on benches and tables in the open air, the light in all cases entering at the front only, and fading away in a few feet from the threshold into a gloom which the eye from without cannot penetrate, but which is generally broken by a ray or two from a feeble lamp at the back of the shop, suspended before a print of the Virgin.

THE VAST TOWER of St. Mark seems to lift itself visibly forth from the level field of chequered stones; and, on each side, the countless arches prolong themselves into ranged symmetry, as if the rugged and irregular houses that pressed together above us in the dark alley had been struck back into sudden obedience and lovely order, and all their rude casements and broken walls had been transformed into arches charged with goodly sculpture, and fluted shafts of delicate stone.

And well may they fall back, for beyond those troops of ordered arches there rises a vision out of the earth, and all the great square seems to have opened from it in a kind of awe, that we may see it far away;—a multitude of pillars and white domes, clustered into a long low pyramid of coloured light; a treasure-heap, it seems, partly of gold, and partly of opal and mother-of-pearl, hollowed beneath into five great vaulted porches, ceiled with fair mosaic, and beset with sculpture of alabaster, clear as amber and delicate as ivory,—sculpture fantastic and involved, of palm leaves and lilies, and grapes and pomegranates, and birds clinging and fluttering among the branches, all twined together into an endless network of buds and plumes; and in the midst of it, the solemn forms of angels, sceptred, and robed to the feet, and leaning to each other across the gates, their figures indistinct among the gleaming of the golden ground through the leaves beside them, interrupted and dim, like the morning light as it faded back among the branches of Eden, when first its gates were angel-guarded long ago. And round the walls of the porches there are set pillars of variegated stones, jasper and porphyry, and deep-green serpentine spotted with flakes of snow, and marbles, that half refuse and half yield to the sunshine, Cleopatra-like, "their bluest veins to kiss"—the shadow, as it steals back from them, revealing line after line of azure undulation, as a receding tide leaves the waved sand; their capitals rich with interwoven tracery, rooted knots of herbage, and drifting leaves of acanthus and vine, and mystical signs, all beginning and ending in the Cross; and above them, in the broad archivolts, a continuous chain of language and of life—angels, and the signs of heaven, and the labours of men, each in its appointed season upon the earth; and above these, another range of glittering pinnacles, mixed with white arches edged with scarlet flowers,—a confusion of delight, amidst which the breasts of the Greek horses are seen blazing in their breadth of golden strength, and the St. Mark's lion, lifted on a blue field covered with stars, until at last, as if in ecstasy, the crests of the arches break into a marble foam, and toss themselves far into the blue sky in flashes and wreaths of sculptured spray, as if the breakers on the Lido shore had been frost-bound before they fell, and the sea-nymphs had inlaid them with coral and amethyst. . . .

PRIEST AND LAYMAN, soldier and civilian, rich and poor, pass by it alike regardlessly. Up to the very recesses of the porches, the meanest tradesmen of the city push their counters; nay, the foundations of its pillars are themselves the seats—not "of them that sell doves" for sacrifice, but of the vendors of toys and caricatures. Round the whole square in front of the church there is almost a continuous line of cafés, where the idle Venetians of the middle classes lounge, and read empty journals; in its centre the Austrian bands play during the time of vespers, their martial music jarring with the organ notes,—the march drowning the miserere, and the sullen crowd thickening round them,—a crowd, which, if it had its will, would stiletto every soldier that pipes to it. And in the recesses of the porches, all day long, knots of men of the lowest classes, unemployed and listless, lie basking in the sun like lizards, and unregarded children,—every heavy glance of their young eyes full of desperation and stony depravity, and their throats hoarse with cursing,—gamble, and fight, and snarl, and sleep, hour after hour, clashing their bruised centesimi upon the marble ledges of the church porch. And the images of Christ and His angels look down upon it continually.

Let us enter the church. It is lost in still deeper twilight, to which the eye must be accustomed for some moments before the form of the building can be traced; and then there opens before us a vast cave, hewn out into the form of a Cross, and divided into shadowy aisles by many pillars. Round the domes of its roof the light enters only through narrow apertures like large stars; and here and there a ray or two from some far-away casement wanders into the darkness, and casts a narrow phosphoric stream upon the waves of marble that heave and fall in a thousand colours along the floor. What else there is of light is from torches, or silver lamps, burning ceaselessly in the recesses of the chapels; the roof sheeted with gold, and the polished walls covered with alabaster, give back at every curve and angle some feeble gleaming to the flames; and the glories round the heads of the sculptured saints flash out upon us as we pass them, and sink again into the gloom. Under foot and over head, a continual succession of crowded imagery, one picture passing into another, as in a dream; forms beautiful and terrible mixed together; dragons and serpents, and ravening beasts of prey, and graceful birds that in the midst of them drink from running fountains and feed from vases of crystal; the passions and the pleasures of human life symbolised together, and the mystery of its redemption; for the mazes of interwoven lines and changeful pictures lead always at last to the Cross, lifted and carved in every place and upon every stone; sometimes with the serpent of eternity wrapt round it, sometimes with doves beneath its arms, and sweet herbage growing forth from its feet; but conspicuous most of all on the great rood that crosses the church before the altar, raised in bright blazonry against the shadow of the apse. . . .

IT IS on its value as a piece of perfect and unchangeable colouring, that the claims of this edifice to our respect are finally rested; and a deaf man might as well pretend to pronounce judgment on the merits of a full orchestra, as an architect trained in the composition of form only, to discern the beauty of St. Mark's. It possesses the charm of colour in common with the greater part of the architecture, as well as of the manufactures, of the East; but the Venetians deserve especial note as the only European people who appear to have sympathized to the full with the great instinct of the Eastern races. They indeed were

compelled to bring artists from Constantinople to design the
mosaics of the vaults of St. Mark's, and to group the colours of
its porches; but they rapidly took up and developed, under more
masculine conditions, the system of which the Greeks had shown
them the example: while the burghers and barons of the North
were building their dark streets and grisly castles of oak and
sandstone, the merchants of Venice were covering their palaces
with porphyry and gold; and at last, when her mighty painters
had created for her a colour more priceless than gold or porphyry, even this, the richest of her treasures, she lavished upon
walls whose foundations were beaten by the sea; and the strong
tide, as it runs beneath the Rialto, is reddened to this day by the
reflection of the frescoes of Giorgione.

PERCY BYSSHE SHELLEY

(1792–1822)

Percy Bysshe Shelley wore a ring with a motto of hope—Il buon tempo verra—"the good time will come." But the "good time" never came for Shelley. His life, much of it spent in self-imposed exile in Italy, was filled with tragedy. Shelley and his wife Mary fled England shortly after their marriage and restlessly moved around Italy. There, though lacking a literary audience, his family life in shambles (he and Mary lost two of their three children and he was denied custody of his children by his first wife), and in poor health, Shelley produced his most memorable work. In 1819 he completed his masterpiece Prometheus Unbound; *a tragedy,* The Cenci; *two satires,* The Mask of Anarchy *and* Peter Bell the Third; *and many poems, including the deeply melancholy* "Stanzas Written in Dejection, Near Naples."*

Shelley found relative contentment when he finally settled at Pisa. A group of friends, "the Pisan Circle," gathered around him—Lord Byron, Edward Trelawney, and a retired lieutenant of the army, Edward Williams. There Shelley unwittingly foreshadowed his own death in his elegy Adonais:

> Far from the shore, far from the trembling throng
> Whose sails were never to the tempest given;
> The massy earth and sphered skies are riven!
> I am borne darkly, fearfully afar;

Shelley and Edward Williams drowned while sailing their open boat in the Gulf of Spezzia. Shelley's ashes were buried in the Protestant Cemetery in Rome near the grave of John Keats.

Stanzas Written in Dejection, Near Naples

1

The sun is warm, the sky is clear,
   The waves are dancing fast and bright,
Blue isles and snowy mountains wear
   The purple noon's transparent might,
   The breath of the moist earth is light,
Around its unexpanded buds;
   Like many a voice of one delight,
The winds, the birds, the ocean floods
The City's voice itself is soft like Solitude's.

2

I see the Deep's untrampled floor
   With green and purple seaweeds strown;
I see the waves upon the shore,
   Like light dissolved in star-showers, thrown:
   I sit upon the sands alone—
The lightning of the noontide ocean
   Is flashing round me, and a tone
Arises from its measured motion,
How sweet! did any heart now share in my emotion.

3

Alas! I have nor hope nor health,
   Nor peace within nor calm around,
Nor that content surpassing wealth
   The sage in meditation found,
    And walked with inward glory crowned—
Nor fame, nor power, nor love, nor leisure.
   Others I see whom these surround—
Smiling they live, and call life pleasure;—
To me that cup has been dealt in another measure.

4

Yet now despair itself is mild,
   Even as the winds and waters are;
I could lie down like a tired child,
   And weep away the life of care
    Which I have borne and yet must bear,
Till death like sleep might steal on me,
   And I might feel in the warm air
My cheek grow cold, and hear the sea
Breathe o'er my dying brain its last monotony.

5

Some might lament that I were cold,
   As I, when this sweet day is gone,
Which my lost heart, too soon grown old,
   Insults with this untimely moan;
    They might lament—for I am one
Whom men love not,—and yet regret,
   Unlike this day, which, when the sun
Shall on its stainless glory set,
Will linger, though enjoyed, like joy in memory yet.

MARY TAYLOR SIMETI

(1941–)

In 1962, fresh from Radcliffe, Mary Taylor did volunteer work in Sicily. There she fell in love with both Italy and Antonio Simeti, an agronomist, and she never left.

Like many Sicilians, the Simetis divide their time between urban Palermo in the winter and their farm in western Sicily in the summer. This bifurcated life is recounted in On Persephone's Island, *Simeti's narrative of one full year in Sicily. Simeti walks a delicate line between America and Italy. Like Tim Parks, she will forever be a foreigner in Italy, although her spouse and her children are Italian. She is both outsider and insider and has never reconciled her American perspective to her Italian home.* On Persephone's Island *weaves folklore, ritual, and the island's Greek roots into the reality of life in modern Sicily.*

from ON PERSEPHONE'S ISLAND

November is a time of beginnings in the double calendar that we follow in our family. Our life here in Sicily is divided between the academic year, which requires our presence in Palermo—where my husband, Tonino, teaches agricultural economics at the university and where our children, Francesco and Natalia, go to school—and the agricultural year, which turns our attention to the vineyards and the olive groves at Bosco, the family farm thirty miles away. Here we take refuge as soon as school lets out for vacation, for a summer of farming after a winter of academic pursuits.

The grapes ripened late this year because of the exceptionally dry summer, so we commuted back and forth from the middle of September, when the schools opened, well into October. But we cannot manage that all year round: quite apart from the exorbitant price of gas here, no one lives on the land in this part of Sicily, we have no neighbors in wintertime, no friends for the children to see, and no guarantee of getting through the mud to the highway once the heavy rains begin.

Every so often the unpleasantness of urban life becomes too much for us and we talk of moving out permanently, but the problems this would create for the children are enormous, so each time we reconcile ourselves to continuing this split existence, at least until our younger child has finished high school.

We are sowing no wheat this year; the fields that last winter held the seed will lie fallow until spring, and October has been dedicated to equipping the children for the winter and to at least the pretense of catching up with the wear and tear on the Palermo apartment, despite our reluctance to invest time and money here when so much remains to be done at Bosco.

That done, I am free to descend to the tiny office on the ground floor of our apartment building where I have spent the last few winters reading about Sicily, research for a book of months that would trace the varying rhythms and calendars—archaic, agrarian, contemporary—that govern the passage of time on the island. But time takes over as I take up my pen; the day I start to write ushers in my twenty-first year in Sicily. What began twenty years ago as a brief visit, an interlude between college and graduate school, has been transformed by choice and circumstance into permanence. Right from the outset, then, the book of months becomes a journal, a chronicle of my Sicilian coming of age, in which these personal beginnings, mine and my family's, coincide with a new year in that classical calendar that provides the structure for my thoughts. For rural Sicily still belongs to Magna Graecia, her crops and her celebrations still echo those of the ancient Greeks, for whom the agricultural year fell into three main divisions, the autumn sowing season followed by the winter, the spring with its first blossoming of fruits and flowers, . . . and the early summer harvest . . . of grain and fruits [to which] was added with the coming of the vine the vintage and the gathering in of the later fruits. . . .

Jane Ellaen Harrison, *Prolegomena to the Study of Greek Religion*

SICILY JOINS ME in celebrating this alternative New Year's and welcomes November and the onset of winter with festivity. All Saints' Day is followed by All Souls' Day, officially known as the "Commemoration of the Defunct," but more familiarly called I Morti, "The Dead." "What are you doing over The Dead this year?" For years I have puzzled over I Morti, convinced that to understand why it is the most beloved of the Sicilian feast days would be to grasp some basic truth about the Sicilian character.

If the inner meaning still eludes me, the outer trappings entrance, since I Morti is to the Sicilian child what Christmas is to the American. During the night the dead come out of the convents and the cemeteries where they are buried and go about the town in procession, leaving behind them presents for those children who have been good and have remembered them in their prayers: hidden troves of elaborate toys, of marzipan and sugar statues.

Just at the time that the countryside turns in upon itself to nurse the dormant seeds and vines, Palermo blossoms forth in this artificial flowering of marzipan, a cornucopia of fruit and vegetables molded out of almond paste. Each pastry shop works hard to outdo its competitors in realism—spiny prickly pears with all their prickles, pomegranates bursting with seeds, roast chestnuts tinged with the bloom of ashes—until the shopwindows rival in miniature the variety and the color of the vegetable stalls in the marketplace.

Here marzipan is known as *pasta reale* or as *frutta di Martorana,* from the convent of the Martorana in Palermo, where the nuns excelled in the preparation of almond paste. It is said that once their mother superior, Sister Gertrude, wishing to celebrate the pastoral visit of the bishop, instructed the nuns to mold the paste into apples, peaches, pears, and oranges, which were then hung on the trees growing in the cloister garden. Strolling in the cloister before dinner with the mother superior, the bishop marveled to see so many different trees bearing fruit all in the same season. Still greater was his surprise when, at the dinner table, he bit into a bright red apple and discovered that it was made of almond paste.

Today it is still possible to play a practical joke with *pasta reale,* even if it would be difficult to invent one as enchanting as Sister Gertrude's: you can buy cakes of soap, sandwiches with the filling dribbling out, even complete meals served on paper plates. I once gave my children fried eggs and peas for supper, and it wasn't until they put their forks to it that they realized it was made of marzipan.

There is a pastry shop in the center of Palermo that used to elaborate on a different theme each year. Once they made marzipan seafood—fish of every size and species, clams and mussels, squid and shrimp, all displayed in the shopwindow on the flat wicker trays the fishmongers use, so lifelike as to make the pastry seeker think he had stopped in front of the wrong store. Another time, in an absolute triumph of patience and dexterity, they produced *semenza,* a window full of baskets of peanuts, hazelnuts, toasted chick-peas and pumpkin seeds, marzipan imitations sold in brown paper cones just like the real *semenza* the Sicilians buy at street-corner stalls to nibble on as they make their way up and down the main street on their evening stroll.

The same gay colors of the marzipan are used to decorate the *pupi di cena,* statues made from melted sugar poured into plaster molds, then painted and stuck with bits of silver paper. The shop windows or tiered street stands selling these *pupi* are dominated by the *paladino,* the knight in armor of the Sicilian puppet

shows, most often mounted on horseback and brandishing a
sword, a snippet of real ostrich plume cascading from his hel-
met. Next to him will stand a peasant girl balancing a basket of
eggs on her hip, a ballerina or a carabiniere in full dress uniform,
traditional figures that have recently been joined by Zorro, Superman, and Mickey Mouse.

The same store of marzipan fame used to make marvelous
pupi di cena, each one individually sculptured and painted with
the greatest attention to detail. The year I discovered this store
one window was filled with sugar peasants, about fifteen inches
high, each selling something different, with baskets of fish or
fruit on their heads or jugs of wine and oil in hand. They were
very expensive, so I bought only one, to give away as a present.
In my ignorance I waited too long to buy one for myself, and
when I went back a few years later the man who made them had
retired, and the store had only run-of-the-mill knights to sell. I
have a knight, a more authentic representative of the tradition
and very beautiful in his crude and brilliant colors. But I regret
those street vendors.

If the culinary delights of I Morti find their highest expression in Palermo, the smaller towns generate a more festive air.
The main street of Alcamo, the town where my husband grew
up, is lined with stalls: in addition to the usual (and this time
genuine) *semenza* sellers, who have their wares spread out on
barrows painted with the bright primary colors of Sicilian carts
and strung with lights and paper garlands, there are the torrone
vendors, their stall shelves groaning under the weight of vast
trays of almonds and hazelnuts in caramelized sugar and spread
with slices of the holiday version of torrone, hazelnuts smothered in tricolor nougat striped pea green, white, and shocking
pink, a travesty of the Italian flag that is reminiscent of the election night scene in *The Leopard* and is so bilious in aspect as to
have discouraged me from ever tasting it. It is nonetheless a gay
addition to the holiday scene, as are the toy booths offering
something for every pocketbook: elegant dolls ripple their long
satiny skirts in the wind, bicycles and push-pedal cars sparkle

next to soccer balls and plastic tea sets and compete with clusters of red plastic donkeys on blue wheels, a local version of the hobby horse that appears to be the most beloved—or most economical—of Sicilian toys: they are ubiquitous, propelled by stout little legs along every street and sticking up from every rubbish dump.

The flower sellers brandish bright masses of color, great bunches of yellow, white, bronze, and purple chrysanthemums, the flowers of the dead, which are destined to decorate the tombs. From both sides of the street the calls of the vendors vie for the attention of the endless stream of families enjoying the *passeggiata* and comparing the wares, dressed in their best and walking arm in arm, pushing baby carriages, cracking *semenza* and leaving a train of peanut shells behind them.

Even on a normal Sunday or at the end of a weekday afternoon the *passeggiata* is a solemn rite, the moment when business is transacted, social ties renewed, news spread, and public opinion formed, not to mention an important occasion for asserting one's economic status and ability to dress. Back and forth, arm in arm, the current of people flows along the Corso, diverted into small eddies as it passes the bars, swelling in front of the churches as new strollers come out from mass, impervious to the few foolhardy drivers who attempt to fend the flood. The *passeggiata* has a morbid fascination: I think of how my husband and his friends, in their rebellious youth, could find nothing more nonconforming to do than to move to another street, where they walked up and down in solitary superiority. The poverty of alternatives, although much alleviated by the economic boom of the last twenty years, is still depressing to me, as is the idea of having to carry out the bulk of one's social relations under the careful scrutiny of the whole town. But my children, who have grown up in the anonymity of a modern residential neighborhood in a big city, are intrigued by the *passeggiata;* when they were younger and we were in Alcamo of a Sunday, they would never refuse their father's invitation to "go as far as the piazza" and would come back wide-eyed with wonder at the number of people their father knew to stop and speak to.

Until a few years ago I Morti was a long holiday: the first of November was All Saints' Day; the second, All Souls' Day; and the fourth was a national holiday celebrating the end of the First World War, so the third crept quietly in to join the party, schools and offices closed for four days, and a bonus came whenever the four days fell on either side of a weekend. Then, in one of its periodic outbursts of efficiency, the Italian government decided to suppress a great many of the nation's twenty-odd national and religious holidays, or to make them into movable feasts that always fall on Sunday, so now only the first of November is officially recognized. Actually, as often happens, the government's efforts in this direction have had ridiculous side effects. All the middle and secondary school teachers in Italy now have four days' vacation, to spread out during the year as they choose, since the government cannot afford to pay them for the work they do on the four days that were formerly holidays. And most Sicilians, whose respect for the dictates of Rome has always been marginal, continue to enjoy I Morti at length.

Be it long or short, the holiday culminates in the visit to the cemetery. The women of the household make a preliminary trip to clean out the family chapel or spruce up the tombs, sweeping, dusting, throwing out dead flowers, and spreading a fresh cloth, rich with lace and embroidery, on the chapel altar. Everything must be clean and in order for the official visit, and a tomb that is neglected causes comment.

On the appointed day, traditionally November 2, the family assembles, arms laden with flowers, to pay their visit. While this is certainly a harrowing experience for those who have recently had a death in the family, on the whole the atmosphere of festivity spreads from the Corso to embrace the cemetery as well. Children play tag around the cemetery paths while the grownups, women to one side and men to another, stand around gossiping, pay visits back and forth between tombs and chapels, observe carefully the quantity and quality of the flowers at each sepulcher, pluck out a few blossoms from their own bunches to lay on the tombs of more distant relatives or friends.

In Partinico, in the years when I was first living in Sicily, the children from the local orphanage were brought to the cemetery to beg contributions for the orphanage funds. No decent funeral in Partinico was without the orphans: a double row of brown rain capes over blue smocks marching at the head of the funeral procession with a fat red-haired woman in attendance. Probably the trips to the cemetery on I Morti were an exciting change in routine for the children, as well as a profitable undertaking for the institution, since anyone would be an easy touch for an orphan on such an occasion. The children themselves did seem cheerful and unperturbed by their constant association with death, and even the funeral processions were rocked by surreptitious shoves and smothered giggles. Nonetheless to me these were scenes straight out of Dickens, and I would be happy to learn that the practice has been discontinued.

Sicilian history is a bitter and bloody succession of wars, conquests, pestilences, and famines. Small wonder, then, that the Sicilians have come to seek consolation and even to luxuriate in the funeral panoply. The coffins still journey in glass-sided carriages drawn by black horses with black plumes nodding on their harnesses, and even the motorized hearses often have large gilt angels weeping on the four corners of the roof. The funeral procession is headed by the priest, together with two or three altar boys; then come the wreaths of flowers, six feet high and bearing black ribbons with gilt letters announcing the names of their donors. A new custom, recently introduced at some funerals in Alcamo, demands that a small group of friends and relatives walk behind the wreath-bearers, carrying armfuls of flowers from which they tear off petals to strew before the coffin. (Although some onlookers derisively describe this, together with chewing gum and other dubious novelties, as an *americanata,* it is in fact a return to the customs of ancient Greece.) The hearse bears the coffin—carved wood for married adults; white for children, spinsters, and bachelors in tribute to their chastity—followed by the family, dressed in black and accompanied by the friends and relatives who bring up the rear of the procession.

A few years ago there was a clamorous case in the Palermo

newspapers, when a young girl was severely beaten by her brothers because she hadn't cried in their father's funeral procession. Yet stranger than the need to feign grief where affection is lacking is the preoccupation with public opinion even among those who have nothing to hide. When her eldest son died, my mother-in-law was prostrated, and no one could have doubted the genuineness of her grief, and yet when we would manage to persuade her to come out for a drive so as to have some air and distraction, she would insist on leaving the house by the back door, lest someone should note these outings and take them as a sign of indifference.

Still strictly observed in most parts of Sicily, although in the big cities and among the middle class it has been much curtailed or even eliminated, mourning has many strange rules. The summer her son died, for example, my mother-in-law would not allow us to turn on the lamp in front of the summer house by the sea; if we wanted to enjoy the cool of the evening in the garden we had to do so in the dark. She herself was married, together with her sister, just a short time after her father's death. Her older brother, finding himself with two nubile but engaged sisters on his hands (their mother had died long before), was in a hurry to get them settled, but since they were in mourning, the double ceremony had to be held very simply, and at four o'clock in the morning.

I am fascinated to read, in a footnote to the Greek myths collected by Robert Graves, that the wearing of black for mourning was originally a message to the dead rather than to the living, a disguise adopted to escape being haunted by the ghost of the deceased. This connection with their most distant history has long since lost its original significance for most Sicilians, but I wonder if in the deepest recesses of the uneducated peasant mind it still lingers, a thread in the peculiar time warp that weaves so much of Sicily's ancient past to its present. Certainly the belief in spirits is still strong: my friend Gabriella, who teaches in a junior high school in one of Palermo's poorest neighborhoods, was instructed by her students to avoid clearing the supper table completely and to leave out some bread and wine overnight "for the spirits." Gabriella was very upset at her failure to dispel this superstition, and yet she occasionally finds herself saying *buon giorno* when she is the first one to come home at noon, greeting out loud the spirits of the empty house as her grandmother taught her to.

The Feast of the Dead always ends on a tragic note, as the newspapers publish accounts of the children who have been wounded or blinded by the BB guns or other weapons that the dead have ill-advisedly brought them. The statistics are always accompanied by articles signed by famous educators on how badly the Italians choose their children's toys, everyone clucks his disapproval, and the Sicilians settle down to the winter.

KATE SIMON

(1912–1990)

Born in Warsaw, Poland, Kate Simon came to the United States when she was four. She wrote travel books about Italy, Mexico, London, Paris, and New York that were applauded as models of the genre. New York Times *critic Stanley Carr wrote that Simon "has made of the guide-book, one of the dullest forms of literature, a brilliant work of art. And to do that requires genius." In 1982 she wrote an autobiography,* Bronx Primitive: Portraits in a Childhood.

Kate Simon called Italy "a Circe dressed in silken landscapes." Her classic travel book Italy: The Places in Between *was a personal travel guide that revealed the less-traveled Italian cities and towns. But she cautioned her readers that if they "want to get to know the people, the real people," they should dispel their image of "large, plump, musical, smiling families, napkins tucked under their chins, heaping platters of steaming spaghetti lovingly placed before them by abundant apronsful of beaming mamas and* nonne *and* zie. *It is not easy to know the people, a very complex people. Nevertheless, the slippery quest is an entertaining game."*

For Women

from ITALY: THE PLACES IN BETWEEN

*—particularly those old enough to have been bitten by a
film called* Summertime, *wherein Katharine
Hepburn lived the apogee of her flat-chested, American life*

Intoxicated by the mists of Venetian canals, her American guardedness lying at her feet like discarded robes, our heroine was ready for Italian Love. It came as a married and undivorceable gentleman of soft-spoken, persuasive charm whose smooth energy was endless; he minded the store, his family, his American love and could, as well, welcome in the dawn on San Marco's piazza. The *Summertime* mirage is still pursued—now timidly, now boldly—by a good number of women. Emphases and pace differ, of course, depending on provenance; the sexually bored Scandinavian may head for southern Italy, where the approach is direct and unequivocal: no prose, no misunderstandings; total Lib. American women, those of a certain age, prefer the slower unguents: the lingering eyes, the world-well-lost-for-love stance and beautifully absurd, unexpected gestures, when the exigencies of job, bambini and card playing permit.

The opening moves are easy. All that is required is a small flag of receptivity, a look that answers a look, a smile that returns a smile. Whether you play the game or stay a spectator, you will find the field immense and variegated and the game capable of diverse moods from ridiculous to mildly funny, from lyrical to bewitching and even—this is rare—menacing. Basic equipment includes, besides nature's gifts, an understanding of a few profound male convictions and how they operate in Italy. One assumes that foreign ladies, English and Americans particularly, because they are tremulous, neurotic bags of bone reduced by sexual malnutrition, find all Italians irresistible. Gentlemen who agree with this premise are often to be found in hotels during *festa* times when numerous visitors, to-ing and fro-ing at odd times, create a nice smörgåsbord. Don Giovanni prowls the hallways, listening to accents and watching the sway of buttocks. He selects a recipient for his gifts and tracks her down to her door. He knocks and keeps knocking, asking for one small moment, pliss. If you've glanced at his wares and found them resistible, lock the door and don't answer. In time he will tire of your silly intransigence and go on to offer his golden moments at another door.

Conviction two: if she wanders the streets alone at night she is offering or selling; consequently, many car doors open to invite her in. Sometimes, she is invited to get the hell off the street, and *subito,* by the pros whose beat she has invaded. The eventful and rarely dangerous night walk, trailed by panting autos, can be quite a sporting event. Try, for instance, a main street in any city, the larger the city the better, and best in Florence and Rome at about 11:00 P.M. The fun is merrier should it be raining; only a *zoccola* or a *troia* (you have just added two extremely base words to your basic Italian) would be out this late in such weather. In small cars, big cars, all polished, one man, two men, three men ride in posses, peering through the slow arcs pulled by the windshield wipers. They spot the quarry, wipers hesitate, hang; the damp purring of tires squeaks to a stop, the door opens. An invitation is voiced as "Don't you want a lift, out of the rain?" with an innocent, host's smile, or "Can I take you home?" with a smile that is a middle-aged, slant-eyed memory of Rudolph Valentino. Occasionally it is a flat "Come on in" using the familiar *tu.* It can be, if your mood is for it, a stimulating half hour's entertainment that encompasses every car on your side of the street, several dozen men in a broad range of ages and looks, a grab bag of becks and nods and leers and never discouragement. Your refusal doesn't send them home to wife, mother and kiddies (who have all decided to agree that he is playing cards). If you won't, the next one will.

Since nothing in Italy is useless, and the male mind always alert for adventure, an open umbrella—yours—might serve as first trysting place. Suddenly a head forces its way into the shelter, complaining winsomely through its shining teeth that its newly pressed suit is being ruined, offers to carry the umbrella, an extraordinary flourish of gallantry, and you're off. "Didn't we meet in Paris?" in vaudeville English, though hackneyed, is still a useful ploy for a woman alone in a sidewalk café. The flattery implied wafts both parties into clouds of international glamour, although his natural horizons stretch from Naples to Rome and hers, normally, from Newark to New York. Already showing symptoms of the *Summertime* syndrome, she sees herself in a Paris salon, speaking exquisite French in a company of enameled gentlemen and jewel-studded odalisques. (Her references are usually old-fashioned literary, leaning heavily on Proust.) While she floats toward Baron Charlus, her new acquaintance eases himself into a chair and *they're* off.

A railroad station is also fertile ground. While you are looking for a cab or bus, showing the usual uncertainties of a stranger, a man appears. Are you looking for a hotel room? He offers to take you to a good inexpensive *albergo,* centrally located, clean and respectably run by his good friends. Be prepared, if you accept his company and advice, to share the bed with him and if he is hard up, as he is likely to be, some of your lire.

Naples seems to play its game with shocking candor; anywhere on the street, "Wanna guy, lady?" What the men are trying to say, however, is "Wanna guide, lady?" In less worldly parts of the south there is no game but the hunt. An unknown woman alone, or two driving a car, are out for sport, surely; especially promising if one wears her hair long and loose, still a prostitute's style in some places. And more especially if one of the women smokes cigarettes. That unleashes the pack. They follow relentlessly, on foot, on motorbikes and cars. They wait at the entrances of museums and restaurants and give chase—passing, permitting themselves to be passed—in nerve-racking, drunken rhythms until they force your car to the edge of the road, all in the serious endeavor to persuade you to go out with them that night. As you turn up the windows and bolt the doors, the thought crosses your mind, where is "out" in this hamlet? The cinema that features a western with John Wayne, young? The "dancing," to be shown in triumph, Cleopatra with the local Caesar, to the girls in their homemade, timid dresses? An abandoned stone farmhouse for love among rustling bats and scurrying mice? Worse still, the narrow back of their car? Each couple to take its turn while the other stands patiently behind the car?

Let us assume that you haven't turned up the windows, you've let the tendrils of attraction creep in and coil about you. What then? The quick mount, sometimes, a practice that derives its satisfactions from how many rather than how well. Several paths of possibility open thereafter. Don Giovanni never shows again. Or he does return and if he is young, full of troubles that may all be soluble with a little cash. His new transistor fell and is irreparably smashed. If he had the money to repair his brother's car, he could go to Bari, where someone promised him a good job. He can't go to his sister's wedding in his worn old suit. If the man is older, the woman sometimes pays in bewildered blank hours while, in addition to other pressing obligations, he must attend his wife's sister's boy's First Communion and tomorrow he must drive his mother to a miracle Virgin in a distant town. Sunday the whole family is driving into the country for a picnic. Monday? His son returns from the university. And so he goes. And so does she, unless we are treating of the anachronism (who should never be loosed on a Latin country) still capable of wailing, "How come he do me like he do do do?" while she hangs on the poisoned cord of a silent phone.

It isn't necessary to pay, always, and there are profits other than sex. A woman may be told repeatedly, with fine Italian tact, that young girls are dull little sprigs of grass; it takes care and time to make the perfect, full rose. For a woman whose native society considers five pounds of avoirdupois the equivalent of five pounds of leprosy, it is a warm boon to hear a man say that he likes a *buona forchetta,* a joyous eater, as he keeps stuffing her the same way his Saracenic ancestors stuffed their women.

Before leaving the subject with much remaining to be said (but this is hardly a manual) several unsung heroes should be lauded, the unconquerable who struggle against incredible odds for a bit of love. There is a superman in Lucca who slows his tired, uncertain bike to stare at a woman, to examine carefully, to make purring noises. At the point where he must dismount or fall off, he speeds up, dashes around the block, returns, slows, slower, slower, inviting, burbling, cooing like a turtle dove. And around the block again, to catch up with his doe on a farther stretch of street for the repeat performance. He cannot possibly expect to carry a woman off on his two-wheeled, one-seated chariot; he looks too poor to afford the opening act of a proffered apéritif and no romance was ever launched on a bottle of mineral water. Undaunted, invincible, he keeps on trying, warbling and wobbling.

An old man with a too-short pegleg haunts the station of Vicenza, a fair walk from the center of town. He picks his lady love from among the descending *turiste* and follows her from station to Palladian palace after palace. Tap, drag; tap, drag; tap, drag; from palace to museum and on to the Olympic theater, whose admission price shuts him out while his Beatrice, his Laura, takes a good, long time over the details of scenery and classic gods. He waits, ready to tap-drag up the hill, always keeping the same distance, to the villas at the top of town. Amused, annoyed, pitying, impatient, his lady returns to town, and, chancing on a funeral cortege about to enter a church, hides in the ranks of the mourners and waits out the service. Futile effort. There it is, cap, leer and wooden peg, waiting. Nothing to do but return to the station and bury one's head in a magazine at the bar until the train makes its rescue.

Then there are the old, old men, who, because their sight is failing, come up close, very close, to stare and drool. You can dismiss them with *vecchio sciocco* (old fool) but that would be vandalism; they are about the last shreds of romanticism, proof that hope still springs eternal. Proof, too, that you never need feel alone in Italy. Ten feet away, around the corner, or observing your reflection in a shopwindow, someone is watching you, if only one of the half-blind, doddering optimists.

So much for *amore.* How about the renowned male *cortesia italiana?* It doesn't exist except as verbiage. Two gentlemen may be all compliments and flirtatious roulades as they stand with two foreign ladies in the anteroom of a small auditorium, but if seats are not reserved they will rush into the hall as soon as the doors are open to sit in the last available chairs while the ladies stand.

A man in a first-class train will compliment a foreign woman extravagantly on her insipid Italian, will look deeply and lovingly at every part of her dress and tear it to shreds with his eyes; advise her about restaurants and hotels, search his *orario* for her train connections. The stop arrives and the time for separation from one's new loving friend, the time also for lifting the heavy valises from the rack above and pushing them out of the window to a porter if there is one close by, or dragging them through the aisle and down the narrow, perilous train steps. If friend is staying his face is lost in the magazine which interested him not at all a half hour ago. If he is leaving, he sits out your struggle and, at the last moment, swings his briefcase down and walks briskly by, without a glance, as you crawl down the platform. His name is Legion. Mrs. Legion, if she is traveling with him, will suggest he help you, the gesture of a member of the no-card, no-fee, universal women's union. The union is strong in Italy. Nevertheless, travel light.

SUSAN SONTAG

(1933–)

Essayist, novelist, philosopher, short story writer, and filmmaker Susan Sontag has been dissecting the human psyche in her essays and fiction for over forty years. Sontag has written on topics as diverse as the meaning of "camp," the need for a less analytical and more intuitive approach to art, an investigation of photography as communication, and an examination of illness in literature and society. She maintains that her work is largely devoid of autobiography. "I've never been tempted to write about my own life," Sontag once said. "Most writers consciously recount and transform their own experiences. But the way in which I found freedom as a writer, and then as a filmmaker, was to invent."

In her novel The Volcano Lover, *published in 1992, Naples' Mt. Vesuvius is the central metaphor. The novel is set in the 1800s; the English Cavaliere is obsessed with the volcano, believing that collecting its fragments will reveal the essence of Vesuvius.*

from THE VOLCANO LOVER

It is my nature to collect, he once told his wife.

"Picture-mad," a friend from his youth called him—one person's nature being another's idea of madness; of immoderate desire.

As a child he collected coins, then automata, then musical instruments. Collecting expresses a free-floating desire that attaches and re-attaches itself—it is a succession of desires. The true collector is in the grip not of what is collected but of collecting. By his early twenties the Cavaliere had already formed and been forced to sell, in order to pay debts, several small collections of paintings.

Upon arriving as envoy he started collecting anew. Within an hour on horseback, Pompeii and Herculaneum were being dug up, stripped, picked over; but everything the ignorant diggers unearthed was supposed to go straight to the storerooms in the nearby royal palace at Portici. He managed to purchase a large collection of Greek vases from a noble family in Rome to whom they had belonged for generations. To collect is to rescue things, valuable things, from neglect, from oblivion, or simply from the ignoble destiny of being in someone else's collection rather than one's own. But buying a whole collection instead of chasing down one's quarry piece by piece—it was not an elegant move. Collecting is also a sport, and its difficulty is part of what gives it honor and zest. A true collector prefers not to acquire in bulk (any more than hunters want the game simply driven past them), is not fulfilled by collecting another's collection: mere acquiring or accumulating is not collecting. But the Cavaliere was impatient. There are not only inner needs and exigencies. And he wanted to get on with what would be but the first of his Neapolitan collections.

No one in England had been surprised that he continued to collect paintings or went after antiquities once he arrived in Naples. But his interest in the volcano displayed a new side of his nature. Being volcano-mad was madder than being picture-mad. Perhaps the sun had gone to his head, or the fabled laxity of the south. Then the passion was quickly rationalized as a scientific interest, and also an aesthetic one, for the eruption of a volcano could be called, stretching the term, beautiful. There was nothing odd in his evenings with guests invited to view the spectacle from the terrace of his country villa near the mountain, like the moonviewing parties of courtiers in Heian Japan. What was odd was that he wanted to be even closer.

The Cavaliere had discovered in himself a taste for the mildly plutonian. He started by riding with one groom out to the sulphurous ground west of the city, and bathing naked in the lake in the cone of a submerged extinct volcano. Walking onto his terrace those first months to see in the distance the well-behaved mountain sitting under the sun might provoke a reverie about the calm that follows catastrophe. Its plume of white smoke, the occasional rumblings and jets of steam seemed *that* perennial, unthreatening. Eighteen thousand villagers in Torre del Greco had died in 1631, an eruption even more lethal than the one in which Herculaneum and Pompeii were entombed and the scholarly admiral of the Roman fleet, the Elder Pliny, famously lost his life, but since then, nothing that could merit the name of disaster.

The mountain had to wake up and start spitting to get the full attention of this much-occupied, much-diverted man. And did so, the year after he arrived. The vapors that drifted up from the summit thickened and grew. Then black smoke mixed with the steam clouds and at night the cone's halo was tinted red. Hitherto absorbed by the hunt for vases and what minor finds from the excavations he could illicitly lay his hands on, he began to climb the mountain and take notes. On his fourth climb, reaching the upper slope, he passed a six-foot hillock of sulphur that hadn't been there the week before. On his next climb up the snow-covered mountain—it was November—the top of the hillock was emitting a blue flame. He drew closer, stood on tiptoe, then a noise like artillery fire above him—behind?—gripped his heart and he leapt backward. Some forty yards higher, at the opening of the crater, a column of black smoke had shot up, followed by an arc of stones, one of which sank near him. Yes.

He was seeing something he had always imagined, always wanted to know.

When an actual eruption began in March of the following year, when a cloud in the shape of a colossal umbrella pine—exactly as described in the letter of Pliny's nephew to Tacitus—poured upward from the mountain, he was at home practicing the cello. Watching from the roof that night, he saw the smoke go flame-red. A few days later there was a thunderous explosion and a gush of red-hot rocks, and that evening at seven o'clock lava began to boil over the top, coursing toward Portici. Taking with him only valet, groom, and local guide, he left the city on horseback and remained all night on the flank of the mountain. Hissing liquid metal on which fiery cinders floated like boats cascaded past him a mere twenty yards away. He experienced himself as fearless, always an agreeable illusion. Dawn rose and he started down. A mile below he caught up with the front of the lava stream, which had pooled in a deep hollow and been stopped.

From then on, the mountain was never free of its smoking wreath, the occasional toss of blazing scoriae, the spurt of fire, the dribble of lava. And now he knew what to do whenever he climbed the mountain. He gathered specimens of cooling lava in a leather pouch lined with lead, he bottled samples of the salts and sulphurs (deep yellow, red, orange) that he fetched from scorchingly hot crevices in the crater top. With the Cavaliere any passion sought the form of, was justified by becoming, a collection. (Soon other people were taking away pieces of the newly interesting volcano, on their one climb up; but accumulating souvenirs is not collecting.) This was pure collecting, shorn of the prospect of profit. Nothing to buy or sell here. Of the volcano he could only make a gift, to his glory and the glory of the volcano.

Fire again appeared at the top: a much more violent display of the mountain's energies was preparing. It grumbled, rattled, and hissed; its emissions of stones more than once obliged even this hardiest of observers to quit the summit. When a great eruption took place the following year, the first full-scale eruption since 1631, he had more booty, a collection of volcanic rocks large and varied enough to be worth presenting to the British Museum, which he shipped back at his own expense. Collecting the volcano was his disinterested passion.

Naples had been added to the Grand Tour, and everybody who came hoped to marvel at the dead cities under the guidance of the learned British envoy. Now that the mountain had shown itself capable of being dangerous again, they wanted to have the great, terrifying experience. It had become another attraction and creator of employment for the ever needy: guides, litter bearers, porters, furnishers of victuals, grooms, and lantern carriers if the ascent was made at night—the best time to see the worst. Anything but impregnable by the standards of real mountains like the Alps, or even of Mount Etna, almost three times as high, Vesuvius offered at most an exertion, sport only for amateurs. The exterminator could be mounted by anyone. For the Cavaliere the volcano was a familiar. He did not find the ascent very strenuous nor the dangers too frightening, whereas most people, underestimating the effort, were appalled by its arduousness, frightened by its vision of injury. Upon their return he would hear the stories of the great risks they had run, of the girandoles of fire, the hail (or shower) of stones, the accompanying racket (cannon, thunder), the infernal, mephitic, sulphurous stench. The very mouth of hell, that's what it is! So people believe it to be here, he would say. Oh, I don't mean literally, the visitor (if English, therefore usually Protestant) would reply.

Yet even as he wished for the volcano not to be profaned by the wheezing, the overweight, and the self-congratulatory, he longed—like any collector—to exhibit it. And was obliged to do so, if the visitor was a friend or relation from England or a foreign dignitary, as long as Vesuvius continued to flaunt its expressiveness. It was expected that he would chaperone an ascent. His eccentric friend from school days at Westminster, Frederick Hervey, about to be made a bishop, came for a long month; he took him up on an Easter Sunday, and Hervey's arm was seared by a morsel of volcanic effluvia; the Cavaliere supposed that he would be boasting about it for the rest of his life.

Hard to imagine that one could feel proprietary about this legendary menace, double-humped, some five thousand feet tall and eight miles from the city, exposed to the view of everyone, indeed the signature feature of the local landscape. No object could be less ownable. Few natural wonders were more famous.

Foreign painters were flocking to Naples: the volcano had many admirers. He set about, by the quality of his attentions, to make it his. He thought about it more than anyone else. My dear mountain. A mountain for a beloved? A monster? With the vases or the paintings or the coins or the statues, he could count on certain conventional recognitions. This passion was about what always surprised, alarmed; what exceeded all expectations; and what never evoked the response that the Cavaliere wanted. But then, to the obsessed collector, the appreciations of other people always seem off-key, withholding, never appreciative enough.

MATTHEW SPENDER

(1945–   )

In the late 1960s sculptor Matthew Spender and his wife, Maro, came to Tuscany: "We came to live near Siena on a whim, tired of the thin blue light of London town. A year or two, we said, not more, or else the hay-seed will germinate in our hair and the red corpuscles in our blood will become stilted with wine lees."

Spender's "year or two" stretched to more than twenty. He, Maro, and their two daughters, Saskia and Cosima, were an "alternative nuclear family." Saskia and Cosima attended a one-room village school while Spender sculpted, painted, and tried to farm.

In the late 1980s, never having written a book, Spender was offered a contract to compose a meditation on his two decades in Tuscany. "I am at the stage of elimination," he wrote. "I know what I cannot do. I cannot write a detailed history; and something without detail, a quick total sketch, can be done better by others . . . I thought I would take just one or two events in the remote past, or even from my own life here, and cover them well, leaving the readers to fill the gaps." The result, Within Tuscany, *is idiosyncratic, personal, and written from an artist's eye.*

San Sano

from WITHIN TUSCANY

We came to live near Siena on a whim, tired of the thin blue light of London town. A year or two, we said, not more, or else the hayseed will germinate in our hair and the red corpuscles in our blood will become silted with wine lees.

We must have had feet that rooted easily. The house had been abandoned for twenty years and still looked friendly. Outside the back door the vines spread from tree to tree in the old style, and we met workmen in the village who could remember who planted them. The sun came through gap-toothed holes in the roof and floors, right down to the stables below. So we latticed them with chestnut rafters, re-tiled and made good, largely with our own hands. The garden grew cabbages and beans, and in the autumn the olives along the dry-stone walls produced fruit that had to be picked and taken to the mill.

Without thinking much about it we acquired two great wheels with which to support the otherwise wholly interior preoccupations of artists. The first was the annual repetition of agricultural duties, shaped by habits that went back to Roman times and punctuated not so much by seasons as by the changing moon and the recurring name-days of saints. Certain things could be seeded on Candlemas, but never before, and a strange piece of doggerel I've now forgotten told you so. This agrarian culture has almost gone, now that the peasants are salaried workers and the eyes of the young are turning to the bright lights of the industrial towns in the valleys.

The second wheel was to have children here, our first daughter, Saskia, and then our second daughter, Cosima, and see the countryside through their eyes, join in the drama of schooling and upbringing, amid a whole flock of once raucous fledglings who are now grown up.

GHOSTS SURROUNDED our first years. We were used to ghosts. In London we had lived in a ramshackle old flat, where Maro, my wife, once saw a red-haired young man staring down at her as she was drifting off to sleep. He proved to be a rare but demanding visitor, this spirit with a hand half raised, like one who has something important to say. (Low corridor, late-eighteenth-century ceiling.)

Here in Tuscany there was the ghost of a malignant sprite, "Like the eye of a chicken," said the bowed man who came to see the house a year or two after we had settled in. "And it followed you from room to room, never left you alone. You'd see it there in front of you, unblinking, just when you'd thought it had gone away! And at night, *una bara,* a coffin, high on the wall in your bedroom. There! See!"

We looked, and saw nothing. Truly, we assured him, we have never lived in a house less filled with anxiety, whatever the weather or season. The old man seemed perplexed. He was down from Montevarchi with his granddaughter, who was evidently bored by country matters. She took his arm to lead him away, but he longed to see every room, searching for the ghosts which had, in the end, driven him from the house, twenty years previously.

"You see," he said, explaining perhaps more to himself than to us, "two families lived here in those days. Fifteen people! And three oxen for the ploughing, seven pigs in the courtyard outside, many sheep on the hill. And so many children! Those animals . . ."

"Maybe it was the ghost of a malevolent chicken," said Maro, and the granddaughter sniggered.

He smiled from politeness, wearily, as if we could never understand. "Were we certain that never . . . ?" and so I took him patiently through the house twice over to make sure that the ghosts were really gone; and then through the garden, where rosemary planted as an ornamental shrub filled him with wonder at the decadence of modern times.

We were Protestants, I told him, and perhaps these ghosts came only to Catholics. A foolish thing to say, but it satisfied him at last. Of course! Protestants! He made it sound as if we had protested against everything, good spirits and bad.

Rebuilding the house retrieved the language for me, first learned up on Lake Garda during summer holidays as a child. I now acquired new words appropriate only to masons. The odd collapsible scaffolds they used were called *"caprette,"* or little goats, as they had small iron horns to stop planks falling off the ends. To do a job quickly, you urged the masons on with the words *"quanto prima,"* a purely Tuscan construction coming straight from the Latin *"quam celerrime."*

And I learned about Tuscan workmen themselves, with their quiet way of moving about the building site, high on humour, low on anger. The image of a long-dead workman comes to mind as I write, who put his feet together like a cricketer when cutting stones. And another who was so terrified of thunder that he went to hide in the cellar during a storm, with his head in his arms. Nobody teased him. In some of those spring tempests, the rain comes rattling over the hills like cavalry on cobbles and the sky for a while seems much too close to the earth.

On a tip from a peasant in the village, I dug for treasure in the cowshed, but found none. The worn stones from its floor were placed in the courtyard around a second-hand ornamental drain. They were of *albarese,* a precipitate limestone that can be cut like flint, with just a hammer, and they came from a pit in the hill-side a hundred yards off.

We altered the structure of the house as little as possible. It had no "original state" to which one could refer. There was supposed to have been an ancient convent on the site, and some bits were definitely older than other bits. But to me the date 1750 carved on the chimney-piece seemed correct: the moment when it became fashionable for Florentines to invest in a new es-tate in the wilds between Florence and Siena, with tax benefits for those who took up the challenge.

In their decline, these buildings were rightly protected. For hygienic reasons it was now illegal to keep cattle in the stalls downstairs, yet it was also illegal to change the stalls to living quarters. In the conversions, which took place twenty-three years ago, these contradictory messages were simply ignored. And recently a law of *condono,* or forgiveness, was passed, allow-ing illegal alterations to be accepted by the government upon payment of a symbolic self-assessed fine—a mystical process that combined repentance from sin with an obol to the government, rather like the sale of indulgences in the sixteenth century, which paid for the Sistine Chapel.

Our only major innovation was a back staircase, rebuilt from a nineteenth-century cowshed we had dismantled. As we were building the staircase, who should come by but Otello, at that time the foreman of Public Works at the local *Comune.* He was just the man the builders most wanted not to see, as of course we had no official permission to build. "Well," he said, "what are you up to here?" Each workman froze in whatever move-ment he happened to be doing, one with a trowel in mid-air, another with slippy-slop cement in a barrow halfway up a ramp. Silence. "Oh well," I said blushing, "you see this staircase was— ah—falling down." Otello acquired a strange interior look of se-rious doubt, then consulted the sky, consulted the ground, and went away. An interesting man, he seldom intervened in life around him, but had an infallible instinct for finding out what went on.

OUR NEAREST NEIGHBOUR was a sharecropper, or *mez-zadro,* called Vittorio Fosi. He told me, in 1968, that the previ-ous year for him had been a good one. He had sold half a *vitellino,* a calf sprung from one of the plough-team, bred for slaughter and kept for most of its brief life in the half-dark of a stall; and the halves of four pigs. The other halves of these ani-mals belonged to the landowner. These sales gave him all the cash he ever needed, he said. He bought shoes and tobacco, and salt from the state monopoly. A little petrol for the motor bike perhaps. Material from the market for his wife to make into clothes. This was as close to self-sufficiency as one could ever imagine in Europe of the late twentieth century.

That first year he ploughed our kitchen garden using the team of white oxen, mother and aunt of the *vitellino.* I remem-ber him talking to them, using odd cow-words to make them start and stop. When I complimented him on their beauty, their patience, their remarkable obedience, he said, "they understand everything: they only lack the power of speech," a remark I found beautiful at the time, as subtle as love, but which I have since discovered was a ritual reply centuries old.

Vittorio and I planted a walnut together in the back garden. Six inches below the surface, we came across a huge rock. Vittorio was delighted. You pull it out, and the hole is made. So the oxen pulled, the tree ten inches high was planted, and today in spring its fragile globe shimmers at the edges for a week or two, before the huge branches fill out with green.

Trees touch their extremities today that I was not even aware I had planted in the same field, twenty years ago.

Looking out at the huge bowl of the walnut yesterday, I heard an echo of long-dead Vittorio's voice, telling me that snakes like its shade, and climb into the branches of walnut trees to mate. This danger could be mitigated by burning at its feet old shoes and rubber tyres.

From Vittorio I learned about the difficult soil I gradually desired to cultivate. When wet, you didn't touch it; you were "better off staying in bed." Shrubs or vegetables planted out in such conditions would bake in a clay pot of your own making, airless in the hardening soil. So we learned to glance at the ground constantly, gauging the state of abrasion or friability as it dried out. When the conditions were perfect, you dropped everything and ploughed—except of course if you had a painting coming along, in which case you postponed it, and then down would come the rain, and away would fly another fortnight while you looked at the ground, waiting.

Eventually I acquired a tractor, but I was never any good at ploughing. The fresh bark of young olives would peel from the trunk as easily as pith off an orange whenever I passed near by. I would postpone the job and it would rain, and when finally I got down to it the couch grass and wild rye would pack the ploughshare at the very moment the furrow was to tip over, clogging the bar that held the brace. Or the far ploughshare would

catch some protruding stone from the eighteenth-century terraces and dump a heap of shale and decayed stone oh-so-neatly
on to the ploughed earth.

Expressionless, or indeed with slight respect, Vittorio would
advise me to keep my hand near the clutch, to disengage if I
were to be so unfortunate as to plough a spur of the living rock
just beneath the topsoil.

Ancestral frugality tinged Vittorio's life. A year after we met I
came across him carving a new yoke for the ox-team from an
oak cut down in the wood. We were restoring the roof at the
time, and, taking advantage of my wonder at his skill as a carpenter, he came up smilingly to talk of little birds, *gli uccellini,*
asking me some favour. Thinking vague thoughts of St. Francis,
I agreed. Whereupon he followed me back to the house, got out
on the roof, and carefully removed from under the tiles all the
young sparrows that were nesting there, tweaking their necks to
make them lie still for the spit.

"Beware of the salamander," said Vittorio. "He is immune to
fire, and his bite is poison."

To feed the family or the animals had the same word: *gov-
ernare.* By contrast, the government, according to Vittorio, did
not "govern," being too busy doing all the eating itself.

From Vittorio we learned how much could be taken from the
hillside, rather than bought in cardboard boxes at the local store.
Pungitopo, a small holly, would clean your chimney if hauled up
and down on a rope or stout string. Acacia was good for the
handles of picks, hoes and *bidenti,* two-pronged mattocks, mentioned in old Latin texts. Pruned trees of *Acer campestre,* the field
maple, could be turned into a living support for the vines. A
weed they called *vetrilla* could be used to polish glass. Some
peasants even grew their own hemp, to make ropes with.

Two years after we came, Vittorio's land was bought by an in-
dustrialist from Brescia who turned him into a salaried worker.
The oxen were sold, the stalls downstairs were closed in accor-
dance with the appropriate regulation on hygiene, and he was
told to work from eight to five every day on a specified wage.

Before this happened, a benevolent government offered him the chance to buy the house he lived in and the land he worked, at an artificially low evaluation, with a loan repayable over forty years, at 2 per cent. In spite of my insistence, he turned this offer down. Forty years, he said, was too long for him to commit himself to an obligation, as he was already fifty years old. He would not die leaving his son in debt.

Too surprised to continue the argument at the time, for a long while I wondered whether this extraordinarily long loan had been offered by the government to *discourage* the survival of a peasant class, while apparently seeming to promote its survival.

Vittorio went into a decline, a kind of culture shock. He had a hunting dog called Whiskers, which, by unfortunate coincidence, was stolen from him about the same time. He went for endless walks in what was to him an apparently vast free time, looking for this dog. I would meet him miles from home, looking miserable.

He survived and became reconciled to his new position, earned much more money than before, lived in the urban metropolis of Gaiole, all one thousand and fifty souls, bought a car. I would see him driving around, always with a good Sunday hat on even inside the car. And if he passed me on the road, I would read his lips saying *"Buon giorno, Signor Matteo,"* as if we had met in the open air, and he behind a pair of white oxen.

When Vittorio died, the postman smiled complacently and told me he had been *"un po' all'antica,"* by which he meant "old-fashioned."

CALVIN TRILLIN

(1935–   )

In his book Third Helpings *Calvin Trillin wrote, "It was at other people's Thanksgiving tables that I first began to articulate my spaghetti carbonara campaign." Trillin's advocacy of Spaghetti Carbonara Day to replace Thanksgiving has a select following, though thus far, he says, Macy's has not come up with a 300-square-foot balloon of spaghetti carbonara for its parade. Trillin's devotion to his cause reflects his enthusiasm for Italian culture; he believes that any society that has handed down spaghetti carbonara is worth revering.*

Trillin has been published in The New York Times Magazine, Travel and Leisure, *and, most often, in* The New Yorker. *Reviewers have found his travel essays refreshing and compare his writing to Twain and Sherwood Anderson.* Travels with Alice, *a collection of essays that includes "Defying Mrs. Tweedie," is set in Europe. In much of Trillin's work, his foil is his sensible wife Alice who, according to her husband, "has seemingly uncontrollable attacks of moderation."*

Defying Mrs. Tweedie

from TRAVELS WITH ALICE

Before Alice and I left for a visit to the Sicilian resort town of Taormina, I consulted *Sunny Sicily* for the observations of Mrs. Alec Tweedie, a rather severe travel writer of late Victorian times who was also the author of *Through Finland in Carts* and, before she caught on to the value of a snappy title, *Danish Versus English Butter Making*. I can't imagine why some people say that I don't have a scholarly approach to travel.

Writing in 1904, Mrs. Tweedie summed up Taormina like this: "The place is being spoilt." It's the sort of comment that can give pause to a traveler who is considering a visit to Taormina somewhat later in the century. Mrs. Tweedie's conclusion that Taormina was being ruined by an influx of English and Americans must have been made, after all, at about the same time the Wright brothers took off at Kitty Hawk—and neither she nor the Wright brothers could have had any notion of the impact of Super-APEX fares. There was no way for me to know whether or not Mrs. Tweedie had been one of those people who simply seem to take great pleasure in telling you that they can recall the time when the place you're about to visit—any place you're about to visit—was actually O.K. ("Pity about the Marquesas. I remember thinking years ago that if that semimonthly prop service from Fiji ever started, that would be it.")

Still, even though Mrs. Tweedie complained bitterly that "the natives have lost their own nice ways," she had to admit that Taormina was "one of the most beautiful spots on earth," an ancient town perched high on a mountain overlooking the Ionian Sea. Also, I had reason to believe that Mrs. Tweedie's standards in matter of spoilage were stricter than my own. She sounded as if she might fit comfortably among those travelers whose measure of authenticity is so exacting that they tend to find even the ruins ruined.

Taormina, in fact, happens to have a noted ruin—a Greek theater where what must have been the cheap seats command such a spectacular view of Mount Etna and the sea and ninety thousand bougainvillea that I can imagine Aristophanes and Euripides sitting around some playwrights' hangout commiserating with each other on how hard it is to hold a Taormina audience's attention. As a matter of fact, Mrs. Tweedie did find that ruin ruined. The Greek theater, she wrote, "is really Roman, as the Romans completely altered it." I have nothing against the Romans myself. How is it possible to dismiss a culture that handed down spaghetti carbonara? Although I don't have much interest in gazing upon volcanic mountains from afar—I find it preferable only to gazing upon them up close—I was, of course, traveling with a connoisseur of views. I always seem to be particularly intent on pleasing Alice during Italian vacations, even if that requires taking in what I would think of as a plethora of views. It may have grown out of my custom of calling her the *principessa* whenever we're traveling in Italy. At some point I found that it improved the service at the hotels.

By Mrs. Tweedie's standards, the natives of Taormina must have lost their own nice ways years before she marched briskly into the piazza, wearing, as I have always envisioned her, a tweed suit, sensible walking shoes, and an authoritative expression. At the time of Mrs. Tweedie's first inspection, the British had been coming to Taormina for thirty years, presumably attracted by an assortment of feasts for the eye—from the long view of Etna and the sea to the constant sight of flowers tumbling over the walls of medieval stone buildings to the sudden surprising slice of sea visible through an alley so narrow that the flower-bedecked balconies on either side almost meet overhead. Those are the sorts of vistas, of course, that only arouse suspicion in somebody with Mrs. Tweedie's keen eye. "Somehow the scene never looks quite real," she complained after taking in a view she found irritatingly gorgeous.

When Mrs. Tweedie was probably still skidding around Finland in a cart, Taormina already had a grand hotel: the San Domenico Palace, which was opened in 1895 in a converted sixteenth-century monastery. Apparently, a visit by Wilhelm II of Prussia made Taormina popular with all sorts of royalty, Vanderbilts and Rothschilds as well as Hohenzollerns—all the more reason to believe, it seemed to me, that the operators of the San Domenico, where we stayed, would know how to treat someone referred to incessantly by her escort as the *principessa*.

Taormina also picked up a reputation as a place that appealed to writers and artists and assorted genteel bohemians. It almost goes without saying that D. H. Lawrence once lived there. Having had D. H. Lawrence residences pointed out to me all over the world, I can only wonder how he got any writing done, what with packing and getting steamship reservations and having to look around for a decent plumber in every new spot. I suspect, though, that Taormina's reputation for harboring exotics comes less from Lawrence than from a German nobleman named Wilhelm von Gloeden, who arrived at about the same time as Wilhelm II and started taking what became well-known photographs of Sicilian boys—some dressed as ancient Greeks, some dressed as girls, and some not dressed at all.

Late in the evening, as I sat in one of the outdoor cafés on Taormina's principal piazza, where one café uses enlargements of von Gloeden photographs to decorate its walls, my thoughts sometimes turned from Sicilian almond pastry to the possibility that von Gloeden and Mrs. Tweedie met in Taormina. The street that dominates the town—the Corso Umberto, a strolling street that bans cars except during early-morning delivery hours— couldn't have changed much from the days when there were no cars to ban, except that in Mrs. Tweedie's time the industrial revolution had not progressed to the point of providing Corso Umberto shops with souvenir T-shirts that say I MAFIOSI TAORMINA. The piazza, known as Piazza Nove Aprile, is a wide spot about halfway down the Corso Umberto where a gap in the buildings along one side of the street for a few hundred feet presents a stunning view of the sea. The jacaranda trees must have been there then, and I suspect the bench alongside the sixteenth-century church was lined with the very same nineteenth-century old folks, sternly watching the evening strollers as if collecting vicarious sins to confess the next day.

I could easily imagine the encounter. Suddenly a man at one of the cafés stands up, trying to keep his composure while gathering up the bulky cameras and tripod he always carries with him. "I really don't see what concern it is of yours, madam," he says in heavily accented English.

Too late. Mrs. Tweedie is bearing down on him, brandishing

the umbrella that made a porter in Palermo sorry that he complained about what had been a perfectly adequate sixpence tip.
Von Gloeden bolts from the café, knocking down a portly mus-
tachioed man (Wilhelm II of Prussia) and caroming off an ice
cream vendor as he races down the street. Mrs. Tweedie is gain-
ing on him.

"Shame! Shame!" she shouts as she waves the lethal umbrella
above her head. "Shame on you, you wicked, wicked man!"

MRS. TWEEDIE couldn't have been the last person to find
Taormina spoiled. I suspect that Tweedie-like comments have
been made about the place pretty steadily ever since. They are
based partly on the belief that Taormina is a European outpost
that is almost unrelated to what Lawrence Durrell called "the
wild precincts of Sicily." It has always been seen as a worldly resort that, by some accident of history, happens to be on the east
coast of Sicily instead of on the Riviera or the Argentario. All of
that is true, of course, even though Taormina seemed stuffed full
of things Sicilian—a vast variety of Sicilian ice cream and Sicilian marzipan and Sicilian pastry, weekly performances of the
traditional Sicilian puppet show, an annual festival celebrating
the intricately painted Sicilian horse cart, and, now and then,
that bracing, life-enhancing smell of pure garlic.

It may be, though, that Taormina has survived as a resort
partly because it always served as a comfortable outpost of Europe on what has traditionally been thought of as a harsh, almost
North African island. The precincts of Sicily are not nearly as
wild as they once were, but the tourist amenities are still spread
pretty thin. A tourist traveling around the island to take in its
Greek and Roman and Byzantine treasures has reason to be
grateful for a place that openly specializes in what the American
army used to call Rest and Rehabilitation. The person who has
been doing the driving on a tour of Sicily may arrive in
Taormina suffering from the sort of nervous exhaustion once
associated with soldiers arriving for R & R in Tokyo from a tour

as artillery spotters in Korea. It is not true, as is often heard in Europe, that Sicilian drivers are unpredictable: they can be counted on to pass. On the highway, Sicilians pass on straight-aways, they pass on hills, they pass on curvy hills and hilly curves. In a large city like Palermo or Catania or Messina, a trav-eler trapped in a motionless line of cars on a conventional two-lane street can suddenly find himself being passed on both the left and the right at the same time.

In Taormina there is no need to drive at all. The layout of the town seems designed for the stroll. The logical way to get to Mazzarò, the beach at the foot of the mountain, is on a funicu-lar, which can't be passed on either side. The big decisions made by visitors to Taormina are on the order of deciding whether to have the grilled shrimp or the grilled swordfish, or deciding whether to take an evening stroll along the Corso Umberto or in the public gardens, where spaces for the benches have been cut out of thick bushes of bougainvillea.

Some friends of ours named Tony and Mary Mackintosh had joined us in Taormina. Mary, a college friend of Alice's, married Tony, who's English, not long after graduation, and they've lived in England ever since. We see them in London or in New York or, now and then, in some third country. As travelers we've al-ways been compatible. They're not the sort of people who are going to push for a stroll in the Corso Umberto if you happen to feel like going to the public gardens instead—they'll just catch up with you in the café later—nor the sort of people who find it troubling that the venue of the evening stroll is the big deci-sion of the day. Which is to say, I suppose, that they're easily en-tertained themselves.

It should be said that once we had made the strolling decision each evening, we did have a couple of other matters to settle. We had to select an appropriate ice cream cone for Alice, and we had to collect entries for our private marzipan contest. As it happens, Alice is even more interested in *gelato*—Italian ice cream—than she is in views. In Taormina we often spent a good part of the evening systematically checking out the various *gela-*

terias, with Alice inspecting the *gelati* displays the way Mrs. Tweedie might have run her eye over a Greek façade that she suspected of having Roman alterations. Our marzipan collection had nothing to do with eating. I'm not sure I know anybody who actually likes to eat marzipan. All of us were simply so astonished at the variety of foodstuffs Sicilians can duplicate in pure marzipan—absolutely realistic bananas and oranges and figs and onions and cucumbers and lobsters—that we thought it only appropriate to give a prize for sheer imagination. For a while we figured the prize would go to a shop near the cathedral that displayed miniature provolone cheeses made of marzipan. Then, on a side street, we discovered the winner. The display consisted of a generous helping of spaghetti, including parsley and cloves of garlic, and next to that a fried egg.

I WASN'T kidding myself. Even though we had taken on those additional responsibilities, Mrs. Tweedie would have accused us of frittering away our time in Taormina, relaxing in a resort when we could have been inspecting ruins or perhaps even studying the difference between Danish and English butter making. If we'd had the sort of gumption Mrs. Tweedie expected from proper tourists, we could have questioned Tony closely on how the English make butter and then picked up the Danish end on some future trip to Scandinavia.

Sitting in a café, I could sometimes imagine Mrs. Tweedie standing before me, like a stern bus-tour guide of vaguely Germanic origins who is outraged at seeing one of her charges having a quiet drink when he's supposed to be on the tour of the glassmaking factory and the eighteenth-century grist mill. "This is not a free morning," she reminds me, in her voice but von Gloeden's accent.

"But Taormina has existed so long as a resort that you can think of it as a historic site itself," I'd say to Mrs. T., edging out of umbrella range as I said it. "Even the cafés."

It's true—or true enough. For instance, a century in the business has left Taormina with a display of just about every sort of hotel that has attracted people to European resorts through changing times and fashions. Between *gelaterias,* we sometimes found ourselves touring hotels—from peaceful, old-fashioned places that conjure up a European resort of the twenties, to those sleek, hard-edged new Italian beach hotels that must retain a couple of porters to go through regularly and remove anything that looks inviting to sit on. In the first few days in Taormina, I seemed to be taking a tour of the San Domenico every time I tried to find my way back to our room—in the "new section," added to the monastery building in 1926. I would wander through courtyards thick with flowers, down high hallways decorated with an occasional icon that seemed to have been left behind by the previous owners, in and out of public rooms that by size and design appeared to have been built for basketball games between the Wilhelm II Royal Five and the Rothschild Bouncing Bankers. Apparently, a lot of people who were not paying guests wanted to take tours of the San Domenico on purpose. A sign outside said, in four languages, IT IS NOT ALLOWED TO VISIT THE HOTEL.

A resort, like an ancient theater, is altered by succeeding occupations. Despite some lingering reputation for elegance and artiness, Taormina had actually become a place that catered mainly to what its more or less official guidebook calls "mass tourism." The English and Americans whose presence troubled Mrs. Tweedie were no longer in evidence; they had been replaced by people on group tours from Italy or Germany or Scandinavia. On a summer Saturday night the Corso Umberto appeared to be dominated by middle-class residents of Catania and Messina who had driven over for a day's outing, making Taormina authentically Sicilian in a way Mrs. Tweedie could never have imagined. Although some prosperous Italian families may always return to the San Domenico for the Christmas holidays, the time had passed when Taormina was the place to observe the sort of chic Europeans seen in resorts like Porto Ercole or Cap Ferrat—the men in spotless white pants and espadrilles, the women looking as if they spend half their time at Gucci and the other half at the gym. Like Greek details in what was eventually converted into a Roman theater, though, the marks of their presence could still be seen in a few hotels and shops; the line of souvenir shops on the Corso Umberto was broken now and then by a fairly elegant antique store or the sort of jewelry store in which purchases are made at a desk rather than a counter, in the manner of negotiating a corporate merger.

The writers' colony had dissolved over the years, leaving as traces a plaque here and there and an occasional art show and some Taormina people's memories of having met Thomas Mann or having had Truman Capote over for dinner. The local people who talked of Taormina's being spoiled were no longer talking about natives losing their own nice ways but about the chic and exotic going elsewhere.

"It used to be much more sophisticated," a man working at one of the hotels told me. "Now the middle classes are traveling more."

I nodded in sympathy. "I was saying as much to the *principessa* today," I said, "as she was selecting her *gelati*."

MARK TWAIN

(1835–1910)

"This book is a record of a pleasure-trip. If it were a record of a solemn scientific expedition, it would have about it that gravity, that profundity, and that impressive incomprehensibility which are so proper to works of that kind, and withal so attractive. . . . I make no apologies for any departures from the usual style of travel writing that may be charged against me—for I think I have seen with impartial eyes, and I am sure I have written at least honestly, whether wisely or not."

So begins Mark Twain's The Innocents Abroad, *a combination travel guide and satirical romp through Europe. Twain was already a well-known author and lecturer before penning* Innocents, *which began as a series of travel letters commissioned by a California newspaper. In 1867 the thirty-two-year old Twain sailed on the cruise ship* The Quaker City *for Europe and the Holy Land. Most of Twain's correspondence is marked by the irreverence and wit that is characteristic of his work. But Pompeii moved him, and his description of "the city of the dead," excerpted here, has a "gravity and profundity" unlike the rest of* The Innocents Abroad.

The Buried City of Pompeii

from THE INNOCENTS ABROAD

They pronounce it Pom-*pay*-e. I always had an idea that you went down into Pompeii with torches, by the way of damp, dark stairways, just as you do in silver mines, and traversed gloomy tunnels with lava overhead and something on either hand like dilapidated prisons gouged out of the solid earth, that faintly resembled houses. But you do nothing of the kind. Fully one-half of the buried city, perhaps, is completely exhumed and thrown open freely to the light of day; and there stand the long rows of solidly-built brick houses (roofless) just as they stood eighteen hundred years ago, hot with the flaming sun; and there lie their floors, clean-swept, and not a bright fragment tarnished or wanting of the labored mosaics that pictured them with the beasts, and birds, and flowers which we copy in perishable carpets to-day; and there are the Venuses, and Bacchuses, and Adonises, making love and getting drunk in many-hued frescoes on the walls of saloon and bed-chamber; and there are the narrow streets and narrower sidewalks, paved with flags of good hard lava, the one deeply rutted with the chariot-wheels, and the other with the passing feet of the Pompeiians of by-gone centuries; and there are the bake-shops, the temples, the halls of justice, the baths, the theatres—all clean-scraped and neat, and suggesting nothing of the nature of a silver mine away down in the bowels of the earth. The broken pillars lying about, the doorless doorways and the crumbled tops of the wilderness of walls, were wonderfully suggestive of the "burnt district" in one of our cities, and if there had been any charred timbers, shattered windows, heaps of debris, and general blackness and smokiness about the place, the resemblance would have been perfect. But no—the sun shines as brightly down on old Pompeii to-day as it did when Christ was born in Bethlehem, and its streets are cleaner a hundred times than ever Pompeiian saw them in her prime. I know whereof I speak—for in the great, chief thoroughfares (Merchant street and the Street of Fortune) have I not seen with my own eyes how for two hundred years at least the pavements were not repaired!—how ruts five and even ten inches deep were worn into the thick flag-stones by the chariot-wheels of generations of swindled tax-payers? And do I not know by these signs that Street Commissioners of Pompeii never attended to their business, and that if they never mended the pavements they never cleaned them? And, besides, is it not the inborn nature of Street Commissioners to avoid their duty whenever they get a chance? I wish I knew the name of the last one that held office in Pompeii so that I could give him a blast. I speak with feeling on this subject, because I caught my foot in one of those ruts, and the sadness that came over me when I saw the first poor skeleton, with ashes and lava sticking to it, was tempered by the reflection that may be that party was the Street Commissioner.

No—Pompeii is no longer a buried city. It is a city of hundreds and hundreds of roofless houses, and a tangled maze of streets where one could easily get lost, without a guide, and have to sleep in some ghostly palace that had known no living tenant since that awful November night of eighteen centuries ago.

We passed through the gate which faces the Mediterranean, (called the "Marine Gate,") and by the rusty, broken image of Minerva, still keeping tireless watch and ward over the possessions it was powerless to save, and went up a long street and stood in the broad court of the Forum of Justice. The floor was level and clean, and up and down either side was a noble colonnade of broken pillars, with their beautiful Ionic and Corinthian columns scattered about them. At the upper end were the vacant seats of the Judges, and behind them we descended into a dungeon where the ashes and cinders had found two prisoners chained on that memorable November night, and tortured them to death. How they must have tugged at the pitiless fetters as the fierce fires surged around them!

Then we lounged through many and many a sumptuous private mansion which we could not have entered without a formal invitation in incomprehensible Latin, in the olden time, when the owners lived there—and we probably wouldn't have got it. These people built their houses a good deal alike. The floors were laid in fanciful figures wrought in mosaics of many-colored marbles. At the threshold your eyes fall upon a Latin sentence of welcome, sometimes, or a picture of a dog, with the legend "Beware of the Dog," and sometimes a picture of a bear or a faun with no inscription at all. Then you enter a sort of vestibule, where they used to keep the hat-rack, I suppose; next a room with a large marble basin in the midst and the pipes of a fountain; on either side are bed-rooms; beyond the fountain is a reception-room, then a little garden, dining-room, and so forth and so on. The floors were all mosaic, the walls were stuccoed, or frescoed, or ornamented with bas-reliefs, and here and there were statues, large and small, and little fish-pools, and cascades of sparkling water that sprang from secret places in the colonnade of handsome pillars that surrounded the court, and kept the flower-beds fresh and the air cool. Those Pompeiians were very luxurious in their tastes and habits. The most exquisite bronzes we have seen in Europe, came from the exhumed cities of Herculaneum and Pompeii, and also the finest cameos and the most delicate engravings on precious stones; their pictures, eighteen or nineteen centuries old, are often much more pleasing than the celebrated rubbish of the old masters of three centuries ago. They were well up in art. From the creation of these works of the first, clear up to the eleventh century, art seems hardly to have existed at all—at least no remnants of it are left— and it was curious to see how far (in some things, at any rate,) these old time pagans excelled the remote generations of masters that came after them. The pride of the world in sculptures seem to be the Laocoön and the Dying Gladiator, in Rome. They are as old as Pompeii, were dug from the earth like Pompeii; but their exact age or who made them can only be conjectured. But worn, and cracked, without a history, and with the blemishing stains of numberless centuries upon them, they still mutely mock at all efforts to rival their perfections.

It was a quaint and curious pastime, wandering through this old silent city of the dead—lounging through utterly deserted streets where thousands and thousands of human beings once bought and sold, and walked and rode, and made the place resound with the noise and confusion of traffic and pleasure. They were not lazy. They hurried in those days. We had evidence of that. There was a temple on one corner, and it was a shorter cut to go between the columns of that temple from one street to the other than to go around—and behold that pathway had been worn deep into the heavy flag-stone floor of the building by generations of time-saving feet! They would not go around when it was quicker to go through. We do that way in our cities.

Every where, you see things that make you wonder how old these old houses were before the night of destruction came—things, too, which bring back those long dead inhabitants and place them living before your eyes. For instance: The steps (two feet thick—lava blocks) that lead up out of the school, and the same kind of steps that lead up into the dress circle of the principal theatre, are almost worn through! For ages the boys hurried out of that school, and for ages their parents hurried into that theatre, and the nervous feet that have been dust and ashes for eighteen centuries have left their record for us to read to-day. I imagined I could see crowds of gentlemen and ladies thronging into the theatre, with tickets for secured seats in their hands, and on the wall, I read the imaginary placard, in infamous grammar, "POSITIVELY NO FREE LIST, EXCEPT MEMBERS OF THE PRESS!" Hanging about the doorway (I fancied,) were slouchy Pompeiian street-boys uttering slang and profanity, and keeping a wary eye out for checks. I entered the theatre, and sat down in one of the long rows of stone benches in the dress circle, and looked at the place for the orchestra, and the ruined stage, and around at the wide sweep of empty boxes, and thought to myself, "This house won't pay." I tried to imagine the music in full blast, the leader of the orchestra beating time, and the "versatile" So-and-So (who had "just returned from a most successful tour in the provinces to play his last and farewell engagement of positively six nights only, in Pompeii, previous to his departure for Herculaneum,") charging around the stage and piling the agony mountains high—but I could not do it with such a "house" as that; those empty benches tied my fancy down to dull reality. I said, these people that ought to be here have been dead, and still, and moldering to dust for ages and ages, and will never care for the trifles and follies of life any more for ever—"Owing to circum-

stances, etc., etc., there will not be any performance tonight."
Close down the curtain. Put out the lights.

And so I turned away and went through shop after shop and
store after store, far down the long street of the merchants, and
called for the wares of Rome and the East, but the tradesmen
were gone, the marts were silent, and nothing was left but the
broken jars all set in cement of cinders and ashes: the wine and
the oil that once had filled them were gone with their owners.

In a bake-shop was a mill for grinding the grain, and the furnaces for baking the bread: and they say that here, in the same
furnaces, the exhumers of Pompeii found nice, well baked
loaves which the baker had not found time to remove from the
ovens the last time he left his shop, because circumstances compelled him to leave in such a hurry.

In one house (the only building in Pompeii which no woman
is now allowed to enter,) were the small rooms and short beds of
solid masonry, just as they were in the old times, and on the
walls were pictures which looked almost as fresh as if they were
painted yesterday, but which no pen could have the hardihood
to describe; and here and there were Latin inscriptions—obscene scintillations of wit, scratched by hands that possibly were
uplifted to Heaven for succor in the midst of a driving storm of
fire before the night was done.

In one of the principal streets was a ponderous stone tank,
and a water-spout that supplied it, and where the tired, heated
toilers from the Campagna used to rest their right hands when
they bent over to put their lips to the spout, the thick stone was
worn down to a broad groove an inch or two deep. Think of the
countless thousands of hands that had pressed that spot in the
ages that are gone, to so reduce a stone that is as hard as iron!

They had a great public bulletin board in Pompeii—a place
where announcements for gladiatorial combats, elections, and
such things, were posted—not on perishable paper, but carved
in enduring stone. One lady, who, I take it, was rich and well
brought up, advertised a dwelling or so to rent, with baths and
all the modern improvements, and several hundred shops, stipu-

lating that the dwellings should not be put to immoral purposes. You can find out who lived in many a house in Pompeii by the carved stone door-plates affixed to them: and in the same way you can tell who they were that occupy the tombs. Every where around are things that reveal to you something of the customs and history of this forgotten people. But what would a volcano leave of an American city, if it once rained its cinders on it? Hardly a sign or a symbol to tell its story.

In one of these long Pompeiian halls the skeleton of a man was found, with ten pieces of gold in one hand and a large key in the other. He had seized his money and started toward the door, but the fiery tempest caught him at the very threshold, and he sank down and died. One more minute of precious time would have saved him. I saw the skeletons of a man, a woman, and two young girls. The woman had her hands spread wide apart, as if in mortal terror, and I imagined I could still trace upon her shapeless face something of the expression of wild despair that distorted it when the heavens rained fire in these streets, so many ages ago. The girls and the man lay with their faces upon their arms, as if they had tried to shield them from the enveloping cinders. In one apartment eighteen skeletons were found, all in sitting postures, and blackened places on the walls still mark their shapes and show their attitudes, like shadows. One of them, a woman, still wore upon her skeleton throat a necklace, with her name engraved upon it—JULIE DI DIOMEDE.

But perhaps the most poetical thing Pompeii has yielded to modern research, was that grand figure of a Roman soldier, clad in complete armor; who, true to his duty, true to his proud name of a soldier of Rome, and full of the stern courage which had given to that name its glory, stood to his post by the city gate, erect and unflinching, till the hell that raged around him *burned out* the dauntless spirit it could not conquer.

We never read of Pompeii but we think of that soldier; we can not write of Pompeii without the natural impulse to grant to him the mention he so well deserves. Let us remember that he was a soldier—not a policeman—and so, praise him. Being a soldier, he staid,—because the warrior instinct forbade him to fly. Had he been a policeman he would have staid, also—because he would have been asleep.

There are not half a dozen flights of stairs in Pompeii, and no other evidences that the houses were more than one story high. The people did not live in the clouds, as do the Venetians, the Genoese and Neapolitans of to-day.

We came out from under the solemn mysteries of this city of the Venerable Past—this city which perished, with all its old ways and its quaint old fashions about it, remote centuries ago, when the Disciples were preaching the new religion, which is as old as the hills to us now—and went dreaming among the trees that grow over acres and acres of its still buried streets and squares, till a shrill whistle and the cry of *"All aboard—last train for Naples!"* woke me up and reminded me that I belonged in the nineteenth century, and was not a dusty mummy, caked with ashes and cinders, eighteen hundred years old. The transition was startling. The idea of a railroad train actually running to old dead Pompeii, and whistling irreverently, and calling for passengers in the most bustling and business-like way, was as strange a thing as one could imagine, and as unpoetical and disagreeable as it was strange.

Compare the cheerful life and the sunshine of this day with the horrors the younger Pliny saw here, the 9th of November, A.D. 79, when he was so bravely striving to remove his mother out of reach of harm, while she begged him, with all a mother's unselfishness, to leave her to perish and save himself.

> "By this time the murky darkness had so increased that one might have believed himself abroad in a black and moonless night, or in a chamber where all the lights had been extinguished. On every hand was heard the complaints of women, the wailing of children, and the cries of men. One called his father, another his son, and another his wife, and only by their voices could they know each other. Many in their despair begged that death would come and end their distress.

"Some implored the gods to succor them, and some believed that this night was the last, the eternal night which should engulf the universe!

"Even so it seemed to me—and I consoled myself for the coming death with the reflection: BEHOLD, THE WORLD IS PASSING AWAY!"

AFTER BROWSING among the stately ruins of Rome, of Baiæ, of Pompeii, and after glancing down the long marble ranks of battered and nameless imperial heads that stretch down the corridors of the Vatican, one thing strikes me with a force it never had before: the unsubstantial, unlasting character of fame. Men lived long lives, in the olden time, and struggled feverishly through them, toiling like slaves, in oratory, in generalship, or in literature, and then laid them down and died, happy in the possession of an enduring history and a deathless name. Well, twenty little centuries flutter away, and what is left of these things? A crazy inscription on a block of stone, which snuffy antiquaries bother over and tangle up and make nothing out of but a bare name (which they spell wrong)— no history, no tradition, no poetry—nothing that can give it even a passing interest. What may be left of General Grant's great name forty centuries hence? This—in the Encyclopedia for A.D. 5868, possibly:

"URIAH S. (or Z.) GRAUNT—popular poet of ancient times in the Aztec provinces of the United States of British America. Some authors say flourished about A.D. 742; but the learned Ah-ah Foo-foo states that he was a contemporary of Scharkspyre, the English poet, and flourished about A.D. 1328, some three centuries *after* the Trojan war instead of before it. He wrote 'Rock me to Sleep, Mother.'"

These thoughts sadden me. I will to bed.

GORE VIDAL

(1925–   )

"I'm exactly as I appear," said Gore Vidal. "There is no lovable person inside. Beneath my cold exterior, once you break the ice, you find cold water." For more than fifty years Vidal has been wielding his acid pen, but Italy, his home for decades, has been largely spared his scorn. Perhaps this is because Vidal has traced his family to a small province outside of Venice. He discovered that the Vidalhaus family of Austria emigrated south in 1590 and became the Vidales of Italy. "I knew ecstasy!" reported Vidal. "The Vidals had gone south to be doges."

Despite his Venetian connection, Vidal avoided visiting Venice for a long time: "Why fall in love with that glorious light which Canaletto and Bellotti and Guardi have dealt with so much better than the retinas of my myopic eyes could ever do?" Finally, in the late 1960s Clare Booth Luce persuaded Vidal to see Venice, and he now returns at least once a year. He wrote and appeared in a two-hour documentary about Venice and wrote the book Vidal in Venice, *from which this excerpt is taken.*

Gore Vidal makes his home in a villa in Ravello, Italy.

The City Today

from VIDAL IN VENICE

Venice Incorporated is still very much in business. The tourists arrive in their hundreds of thousands from all over the world. In fact, it seems to be an integral law of tourism that the smaller the place, the bigger the crowd. Today there are only 83,000 Venetians residing in historic Venice. The modern Venetian, though detesting the crowded *vaporetti* and streets as much as the visitors do, has adapted himself to the situation. "Venetians are like aquatic birds, now on sea, now on land," Cassiodorus wrote in the sixth century. Always bobbing about for a morsel or for prey. Since few of today's Venetian birds can afford to migrate to equally bountiful climes when winter comes, their sometimes pelican-like appetite during the warmer months, when the tourists also are bobbing about on the lagoon, may be explained as their natural way of storing up enough nourishing funds for the leaner months. Few are the Venetian families of any class who do not benefit, directly or indirectly, from the annual invasion of tourists. In fact, many spend the winter months preening themselves for the onslaught. If they are hotelkeepers that might take the form of devising ways of turning two single bedrooms into three.

Survival, and success, began and ended with boats—with rowing, with the great galleys. Fathers taught sons, generation after generation. The Voga Longa, or "Long Row," is not a race so much as a commemoration, a reminder to Venetians of who they once were—and are. Each spring, all Venetians who want to take part in the newly-established Voga Longa can do so. The route round the lagoon and back to the Grand Canal is twenty miles long. Venetians row standing up so that they can study the water and the treacherous mud. Venetians, by nature, are watchful.

They also stand up to row because the shallowness of most of the small canals gives them the chance to use their oars as poles. They invented the gondola, with its flat bottom, to allow them to glide along the surface of the water, and to free the boat more easily from mudbanks. Even the *vaporetti* have been designed especially by Venetians for local needs; but they are, of course, no longer propelled by steam (*vapore*), but diesel oil. The American novelist, William Dean Howells, as a young American consul in Venice in the 1860s, said that the first steam-operated public transport boats were called "omnibuses," so our seemingly silly translation of "water-bus" for *vaporetto* has a precedent.

Surely the last book to recommend that visitors should see Venice by the traditional means of transport, rather than as a special treat, was published in London as late as 1954. The sentence "Your gondola passes among these humble folk [on the Giudecca] as in a dream," brings today's reader up with a start, as if the author, Edward Hutton, had suddenly transferred himself backwards into the last century.

There were once more than 10,000 gondolas in Venice, which conjures up the image of frequent traffic jams. By the mid-1600s, the number was reduced to about 8,500, and today there are said to be some 350 gondolas in Venice, though many of those may be in semi-permanent drydock. Once a gondola's oars were handed down from father to son, as the boat's life span was half a century. Now, because of the damage done by the waves of motorboats and water-taxis, a gondola becomes firewood after twenty years. A few years ago, a private German-Italian committee was set up to save the gondola from total extinction. In plain words, this meant subsidising the last remaining gondola shipyard, which is near the S. Trovaso Church. It also meant finding and training young men to build the boats, which is still the Committee's main problem. A fully-fitted gondola, with all accessories, none of them really optional, costs between 12,000 and 15,000 dollars. If one could persuade Arab or Texan oil millionaires that life is but an incomplete dream without a gondola moored by the front porch, the craft might attract more young builders and guarantee the continuous presence of the gondola in the city of its invention.

If any Venetian family still owns a private gondola, it almost certainly does not maintain its own gondolier any longer. (The Cassa di Risparmio, the powerful local Savings Bank, has a splendid gondola, brought out on great occasions, but rowed by a professional gondolier hired for the day.) It now officially costs 50,000 lire to hire a manned gondola for a 50-minute hour, though that is likely to be your starting price; the final fee will be agreed upon when you near the gondolier's own estimate. Divided between four or six passengers, the price is right for a rare experience.

You can also say you have been on a gondola ride by taking one of the gondola ferries, which will pole you across the Grand Canal at six authorised and often essential points. The current charge for the 90-second shuttle, which one Venetian said recently used to be roughly the same as the cost of a pack of cigarettes, is now ridiculously low—200 lire, or one-tenth the cost of a pack. These ferries are primarily for local use, by countesses, their poodles, and delivery boys. Passengers are expected to stand up, perfectly balanced, during the brief crossing. They are not recommended for vertiginous tourists.

Life goes on, with or without an empire. There are no doges now, there is no fleet, there are no victorious admirals. But there are still Venetian heroes. . . . Like Arrigo Cipriani, hereditary proprietor of the world's most famous bar, Harry's Bar. Cipriani is a new representative of an old tradition, that is to say, he is a highly ingenious creator of what the Venetians still most respect—wealth for their city.

Harry's Bar may be Venice's most successful invention since Venice itself. In 1931, an American lamented with his favourite hotel bartender, the late Giuseppe Cipriani, that what Venice lacked was a good bar. The American, whose name was Harry, probably was not the first refugee from American Prohibition to make that observation, although the lengthy Venetian chronicles of two other Americans, Henry James and William Dean Howells, carry no mention of the city's lack of saloons. But Harry was the first to follow the inbred American tradition of wanting to set right a wrong. This was done in the form of financial backing to Cipriani, who found a rope storeroom next to the St. Mark's *vaporetto* stop and there opened what he called Harry's Bar.

Even without knowing the origin of its history, some American visitors today consider Harry's Bar as being almost extraterritorially *theirs*. Since the closing of the American consulate in the 1970s, it is indeed sometimes the only place for Americans in acute distress to go for comfort and advice. However, Harry's Bar was and remains an entirely Venetian operation, though the babble of barbaric voices on summer days and nights is predominantly American. Most important, it is an innovation, perhaps the only one in the ancient city, which has been accepted by the Venetians. It has become one of their own monuments. Like most natives everywhere, they may shy away from actually visiting their monuments (call it the Grant's Tomb or Tower of London syndrome), but they like to know that it is there, and that it is appreciated and frequented by foreign visitors. The bar and the restaurant are always under the watchful eye of Arrigo (the nearest Italian equivalent of Harry), and when he and his son, Roberto, rowed in the Voga Longa race, they were cheered by the Venetians lining the embankments as local heroes. Nothing succeeds like success, and in Venice nothing succeeds like selling Venice, particularly to satisfied customers.

The only legal gambling today in Venice is still run by the local government, at the winter casino in the Vendramin Palace and at the summer casino on the Lido. Carnival faded away with the Republic itself; but an attempt to revive it, as a tourist attraction, came in with the new Communist-Socialist city council in the early 1980s. In 1985, they also planned to revive bull-fighting in Campo S. Polo, guaranteeing that it would be bloodless, with imported torreros only "worrying" the bulls. Meanwhile, until the bulls arrive, as a distraction, they held a "Miss Courtesan of 1985" contest.

If each Carnival visitor was obliged to take home one Venetian pigeon, the pigeon problem could have been resolved. For pigeon droppings can, and do, corrode marble. The city fathers now plan to import jackdaws (the *corvus monedula*) from Holland, giving them a municipal roost in the eaves of the Frari Church. The jackdaw is a noted thief, with a passion for other birds' nests. It is reckoned that in five years' time, the pigeons will be permanently and "naturally" evicted by the thieving birds from St. Mark's Square, itself a showcase for stolen treasures from the past. The bailiffs who stand guard outside the church will, doubtless, be warned that the jackdaw reputedly likes to steal gold coins. Otherwise, the final solution to Venice's pigeon problem might well bring an end to the church's gold mosaics, as chip by chip they are spirited away to stolen nests.

Why do people still come to Venice, a city not easy of access and certainly not easy on the tourist's budget? What am I doing in St. Mark's Square when I've never met a pigeon that I liked? What are *they* doing here—all these people? Millions come here every year, and thousands came in past centuries. (And I am improvising, rather desperately, dialogue to a camera in the far distance as pigeons and tourists stare in horror at the man talking loudly to himself.) Well, I have a hunch that most of the people who come here hope to find something that they've never known before. For the visitor it is a sort of waking dream. Naturally, no Venetian ever dreams this Venice, but every Venetian works to evoke it for others.

Water gave birth to Venice. Water protected Venice from enemies. Water made Venice rich, first through the salt trade, then with ships and commerce. Now it is the tourists who make Venice rich, who come to see themselves reflected. Venetian glass is like Venetian water. You are reflected. The reflection is real, but is the thing reflected real? Venetians tend to prefer reflections to the flesh and the mask to either. As the twentieth century draws to a close, no one knows quite what to expect, if anything, of the future. There is a strong need for magic, for a place that is outside of time, for a postponement of reality. For Venice.

EDITH WHARTON

(1862–1937)

Italy's terrain was imprinted on Edith Wharton in childhood. In the 1860s her family, members of New York's social aristocracy, lived in Rome and Florence. Although she eventually made her home in France, Italy was one of Wharton's favorite destinations and literary settings. Her first real success was The Valley of Decision, *published in 1902 and set in eighteenth-century Italy. The next year Wharton traveled throughout northern Italy researching a series of articles commissioned by* Century Magazine. *Her impressions were published in her book* Italian Backgrounds *in 1905. About the same time, Wharton bought her first car and learned to drive. She was an enthusiastic fan of "motorflight" and often organized elaborate, extended trips through Italy.*

At first glance Wharton's short story "Roman Fever" seems to owe more to O. Henry than to her mentor Henry James. However, the finely wrought New York widows Mrs. Ansley and Mrs. Slade are typical Wharton characters, hiding secrets beneath a veneer of civility.

Roman Fever

I

From the table at which they had been lunching two American ladies of ripe but well-cared-for middle age moved across the lofty terrace of the Roman restaurant and, leaning on its parapet, looked first at each other, and then down on the outspread glories of the Palatine and the Forum, with the same expression of vague but benevolent approval.

As they leaned there a girlish voice echoed up gaily from the stairs leading to the court below. "Well, come along, then," it cried, not to them but to an invisible companion, "and let's leave the young things to their knitting"; and a voice as fresh laughed back: "Oh, look here, Babs, not actually *knitting*—" "Well, I mean figuratively," rejoined the first. "After all, we haven't left our poor parents much else to do . . ." and at that point the turn of the stairs engulfed the dialogue.

The two ladies looked at each other again, this time with a tinge of smiling embarrassment, and the smaller and paler one shook her head and coloured slightly.

"Barbara!" she murmured, sending an unheard rebuke after the mocking voice in the stairway.

The other lady, who was fuller, and higher in colour, with a small determined nose supported by vigorous black eyebrows, gave a good-humoured laugh. "That's what our daughters think of us!"

Her companion replied by a deprecating gesture. "Not of us individually. We must remember that. It's just the collective modern idea of Mothers. And you see—" Half guiltily she drew from her handsomely mounted black hand-bag a twist of crimson silk run through by two fine knitting needles. "One never knows," she murmured. "The new system has certainly given us a good deal of time to kill; and sometimes I get tired just look-ing—even at this." Her gesture was now addressed to the stu-pendous scene at their feet.

The dark lady laughed again, and they both relapsed upon the view, contemplating it in silence, with a sort of diffused serenity which might have been borrowed from the spring effulgence of the Roman skies. The luncheon-hour was long past, and the two had their end of the vast terrace to themselves. At its oppo-site extremity a few groups, detained by a lingering look at the outspread city, were gathering up guide-books and fumbling for tips. The last of them scattered, and the two ladies were alone on the air-washed height.

"Well, I don't see why we shouldn't just stay here," said Mrs. Slade, the lady of the high colour and energetic brows. Two derelict basket-chairs stood near, and she pushed them into the angle of the parapet, and settled herself in one, her gaze upon the Palatine. "After all, it's still the most beautiful view in the world."

"It always will be, to me," assented her friend Mrs. Ansley, with so slight a stress on the "me" that Mrs. Slade, though she noticed it, wondered if it were not merely accidental, like the random underlinings of old-fashioned letter-writers.

"Grace Ansley was always old-fashioned," she thought; and added aloud, with a retrospective smile: "It's a view we've both been familiar with for a good many years. When we first met here we were younger than our girls are now. You remember?"

"Oh, yes, I remember," murmured Mrs. Ansley, with the same undefinable stress.—"There's that head-waiter wondering," she interpolated. She was evidently far less sure than her companion of herself and of her rights in the world.

"I'll cure him of wondering," said Mrs. Slade, stretching her hand toward a bag as discreetly opulent-looking as Mrs. Ansley's. Signing to the head-waiter, she explained that she and her friend were old lovers of Rome, and would like to spend the end of the afternoon looking down on the view—that is, if it did not disturb the service? The head-waiter, bowing over her gratuity, assured her that the ladies were most welcome, and would be still more so if they would condescend to remain for dinner. A full moon night, they would remember . . .

Mrs. Slade's black brows drew together, as though references to the moon were out-of-place and even unwelcome. But she smiled away her frown as the head-waiter retreated. "Well, why not? We might do worse. There's no knowing, I suppose, when the girls will be back. Do you even know back from *where?* I don't!"

Mrs. Ansley again coloured slightly. "I think those young Italian aviators we met at the Embassy invited them to fly to Tarquinia for tea. I suppose they'll want to wait and fly back by moonlight."

"Moonlight—moonlight! What a part it still plays. Do you suppose they're as sentimental as we were?"

"I've come to the conclusion that I don't in the least know what they are," said Mrs. Ansley. "And perhaps we didn't know much more about each other."

"No; perhaps we didn't."

Her friend gave her a shy glance. "I never should have supposed you were sentimental, Alida."

"Well, perhaps I wasn't." Mrs. Slade drew her lids together in retrospect; and for a few moments the two ladies, who had been intimate since childhood, reflected how little they knew each other. Each one, of course, had a label ready to attach to the other's name; Mrs. Delphin Slade, for instance, would have told herself, or any one who asked her, that Mrs. Horace Ansley, twenty-five years ago, had been exquisitely lovely—no, you wouldn't believe it, would you? . . . though, of course, still charming, distinguished . . . Well, as a girl she had been exquisite; far more beautiful than her daughter Barbara, though certainly Babs, according to the new standards at any rate, was more effective—had more *edge,* as they say. Funny where she got it, with those two nullities as parents. Yes; Horace Ansley was—well, just the duplicate of his wife. Museum specimens of old New York. Good-looking, irreproachable, exemplary. Mrs. Slade and Mrs. Ansley had lived opposite each other—actually as well as figuratively—for years. When the drawing-room curtains in No. 20 East 73rd Street were renewed, No. 23, across the way, was always aware of it. And of all the movings, buyings, travels, anniversaries, illnesses—the tame chronicle of an estimable pair. Little of it escaped Mrs. Slade. But she had grown bored with it by the time her husband made his big *coup* in Wall Street, and when they bought in upper Park Avenue had already begun to think: "I'd rather live opposite a speak-easy for a change; at least one might see it raided." The idea of seeing Grace raided was so amusing that (before the move) she launched it at a woman's lunch. It made a hit, and went the rounds—she sometimes wondered if it had crossed the street, and reached Mrs. Ansley. She hoped not, but didn't much mind. Those were the days when respectability was at a discount, and it did the irreproachable no harm to laugh at them a little.

A few years later, and not many months apart, both ladies lost their husbands. There was an appropriate exchange of wreaths and condolences, and a brief renewal of intimacy in the half-shadow of their mourning; and now, after another interval, they had run across each other in Rome, at the same hotel, each of them the modest appendage of a salient daughter. The similarity of their lot had again drawn them together, lending itself to mild jokes, and the mutual confession that, if in old days it must have been tiring to "keep up" with daughters, it was now, at times, a little dull not to.

No doubt, Mrs. Slade reflected, she felt her unemployment more than poor Grace ever would. It was a big drop from being the wife of Delphin Slade to being his widow. She had always regarded herself (with a certain conjugal pride) as his equal in social gifts, as contributing her full share to the making of the exceptional couple they were: but the difference after his death was irremediable. As the wife of the famous corporation lawyer, always with an international case or two on hand, every day brought its exciting and unexpected obligation: the impromptu entertaining of eminent colleagues from abroad, the hurried dashes on legal business to London, Paris or Rome, where the entertaining was so handsomely reciprocated; the amusement of hearing in her wake: "What, that handsome woman with the good clothes and the eyes is Mrs. Slade—*the* Slade's wife? Really? Generally the wives of celebrities are such frumps."

Yes; being *the* Slade's widow was a dullish business after that. In living up to such a husband all her faculties had been engaged; now she had only her daughter to live up to, for the son who seemed to have inherited his father's gifts had died suddenly in boyhood. She had fought through that agony because her husband was there, to be helped and to help; now, after the father's death, the thought of the boy had become unbearable. There was nothing left but to mother her daughter; and dear Jenny was such a perfect daughter that she needed no excessive mothering. "Now with Babs Ansley I don't know that I *should* be so quiet," Mrs. Slade sometimes half-enviously reflected; but

Jenny, who was younger than her brilliant friend, was that rare accident, an extremely pretty girl who somehow made youth and prettiness seem as safe as their absence. It was all perplexing—and to Mrs. Slade a little boring. She wished that Jenny would fall in love—with the wrong man, even; that she might have to be watched, out-manoeuvred, rescued. And instead, it was Jenny who watched her mother, kept her out of draughts, made sure that she had taken her tonic . . .

Mrs. Ansley was much less articulate than her friend, and her mental portrait of Mrs. Slade was slighter, and drawn with fainter touches. "Alida Slade's awfully brilliant; but not as brilliant as she thinks," would have summed it up; though she would have added, for the enlightenment of strangers, that Mrs. Slade had been an extremely dashing girl; much more so than her daughter, who was pretty, of course, and clever in a way, but had none of her mother's—well, "vividness," some one had once called it. Mrs. Ansley would take up current words like this, and cite them in quotation marks, as unheard-of audacities. No; Jenny was not like her mother. Sometimes Mrs. Ansley thought Alida Slade was disappointed; on the whole she had had a sad life. Full of failures and mistakes; Mrs. Ansley had always been rather sorry for her . . .

So these two ladies visualized each other, each through the wrong end of her little telescope.

II

For a long time they continued to sit side by side without speaking. It seemed as though, to both, there was a relief in laying down their somewhat futile activities in the presence of the vast Memento Mori which faced them. Mrs. Slade sat quite still, her eyes fixed on the golden slope of the Palace of the Caesars, and after a while Mrs. Ansley ceased to fidget with her bag, and she too sank into meditation. Like many intimate friends, the two ladies had never before had occasion to be silent together, and Mrs. Ansley was slightly embarrassed by what seemed, after so many years, a new stage in their intimacy, and one with which she did not yet know how to deal.

Suddenly the air was full of that deep clangour of bells which periodically covers Rome with a roof of silver. Mrs. Slade glanced at her wristwatch. "Five o'clock already," she said, as though surprised.

Mrs. Ansley suggested interrogatively: "There's bridge at the Embassy at five." For a long time Mrs. Slade did not answer. She appeared to be lost in contemplation, and Mrs. Ansley thought the remark had escaped her. But after a while she said, as if speaking out of a dream: "Bridge, did you say? Not unless you want to . . . But I don't think I will, you know."

"Oh, no," Mrs. Ansley hastened to assure her. "I don't care to at all. It's so lovely here; and so full of old memories, as you say." She settled herself in her chair, and almost furtively drew forth her knitting. Mrs. Slade took sideway note of this activity, but her own beautifully cared-for hands remained motionless on her knee.

"I was just thinking," she said slowly, "what different things Rome stands for to each generation of travellers. To our grand-mothers, Roman fever; to our mothers, sentimental dangers—how we used to be guarded! —to our daughters, no more dangers than the middle of Main Street. They don't know it—but how much they're missing!"

The long golden light was beginning to pale, and Mrs. Ans-ley lifted her knitting a little closer to her eyes "Yes; how we were guarded!"

"I always used to think," Mrs. Slade continued, "that our mothers had a much more difficult job than our grandmothers. When Roman fever stalked the streets it must have been com-paratively easy to gather in the girls at the danger hour; but when you and I were young, with such beauty calling us, and the spice of disobedience thrown in, and no worse risk than catching cold during the cool hour after sunset, the mothers used to be put to it to keep us in—didn't they?"

She turned again toward Mrs. Ansley, but the latter had

reached a delicate point in her knitting. "One, two, three—slip two; yes, they must have been," she assented, without looking up.

Mrs. Slade's eyes rested on her with a deepened attention. "She can knit—in the face of *this!* How like her . . ."

Mrs. Slade leaned back, brooding, her eyes ranging from the ruins which faced her to the long green hollow of the Forum, the fading glow of the church fronts beyond it, and the outlying immensity of the Colosseum. Suddenly she thought: "It's all very well to say that our girls have done away with sentiment and moonlight. But if Babs Ansley isn't out to catch that young aviator—the one who's a Marchese—then I don't know anything. And Jenny has no chance beside her. I know that too. I wonder if that's why Grace Ansley likes the two girls to go everywhere together? My poor Jenny as a foil—!" Mrs. Slade gave a hardly audible laugh, and at the sound Mrs. Ansley dropped her knitting.

"Yes—?"

"I—oh, nothing. I was only thinking how your Babs carries everything before her. That Campolieri boy is one of the best matches in Rome. Don't look so innocent, my dear—you know he is. And I was wondering, ever so respectfully, you understand . . . wondering how two such exemplary characters as you and Horace had managed to produce anything quite so dynamic." Mrs. Slade laughed again, with a touch of asperity.

Mrs. Ansley's hands lay inert across her needles. She looked straight out at the great accumulated wreckage of passion and splendour at her feet. But her small profile was almost expressionless. At length she said: "I think you overrate Babs, my dear."

Mrs. Slade's tone grew easier. "No; I don't. I appreciate her. And perhaps envy you. Oh, my girl's perfect; if I were a chronic invalid I'd— well, I think I'd rather be in Jenny's hands. There must be times . . . but there! I always wanted a brilliant daughter . . . and never quite understood why I got an angel instead."

Mrs. Ansley echoed her laugh in a faint murmur. "Babs is an angel too."

"Of course—of course! But she's got rainbow wings. Well,

they're wandering by the sea with their young men; and here we sit . . . and it all brings back the past a little too acutely."

Mrs. Ansley had resumed her knitting. One might almost have imagined (if one had known her less well, Mrs. Slade reflected) that, for her also, too many memories rose from the lengthening shadows of those august ruins. But no; she was simply absorbed in her work. What was there for her to worry about? She knew that Babs would almost certainly come back engaged to the extremely eligible Campolieri. "And she'll sell the New York house, and settle down near them in Rome, and never be in their way . . . she's much too tactful. But she'll have an excellent cook, and just the right people in for bridge and cocktails . . . and a perfectly peaceful old age among her grandchildren."

Mrs. Slade broke off this prophetic flight with a recoil of self-disgust. There was no one of whom she had less right to think unkindly than of Grace Ansley. Would she never cure herself of envying her? Perhaps she had begun too long ago.

She stood up and leaned against the parapet, filling her troubled eyes with the tranquillizing magic of the hour. But instead of tranquillizing her the sight seemed to increase her exasperation. Her gaze turned toward the Colosseum. Already its golden flank was drowned in purple shadow, and above it the sky curved crystal clear, without light or colour. It was the moment when afternoon and evening hang balanced in mid-heaven.

Mrs. Slade turned back and laid her hand on her friend's arm. The gesture was so abrupt that Mrs. Ansley looked up, startled.

"The sun's set. You're not afraid, my dear?"

"Afraid—?"

"Of Roman fever or pneumonia? I remember how ill you were that winter. As a girl you had a very delicate throat, hadn't you?"

"Oh, we're all right up here. Down below, in the Forum, it does get deathly cold, all of a sudden . . . but not here."

"Ah, of course you know because you had to be so careful." Mrs. Slade turned back to the parapet. She thought: "I must make one more effort not to hate her." Aloud she said: "Whenever I look at the Forum from up here I remember that story about a great-aunt of yours, wasn't she? A dreadfully wicked great-aunt?"

"Oh yes; Great-aunt Harriet. The one who was supposed to have sent her young sister out to the Forum after sunset to gather a night-blooming flower for her album. All our great-aunts and grandmothers used to have albums of dried flowers."

Mrs. Slade nodded. "But she really sent her because they were in love with the same man—"

"Well, that was the family tradition. They said Aunt Harriet confessed it years afterward. At any rate, the poor little sister caught the fever and died. Mother used to frighten us with the story when we were children."

"And you frightened *me* with it, that winter when you and I were here as girls. The winter I was engaged to Delphin."

Mrs. Ansley gave a faint laugh. "Oh, did I? Really frightened you? I don't believe you're easily frightened."

"Not often; but I was then. I was easily frightened because I was too happy. I wonder if you know what that means?"

"I—yes . . ." Mrs. Ansley faltered.

"Well, I suppose that was why the story of your wicked aunt made such an impression on me. And I thought: 'There's no more Roman fever, but the Forum is deathly cold after sunset—especially after a hot day. And the Colosseum's even colder and damper.'"

"The Colosseum—?"

"Yes. It wasn't easy to get in, after the gates were locked for the night. Far from easy. Still, in those days it could be managed; it was managed, often. Lovers met there who couldn't meet elsewhere. You knew that?"

"I—I daresay. I don't remember."

"You don't remember? You don't remember going to visit some ruins or other one evening, just after dark, and catching a bad chill? You were supposed to have gone to see the moon rise. People always said that expedition was what caused your illness."

There was a moment's silence; then Mrs. Ansley rejoined: "Did they? It was all so long ago."

"Yes. And you got well again—so it didn't matter. But I suppose it struck your friends—the reason given for your illness, I mean—because everybody knew you were so prudent on account of your throat, and your mother took such care of you . . . You *had* been out late sight-seeing, hadn't you, that night?"

"Perhaps I had. The most prudent girls aren't always prudent. What made you think of it now?"

Mrs. Slade seemed to have no answer ready. But after a moment she broke out: "Because I simply can't bear it any longer—!"

Mrs. Ansley lifted her head quickly. Her eyes were wide and very pale. "Can't bear what?"

"Why—your not knowing that I've always known why you went."

"Why I went—?"

"Yes. You think I'm bluffing, don't you? Well, you went to meet the man I was engaged to—and I can repeat every word of the letter that took you there."

While Mrs. Slade spoke Mrs. Ansley had risen unsteadily to her feet. Her bag, her knitting and gloves, slid in a panic-stricken heap to the ground. She looked at Mrs. Slade as though she were looking at a ghost.

"No, no—don't," she faltered out.

"Why not? Listen, if you don't believe me. 'My one darling, things can't go on like this. I must see you alone. Come to the Colosseum immediately after dark tomorrow. There will be somebody to let you in. No one whom you need fear will suspect'—but perhaps you've forgotten what the letter said?"

Mrs. Ansley met the challenge with an unexpected composure. Steadying herself against the chair she looked at her friend, and replied: "No; I know it by heart too."

"And the signature? 'Only *your* D.S.' Was that it? I'm right, am I? That was the letter that took you out that evening after dark?"

Mrs. Ansley was still looking at her. It seemed to Mrs. Slade that a slow struggle was going on behind the voluntarily controlled mask of her small quiet face. "I shouldn't have thought she had herself so well in hand," Mrs. Slade reflected, almost resentfully. But at this moment Mrs. Ansley spoke. "I don't know how you knew. I burnt that letter at once."

"Yes; you would, naturally—you're so prudent!" The sneer was open now. "And if you burnt the letter you're wondering how on earth I know what was in it. That's it, isn't it?"

Mrs. Slade waited, but Mrs. Ansley did not speak.

"Well, my dear, I know what was in that letter because I wrote it!"

"You wrote it?"

"Yes."

The two women stood for a minute staring at each other in the last golden light. Then Mrs. Ansley dropped back into her chair. "Oh," she murmured, and covered her face with her hands.

Mrs. Slade waited nervously for another word or movement. None came, and at length she broke out: "I horrify you."

Mrs. Ansley's hands dropped to her knee. The face they uncovered was streaked with tears. "I wasn't thinking of you. I was thinking—it was the only letter I ever had from him!"

"And I wrote it. Yes; I wrote it! But I was the girl he was engaged to. Did you happen to remember that?"

Mrs. Ansley's head drooped again. "I'm not trying to excuse myself . . . I remembered . . ."

"And still you went?"

"Still I went."

Mrs. Slade stood looking down on the small bowed figure at her side. The flame of her wrath had already sunk, and she wondered why she had ever thought there would be any satisfaction in inflicting so purposeless a wound on her friend. But she had to justify herself.

"You do understand? I'd found out—and I hated you, hated you. I knew you were in love with Delphin—and I was afraid; afraid of you, of your quiet ways, your sweetness . . . your . . . well, I wanted you out of the way, that's all. Just for a few weeks; just till I was sure of him. So in a blind fury I wrote that letter . . . I don't know why I'm telling you now."

"I suppose," said Mrs. Ansley slowly, "it's because you've always gone on hating me."

"Perhaps. Or because I wanted to get the whole thing off my mind." She paused. "I'm glad you destroyed the letter. Of course I never thought you'd die."

Mrs. Ansley relapsed into silence, and Mrs. Slade, leaning above her, was conscious of a strange sense of isolation, of being cut off from the warm current of human communion. "You think me a monster!"

"I don't know . . . It was the only letter I had, and you say he didn't write it?"

"Ah, how you care for him still!"

"I cared for that memory," said Mrs. Ansley.

Mrs. Slade continued to look down on her. She seemed physically reduced by the blow—as if, when she got up, the wind might scatter her like a puff of dust. Mrs. Slade's jealousy suddenly leapt up again at the sight. All these years the woman had been living on that letter. How she must have loved him, to treasure the mere memory of its ashes! The letter of the man her friend was engaged to. Wasn't it she who was the monster?

"You tried your best to get him away from me, didn't you? But you failed; and I kept him. That's all."

"Yes. That's all."

"I wish now I hadn't told you. I'd no idea you'd feel about it as you do; I thought you'd be amused. It all happened so long ago, as you say; and you must do me the justice to remember that I had no reason to think you'd ever taken it seriously. How could I, when you were married to Horace Ansley two months afterward? As soon as you could get out of bed your mother rushed you off to Florence and married you. People were rather surprised—they wondered at its being done so quickly; but I thought I knew. I had an idea you did it out of *pique*—to be able to say you'd got ahead of Delphin and me. Girls have such silly reasons for doing the most serious things. And your marrying so soon convinced me that you'd never really cared."

"Yes. I suppose it would," Mrs. Ansley assented.

The clear heaven overhead was emptied of all its gold. Dusk spread over it, abruptly darkening the Seven Hills. Here and there lights began to twinkle through the foliage at their feet. Steps were coming and going on the deserted terrace—waiters looking out of the doorway at the head of the stairs, then reappearing with trays and napkins and flasks of wine. Tables were moved, chairs straightened. A feeble string of electric lights flickered out. Some vases of faded flowers were carried away, and brought back replenished. A stout lady in a dust-coat suddenly appeared, asking in broken Italian if any one had seen the elastic band which held together her tattered Baedeker. She poked with her stick under the table at which she had lunched, the waiters assisting.

The corner where Mrs. Slade and Mrs. Ansley sat was still shadowy and deserted. For a long time neither of them spoke. At length Mrs. Slade began again: "I suppose I did it as a sort of joke—"

"A joke?"

"Well, girls are ferocious sometimes, you know. Girls in love especially. And I remember laughing to myself all that evening at the idea that you were waiting around there in the dark, dodging out of sight, listening for every sound, trying to get in—. Of course I was upset when I heard you were so ill afterward."

Mrs. Ansley had not moved for a long time. But now she turned slowly toward her companion. "But I didn't wait. He'd arranged everything. He was there. We were let in at once," she said.

Mrs. Slade sprang up from her leaning position. "Delphin there? They let you in?— Ah, now you're lying!" she burst out with violence.

Mrs. Ansley's voice grew clearer, and full of surprise. "But of course he was there. Naturally he came—"

"Came? How did he know he'd find you there? You must be raving!"

Mrs. Ansley hesitated, as though reflecting. "But I answered the letter. I told him I'd be there. So he came."

Mrs. Slade flung her hands up to her face. "Oh, God—you answered! I never thought of your answering . . ."

"It's odd you never thought of it, if you wrote the letter."

"Yes. I was blind with rage."

Mrs. Ansley rose, and drew her fur scarf about her. "It is cold here. We'd better go . . . I'm sorry for you," she said, as she clasped the fur about her throat.

The unexpected words sent a pang through Mrs. Slade. "Yes; we'd better go." She gathered up her bag and cloak. "I don't know why you should be sorry for me," she muttered.

Mrs. Ansley stood looking away from her toward the dusky secret mass of the Colosseum. "Well—because I didn't have to wait that night."

Mrs. Slade gave an unquiet laugh. "Yes; I was beaten there. But I oughtn't to begrudge it to you, I suppose. At the end of all these years. After all, I had everything; I had him for twenty-five years. And you had nothing but that one letter that he didn't write."

Mrs. Ansley was again silent. At length she turned toward the door of the terrace. She took a step, and turned back, facing her companion.

"I had Barbara," she said, and began to move ahead of Mrs. Slade toward the stairway.

RICHARD WILBUR

(1921–   )

"Poems" said Richard Wilbur, "are not addressed to anybody in particular . . . they are conflicts with disorder, not messages from one person to another." Formality, urbanity, and wit characterize Richard Wilbur's poetry.

Wilbur was born in New York City. He was profoundly affected by his service in World War II. "It was not until World War II took me to Cassino, Anzio, and the Siegfried Line that I began to versify in earnest," he said. "One does not use poetry for its major purposes, as a means to organize oneself and the world, until one's world somehow gets out of hand." His response to war was his first volume of poetry, The Beautiful Changes. *A second volume,* Ceremony and Other Poems, *followed in 1950. After the publication of* Things of This World *in 1957, from which "A Baroque Wall-Fountain in the Villa Sciarra" is taken, Wilbur was awarded the Pulitzer Prize and the National Book Award. In 1987, Wilbur succeeded Robert Penn Warren as America's poet laureate.*

"A Baroque Wall-Fountain in the Villa Sciarra" is characteristic of Wilbur's work. Rhymed and metrically regular, it is elegant, fresh and tightly wrought.

A Baroque Wall-Fountain in the Villa Sciarra
for Dore and Adja

from THE POEMS OF RICHARD WILBUR

Under the bronze crown
Too big for the head of the stone cherub whose feet
    A serpent has begun to eat,
Sweet water brims a cockle and braids down

    Past spattered mosses, breaks
On the tipped edge of a second shell, and fills
    The massive third below. It spills
In threads then from the scalloped rim, and makes

    A scrim or summery tent
For a faun-ménage and their familiar goose.
    Happy in all that ragged, loose
Collapse of water, its effortless descent

    And flatteries of spray,
The stocky god upholds the shell with ease,
    Watching, about his shaggy knees,
The goatish innocence of his babes at play;

    His fauness all the while
Leans forward, slightly, into a clambering mesh
    Of water-lights, her sparkling flesh
In a saecular ecstasy, her blinded smile

Bent on the sand floor
Of the trefoil pool, where ripple-shadows come
    And go in swift reticulum,
More addling to the eye than wine, and more

    Interminable to thought
Than pleasure's calculus. Yet since this all
    Is pleasure, flash, and waterfall,
Must it not be too simple? Are we not

    More intricately expressed
In the plain fountains that Maderna set
    Before St. Peter's—the main jet
Struggling aloft until it seems at rest

    In the act of rising, until
The very wish of water is reversed,
    That heaviness borne up to burst
In a clear, high, cavorting head, to fill

    With blaze, and then in gauze
Delays, in a gnatlike shimmering, in a fine
    Illumined version of itself, decline,
And patter on the stones its own applause?

    If that is what men are
Or should be, if those water-saints display
    The pattern of our areté,
What of these showered fauns in their bizarre,

    Spangled, and plunging house?
They are at rest in fulness of desire
    For what is given, they do not tire
Of the smart of the sun, the pleasant water-douse

    And riddled pool below,
Reproving our disgust and our ennui
    With humble insatiety.
Francis, perhaps, who lay in sister snow

Before the wealthy gate
Freezing and praising, might have seen in this
  No trifle, but a shade of bliss—
That land of tolerable flowers, that state

  As near and far as grass
Where eyes become the sunlight, and the hand
  Is worthy of water: the dreamt land
Toward which all hungers leap, all pleasures pass.

CHARLES WRIGHT
(1935–   )

Charles Wright's life has two poles—the American South, where he grew up, and Italy, where he first discovered poetry. In 1957 he went into the Army and spent three of his four years of service in Italy. While living in Verona he was given the Selected Poems of Ezra Pound.

"I was told, by a friend, to take the Pound book out to Sirmione on Lake Garda where the Latin poet Catullus supposedly had a villa, and to read it there. It was, and continues to be, one of the most beautiful places I have ever been or expect to go to. Lake Garda in front of you, the Italian Alps on three sides of you, the ruined and romantic villa around you, and I read a poem 'Blandula, Tenulla, Vagula' that Pound had written about the place, about how Sirmione was more beautiful and desirable than Paradise itself, and my life was changed forever, at the age of twenty-three."

"Roma I" is taken from Wright's The World of 10,000 Things: Poems 1980–1990. *It displays Wright's trademark of cataloguing people and events and compiling images. A critic for the* Washington Post *wrote that reading Wright's poetry is "like watching the changing fragments of a kaleidoscope."*

Roma I

from THE WORLD OF 10,000 THINGS

To start with, it looked abstract
                              that first year from the balcony
Over the Via del Babuino,
Local color as far as the eye could see,
                              and mumbled in slaps and clumps
Of gouaches constantly to itself,
A gentian snood of twilight in winter,
                                        blood orange in spring,
And ten thousand yards of glass in the summer sky.
Wherever you looked in October, the night was jigged.

(In front of the Ristorante Bolognese,
Monica Vitti and Michelangelo Antonioni are having an
     aperitif,
Watched by a hundred people.
                              On the marble plaque
On the building across the street from my room to the Polish
     patriot
Whose name escapes me forever,
The words start to disappear in the April nightswell.
The river of cars turns its small lights on,
                    and everyone keeps on looking at everyone else.)

Rome in Rome? We're all leading afterlives
                                        of one sort or another,

Wrapped in bird feathers, pecking away at our gathered seed,
The form inside the form inside.
And nothing's more common by now than the obelisk
At one end of the street
                            and the stone boat at the other . . .
The smell of a dozen dinners is borne up
On exhaust fumes,
                        timeless, somehow, and vaguely reassuring.

Trust by a deed of Trust of Mary Hemingway 16 of March 1962. Reprinted by permission of Scribner, a division of Simon & Schuster and Hemingway Foreign Rights Trust.

Scribner and *Watkins/Loomis Agency, Inc.:* "Roman Fever" from *Roman Fever and Other Stories* by Edith Wharton, copyright © 1934 by Liberty Magazine, copyright renewed 1962 by William R. Tyler. Reprinted by permission of Scribner, a division of Simon & Schuster, and Watkins/Loomis Agency, Inc., and the Estate of Edith Wharton.

Simon & Schuster: "Queen of the Bogs" from *The Last Italian* by William Murray (*The Traveler Magazine,* June 1988), copyright © 1991 by William Murray. Reprinted by permission of Simon & Schuster.

Viking Penguin: Excerpt from *The Uncle from Rome* by Joseph Caldwell, copyright © 1992 by Joseph Caldwell. Reprinted by permission of Viking Penguin, a division of Penguin Books USA Inc.

Viking Penguin and *Laurence Pollinger Limited:* Excerpt from "To Sorgonno" from *Sea and Sardinia* by D. H. Lawrence, copyright © 1921 by Thomas Seltzer, Inc., copyright renewed 1949 by Frieda Lawrence. Rights in the United Kingdom from *The Portable D. H. Lawrence* administered by Laurence Pollinger Limited, London. Reprinted by permission of Viking Penguin, a division of Penguin Books USA Inc., and Laurence Pollinger Limited.

Viking Penguin and *Viking UK:* "Pitigliano" and "San Sano" from *Within Tuscany* by Matthew Spender, copyright © 1991, 1992 by Matthew Spender. Rights in Canada administered by Viking, London. Reprinted by permission of Viking Penguin, a division of Penguin Books USA Inc., and Viking, a division of Penguin UK.

Wallace Literary Agency: Excerpt from *Women of the Shadows* by Ann Cornelisen, copyright © 1976 by Ann Cornelisen. Reprinted by permission of the Wallace Literary Agency, Inc.

Weidenfeld & Nicolson: "The City Today" from *Vidal in Venice* by Gore Vidal. Reprinted by permission of Weidenfeld & Nicolson, an imprint of The Orion Publishing Group Ltd., London.